W9-ANB-241

WITHDRAWN

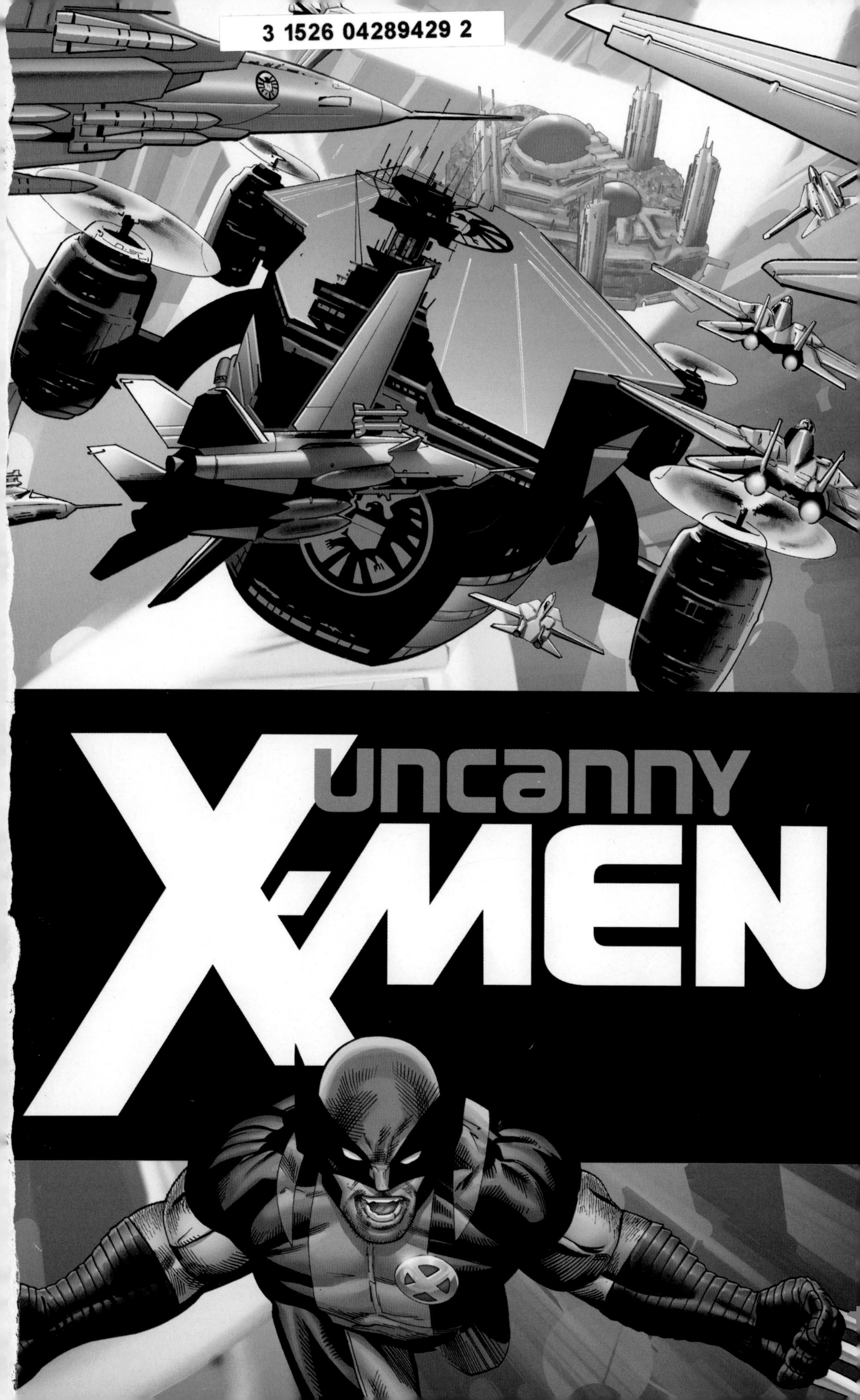
UNCANNY
X-MEN

WRITER: **KIERON GILLEN**

#11-12 PENCILS: **GREG LAND**
INKS: **JAY LEISTEN** • COLORS: **GURU-eFX**

#13 PENCILS: **BILLY TAN**
INKS: **CAM SMITH** & **CRAIG YEUNG**
COLORS: **GURU-eFX**

#14 ARTIST: **DUSTIN WEAVER**
COLORS: **JIM CHARALAMPIDIS**

LETTERS: **VC'S JOE CARAMAGNA** • COVER ART: **GREG LAND** WITH **GURU-eFX** &
WIL QUINTANA (#11-12); **ADAM KUBERT** WITH **MORRY HOLLOWELL** (#13); AND
STUART IMMONEN WITH **JIM CHARALAMPIDIS** (#14)
ASSISTANT EDITOR: **JORDAN D. WHITE**
ASSOCIATE EDITOR: **DANIEL KETCHUM** • EDITOR: **NICK LOWE**

COLLECTION EDITOR: **JENNIFER GRÜNWALD** • ASSISTANT EDITORS: **ALEX STARBUCK** & **NELSON RIBEIRO**
EDITOR, SPECIAL PROJECTS: **MARK D. BEAZLEY** • SENIOR EDITOR, SPECIAL PROJECTS: **JEFF YOUNGQUIST**
SENIOR VICE PRESIDENT OF SALES: **DAVID GABRIEL**
SVP OF BRAND PLANNING & COMMUNICATIONS: **MICHAEL PASCIULLO**
BOOK DESIGNER: **RODOLFO MURAGUCHI**

EDITOR IN CHIEF: **AXEL ALONSO** • CHIEF CREATIVE OFFICER: **JOE QUESADA**
PUBLISHER: **DAN BUCKLEY** • EXECUTIVE PRODUCER: **ALAN FINE**

UNCANNY X-MEN BY KIERON GILLEN VOL. 3. Contains material originally published in magazine form as UNCANNY X-MEN #11-14. First printing 2012. Hardcover ISBN# 978-0-7851-5997-1. Softcover ISBN# 978-0-7851-5998-8. Published by MARVEL WORLDWIDE, INC., a subsidiary of MARVEL ENTERTAINMENT, LLC. OFFICE OF PUBLICATION: 135 West 50th Street, New York, NY 10020. Copyright © 2012 Marvel Characters, Inc. All rights reserved. Hardcover: $19.99 per copy in the U.S. and $21.99 in Canada (GST #R127032852). Softcover: $16.99 per copy in the U.S. and $18.99 in Canada (GST #R127032852). Canadian Agreement #40668537. All characters featured in this issue and the distinctive names and likenesses thereof, and all related indicia are trademarks of Marvel Characters, Inc. No similarity between any of the names, characters, persons, and/or institutions in this magazine with those of any living or dead person or institution is intended, and any such similarity which may exist is purely coincidental. **Printed in the U.S.A.** ALAN FINE, EVP - Office of the President, Marvel Worldwide, Inc. and EVP & CMO Marvel Characters B.V.; DAN BUCKLEY, Publisher & President - Print, Animation & Digital Divisions; JOE QUESADA, Chief Creative Officer; TOM BREVOORT, SVP of Publishing; DAVID BOGART, SVP of Operations & Procurement, Publishing; RUWAN JAYATILLEKE, SVP & Associate Publisher, Publishing; C.B. CEBULSKI, SVP of Creator & Content Development; DAVID GABRIEL, SVP of Publishing Sales & Circulation; MICHAEL PASCIULLO, SVP of Brand Planning & Communications; JIM O'KEEFE, VP of Operations & Logistics; DAN CARR, Executive Director of Publishing Technology; SUSAN CRESPI, Editorial Operations Manager; ALEX MORALES, Publishing Operations Manager; STAN LEE, Chairman Emeritus. For information regarding advertising in Marvel Comics or on Marvel.com, please contact Niza Disla, Director of Marvel Partnerships, at ndisla@marvel.com. For Marvel subscription inquiries, please call 800-217-9158. **Manufactured between 7/23/2012 and 9/3/2012 (hardcover), and 7/23/2012 and 2/18/2013 (softcover), by R.R. DONNELLEY, INC., SALEM, VA, USA.**

10 9 8 7 6 5 4 3 2 1

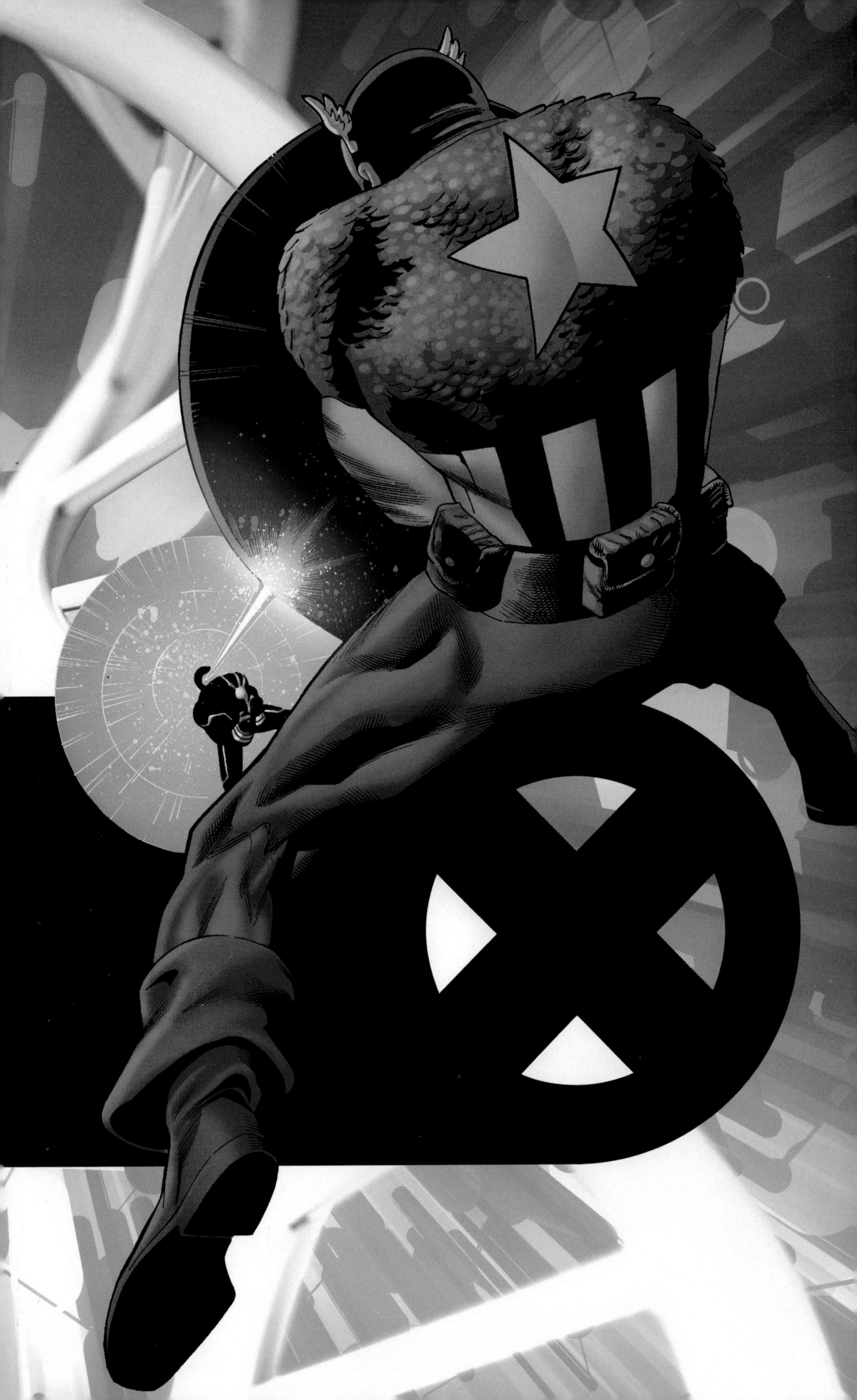

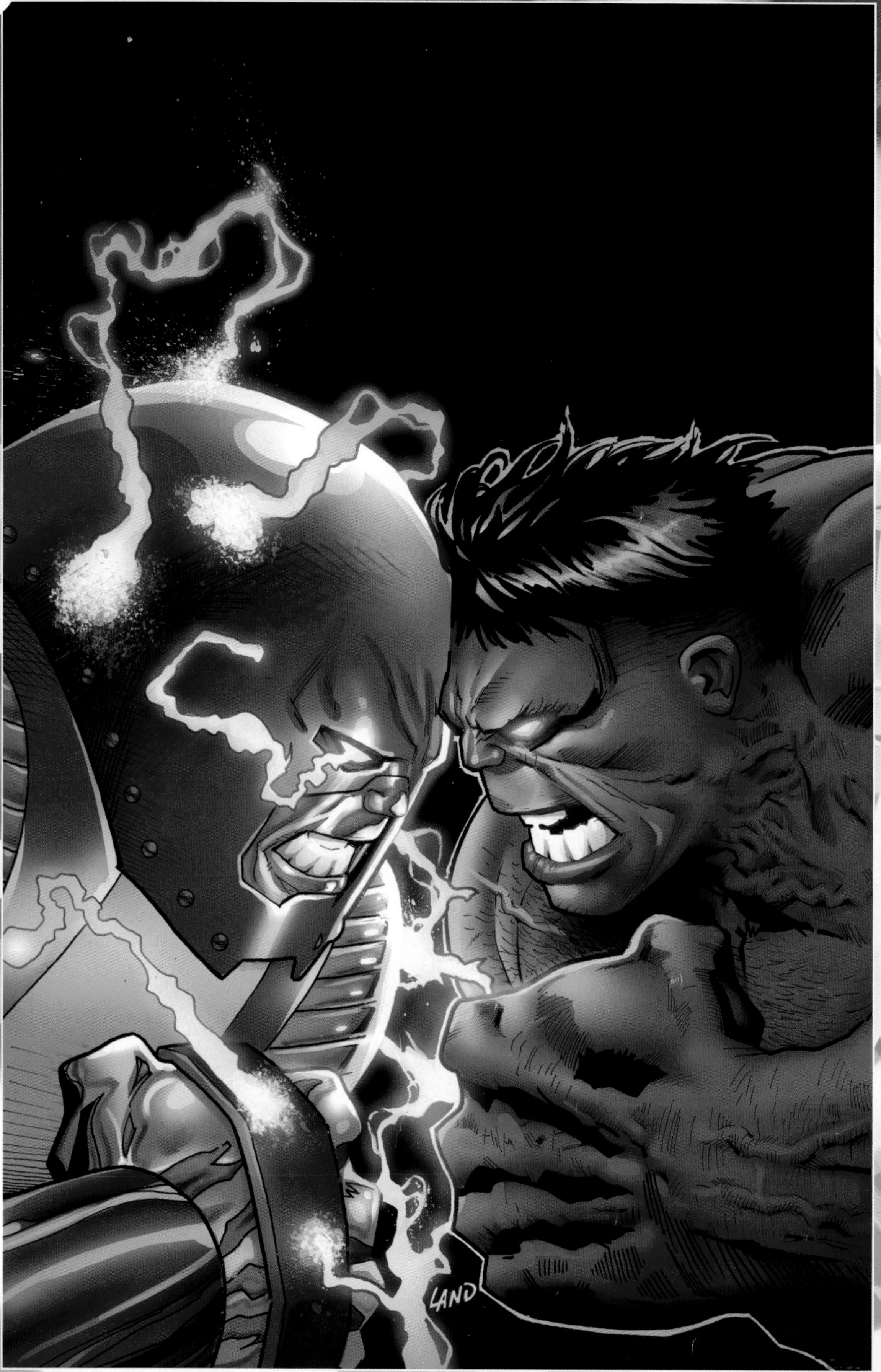
LAND

UNCANNY X-MEN

Born with powers and abilities beyond those of normal humans, mutantkind has long been hated and feared by those they sought to protect. Now, from their island nation of Utopia, Cyclops leads the most powerful group of mutants ever assembled to protect what is left of his dwindling species. Hated and feared? When you are as powerful as the Uncanny X-Men, does it matter?

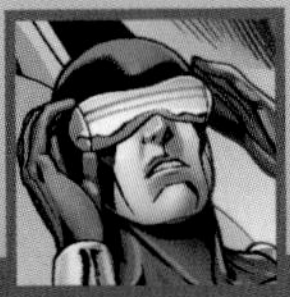

CYCLOPS
eye-blasting leader

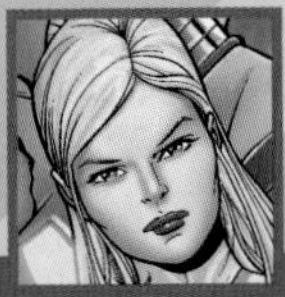

EMMA FROST
telepath with diamond form

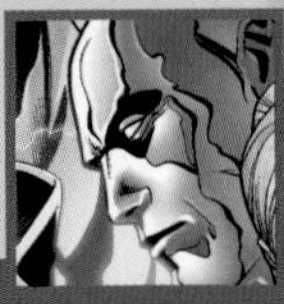

COLOSSUS
steel-skinned juggernaut

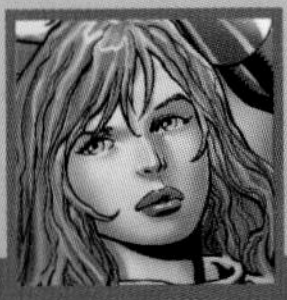

HOPE
power copycat

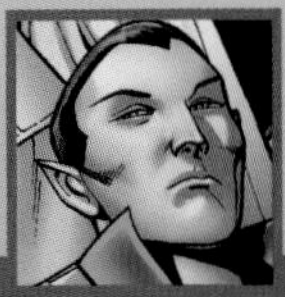

NAMOR
king of Atlantis

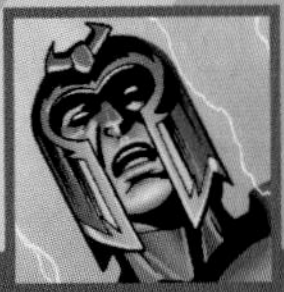

MAGNETO
master of magnetism

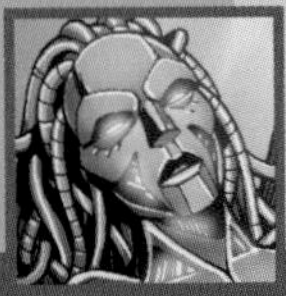

DANGER
light-shaping AI

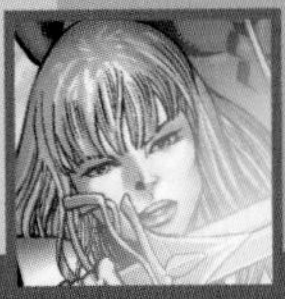

MAGIK
magic-using teleporter

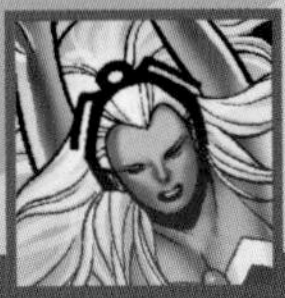

STORM
weather witch

PREVIOUSLY

Cyclops' X-Men may fight for the good of human and mutant alike, but to their point of view, mutants need more help than humans do—that's why he assembled such a powerful team. Colossus, now transformed into the Juggernaut by the dark god Cyttorak, has had himself locked in the X-Brig between missions, worried he cannot control his destructive urges. Meanwhile, the teenaged "Mutant Messiah," Hope, is seeking counsel from another new addition to the X-Brig, the galactic war-criminal alien robot known as Unit. Little does Hope know that Unit has allowed himself to be captured and has complete control of his jailer, Danger.

The Avengers, meanwhile, received an urgent message from deep space when the cosmic hero Nova crash lands in New York City, saying "It's coming..." Thus Earth's Mightiest Heroes learn that the Phoenix Force is cutting a swath across the stars, destroying anything in its path. When they then detect a sudden burst of Phoenix energy emanating from Hope, the Avengers go to the mutants' island home of Utopia to retrieve the girl in fear of what Phoenix Force will do to Earth once it finds her...

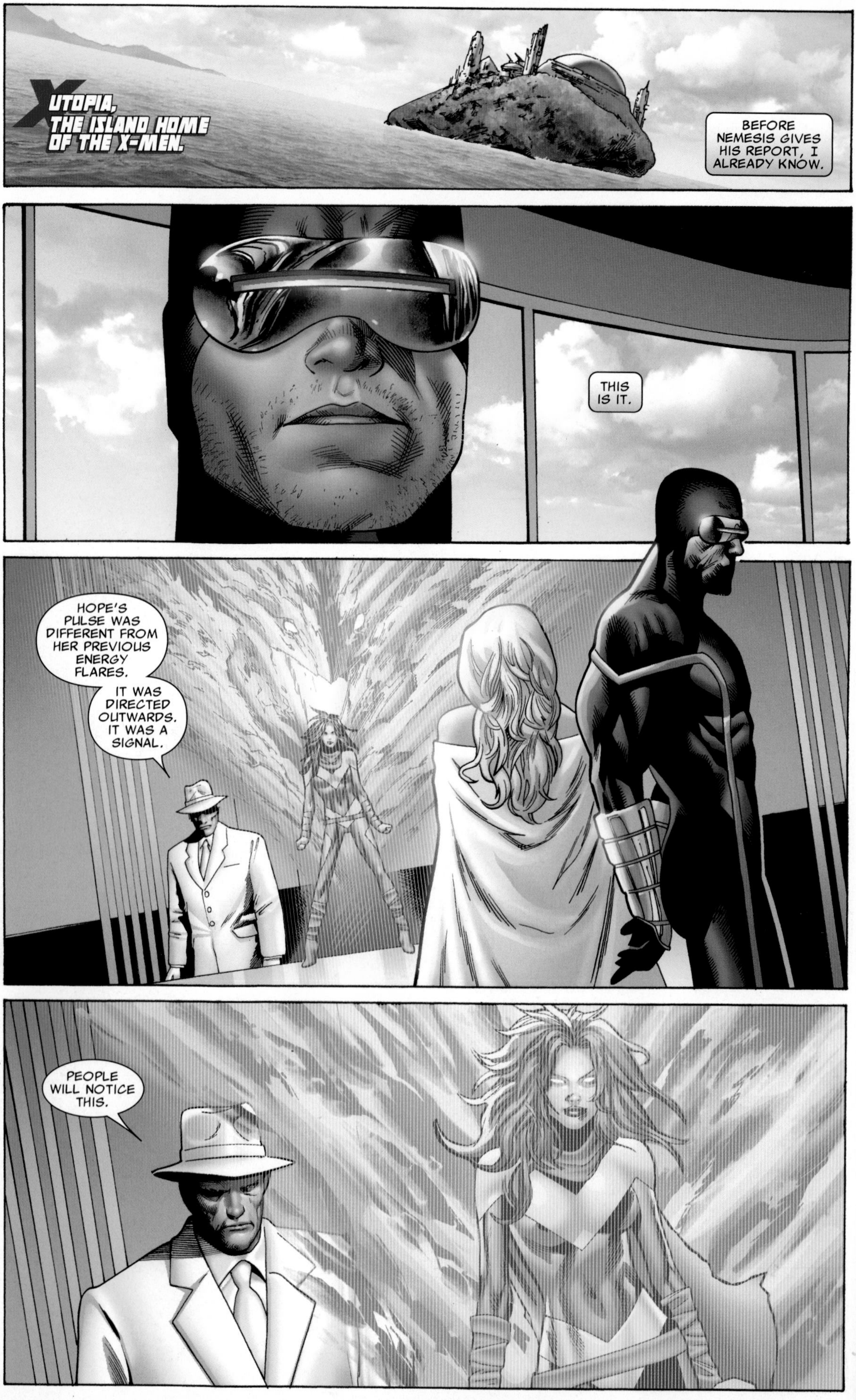
UTOPIA, THE ISLAND HOME OF THE X-MEN.
BEFORE NEMESIS GIVES HIS REPORT, I ALREADY KNOW.
THIS IS IT.
HOPE'S PULSE WAS DIFFERENT FROM HER PREVIOUS ENERGY FLARES.
IT WAS DIRECTED OUTWARDS. IT WAS A SIGNAL.
PEOPLE WILL NOTICE THIS.

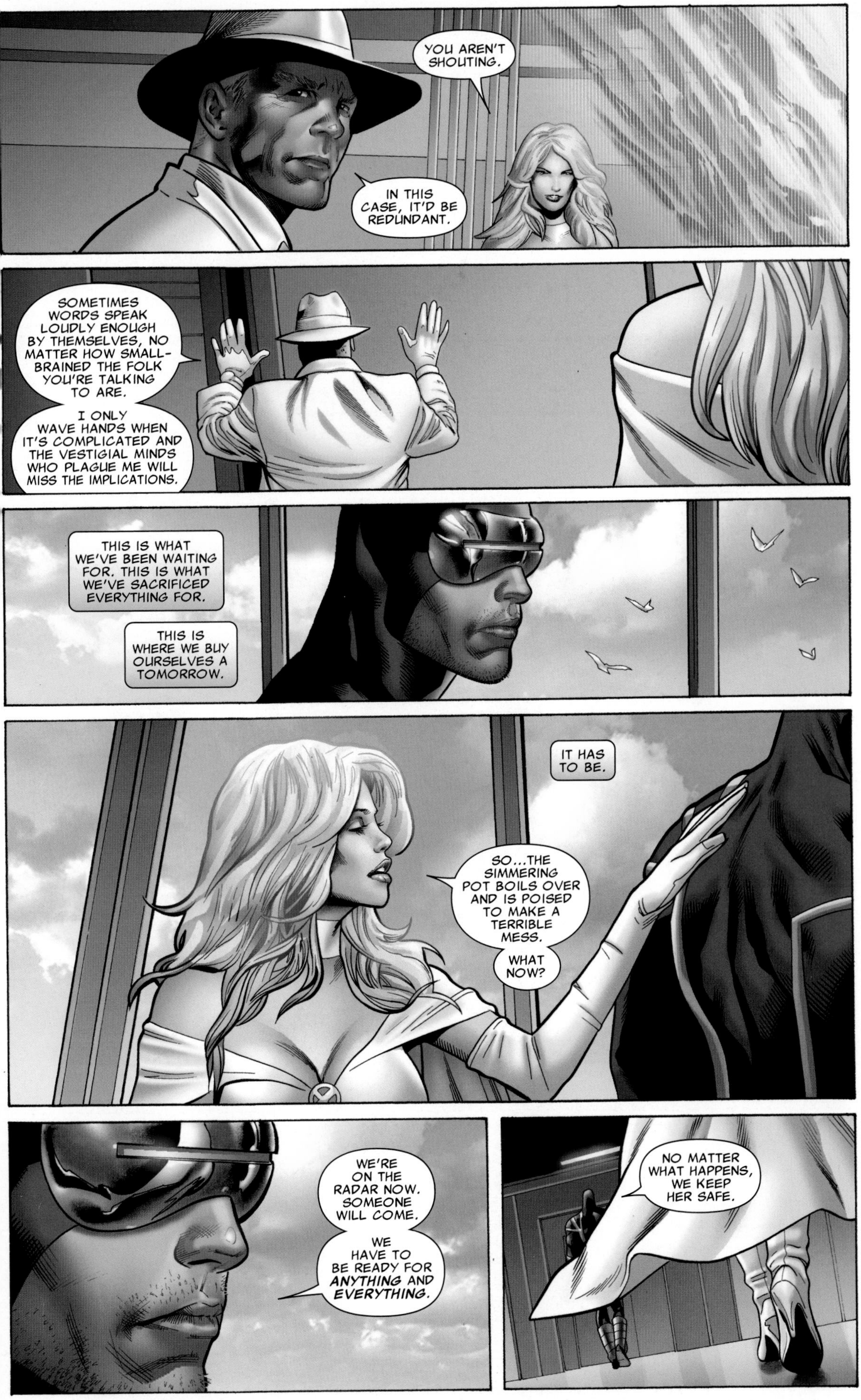

YOU AREN'T SHOUTING.
IN THIS CASE, IT'D BE REDUNDANT.
SOMETIMES WORDS SPEAK LOUDLY ENOUGH BY THEMSELVES, NO MATTER HOW SMALL-BRAINED THE FOLK YOU'RE TALKING TO ARE.
I ONLY WAVE HANDS WHEN IT'S COMPLICATED AND THE VESTIGIAL MINDS WHO PLAGUE ME WILL MISS THE IMPLICATIONS.
THIS IS WHAT WE'VE BEEN WAITING FOR. THIS IS WHAT WE'VE SACRIFICED EVERYTHING FOR.
THIS IS WHERE WE BUY OURSELVES A TOMORROW.
IT HAS TO BE.
SO...THE SIMMERING POT BOILS OVER AND IS POISED TO MAKE A TERRIBLE MESS.
WHAT NOW?
WE'RE ON THE RADAR NOW. SOMEONE WILL COME.
WE HAVE TO BE READY FOR *ANYTHING* AND *EVERYTHING*.
NO MATTER WHAT HAPPENS, WE KEEP HER SAFE.

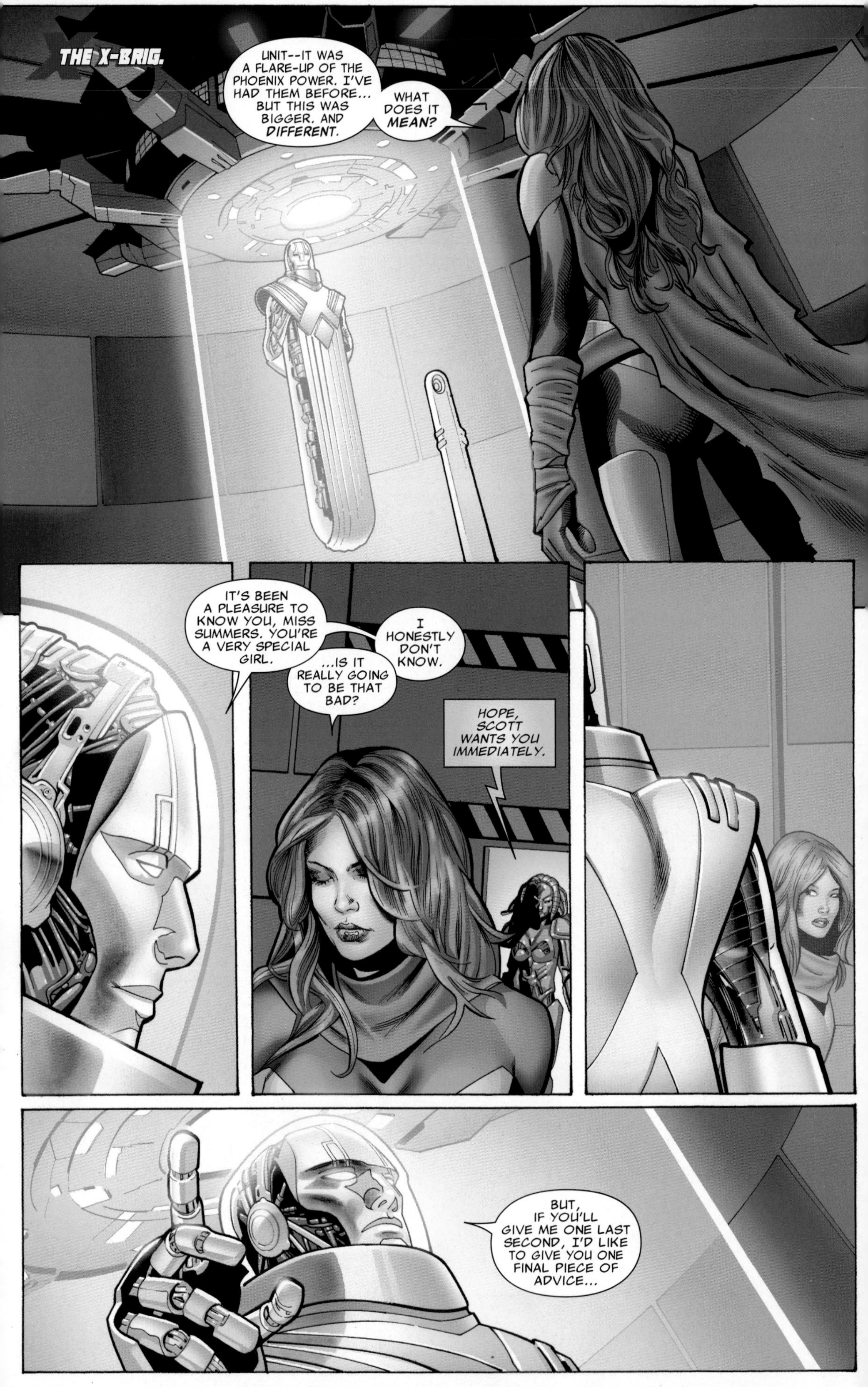
THE X-BRIG.
UNIT--IT WAS A FLARE-UP OF THE PHOENIX POWER. I'VE HAD THEM BEFORE... BUT THIS WAS BIGGER. AND DIFFERENT.
WHAT DOES IT MEAN?
I HONESTLY DON'T KNOW.
...IS IT REALLY GOING TO BE THAT BAD?
IT'S BEEN A PLEASURE TO KNOW YOU, MISS SUMMERS. YOU'RE A VERY SPECIAL GIRL.
HOPE, SCOTT WANTS YOU IMMEDIATELY.
BUT, IF YOU'LL GIVE ME ONE LAST SECOND, I'D LIKE TO GIVE YOU ONE FINAL PIECE OF ADVICE...

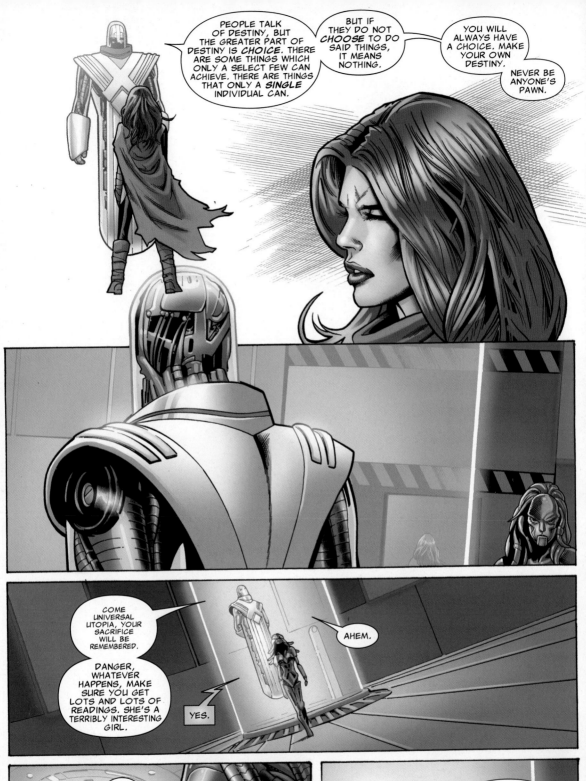

PEOPLE TALK OF DESTINY, BUT THE GREATER PART OF DESTINY IS *CHOICE*. THERE ARE SOME THINGS WHICH ONLY A SELECT FEW CAN ACHIEVE. THERE ARE THINGS THAT ONLY A *SINGLE* INDIVIDUAL CAN.

BUT IF THEY DO NOT *CHOOSE* TO DO SAID THINGS, IT MEANS NOTHING.

YOU WILL ALWAYS HAVE A CHOICE. MAKE YOUR OWN DESTINY.

NEVER BE ANYONE'S PAWN.

COME UNIVERSAL UTOPIA, YOUR SACRIFICE WILL BE REMEMBERED.

AHEM.

DANGER, WHATEVER HAPPENS, MAKE SURE YOU GET LOTS AND LOTS OF READINGS. SHE'S A TERRIBLY INTERESTING GIRL.

YES.

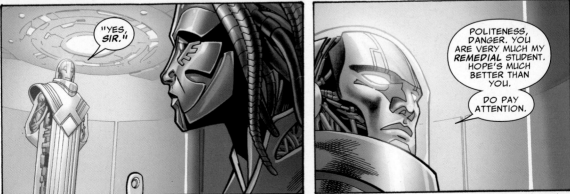

"YES, *SIR*."

POLITENESS, DANGER, YOU ARE VERY MUCH MY *REMEDIAL* STUDENT. HOPE'S MUCH BETTER THAN YOU.

DO PAY ATTENTION.

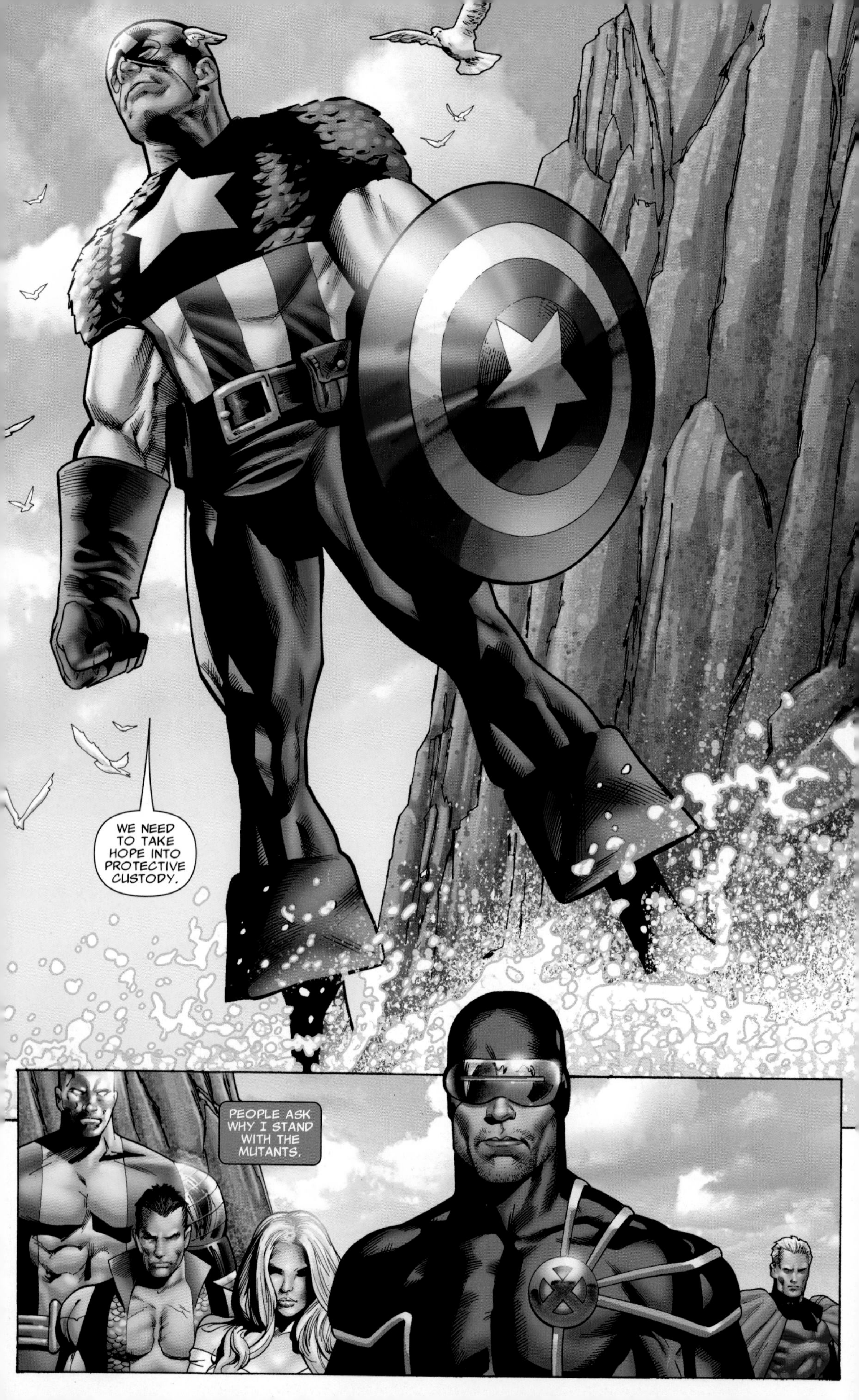
WE NEED TO TAKE HOPE INTO PROTECTIVE CUSTODY.
PEOPLE ASK WHY I STAND WITH THE MUTANTS.

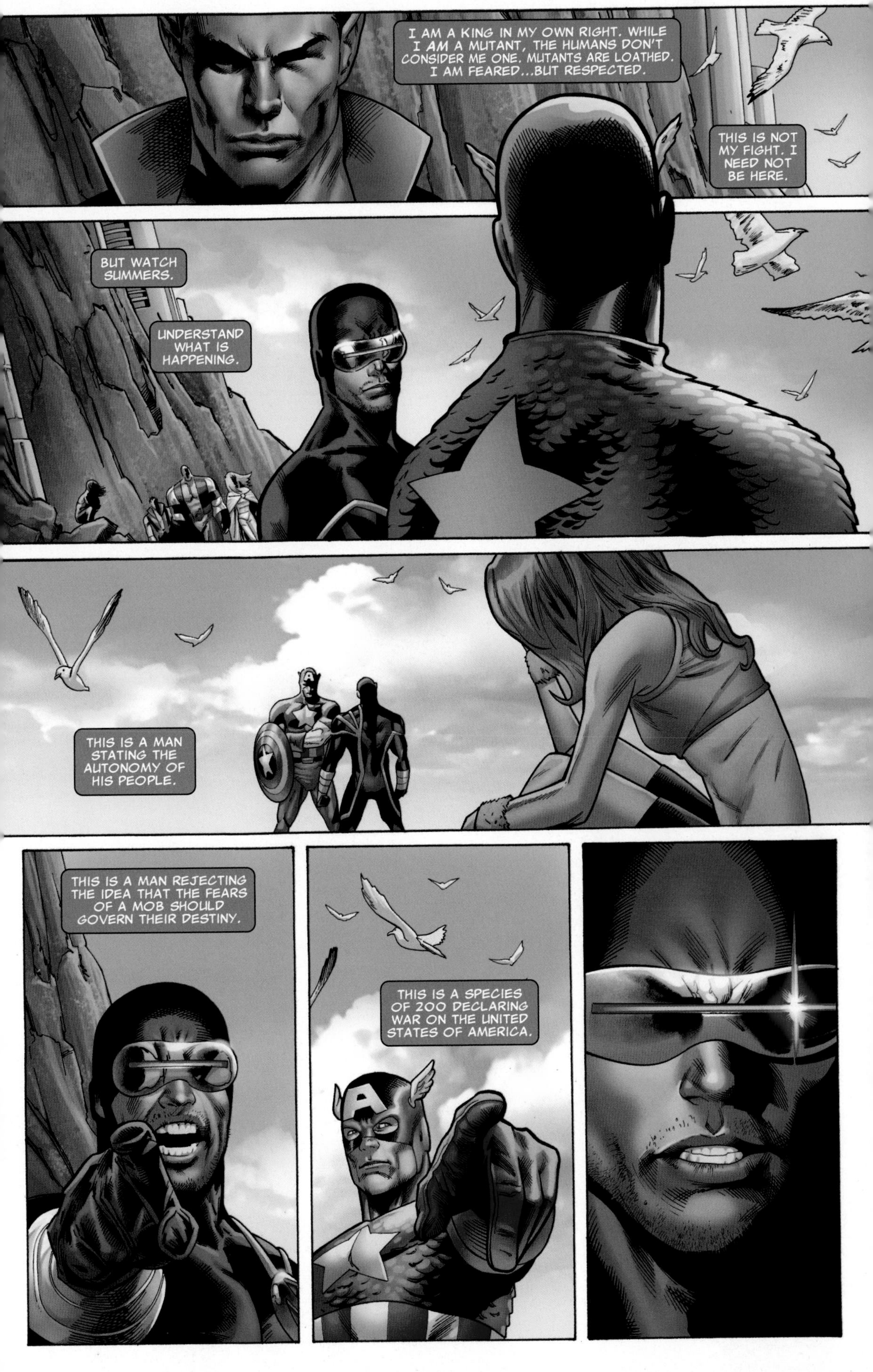
I AM A KING IN MY OWN RIGHT. WHILE I AM A MUTANT, THE HUMANS DON'T CONSIDER ME ONE. MUTANTS ARE LOATHED. I AM FEARED...BUT RESPECTED.
THIS IS NOT MY FIGHT. I NEED NOT BE HERE.
BUT WATCH SUMMERS.
UNDERSTAND WHAT IS HAPPENING.
THIS IS A MAN STATING THE AUTONOMY OF HIS PEOPLE.
THIS IS A MAN REJECTING THE IDEA THAT THE FEARS OF A MOB SHOULD GOVERN THEIR DESTINY.
THIS IS A SPECIES OF 200 DECLARING WAR ON THE UNITED STATES OF AMERICA.

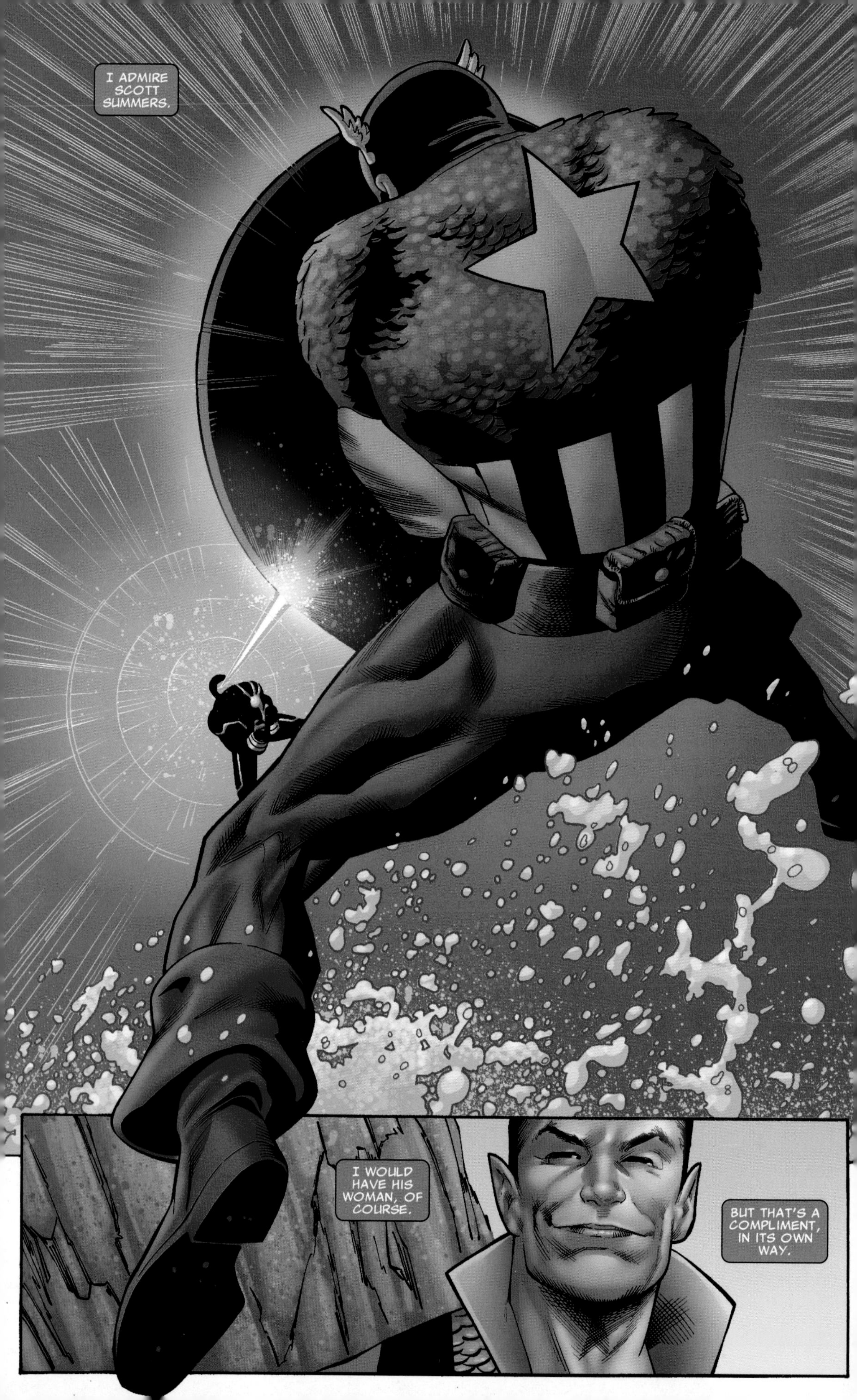
I ADMIRE SCOTT SUMMERS.
I WOULD HAVE HIS WOMAN, OF COURSE.
BUT THAT'S A COMPLIMENT, IN ITS OWN WAY.

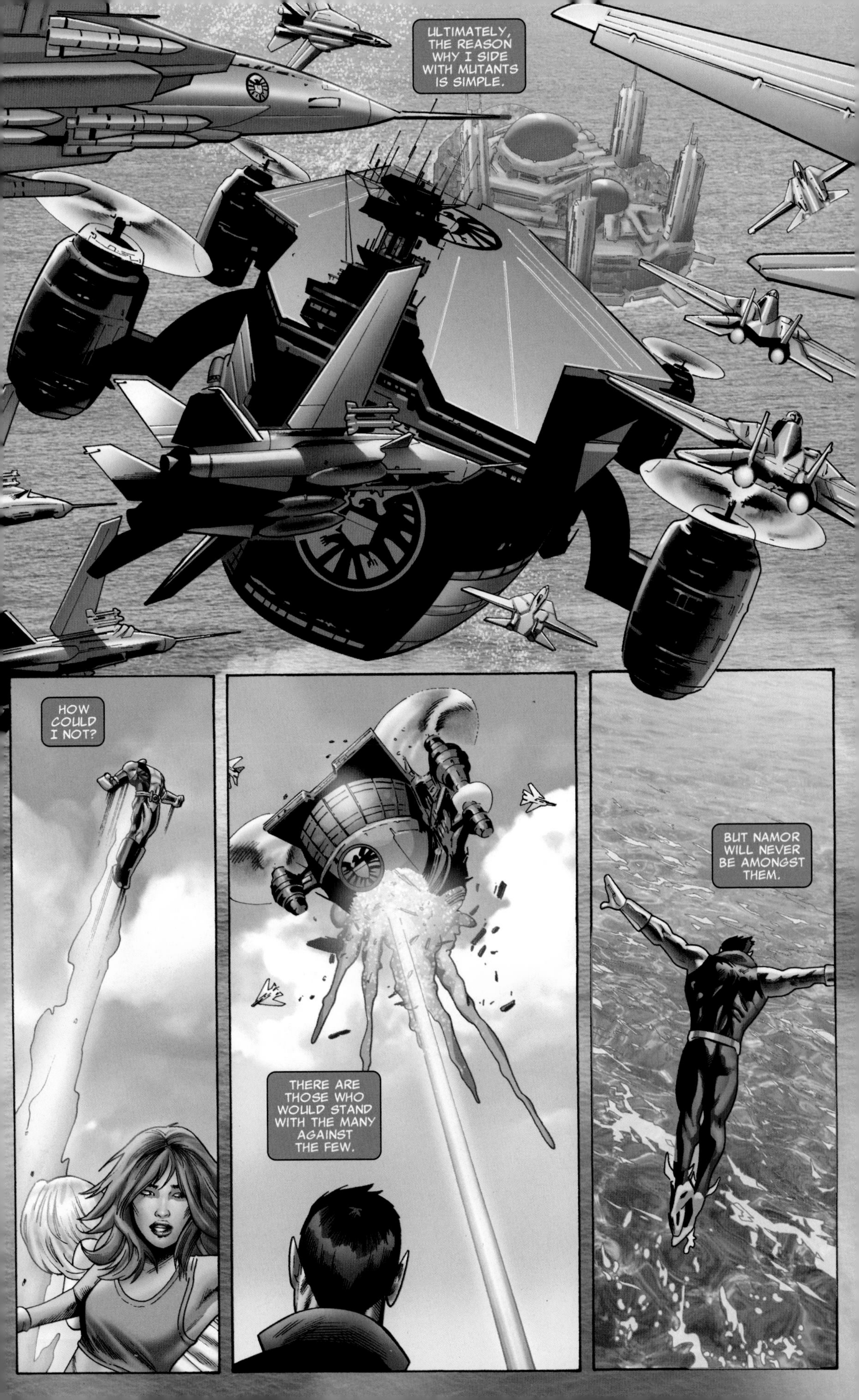
ULTIMATELY, THE REASON WHY I SIDE WITH MUTANTS IS SIMPLE.
HOW COULD I NOT?
THERE ARE THOSE WHO WOULD STAND WITH THE MANY AGAINST THE FEW.
BUT NAMOR WILL NEVER BE AMONGST THEM.

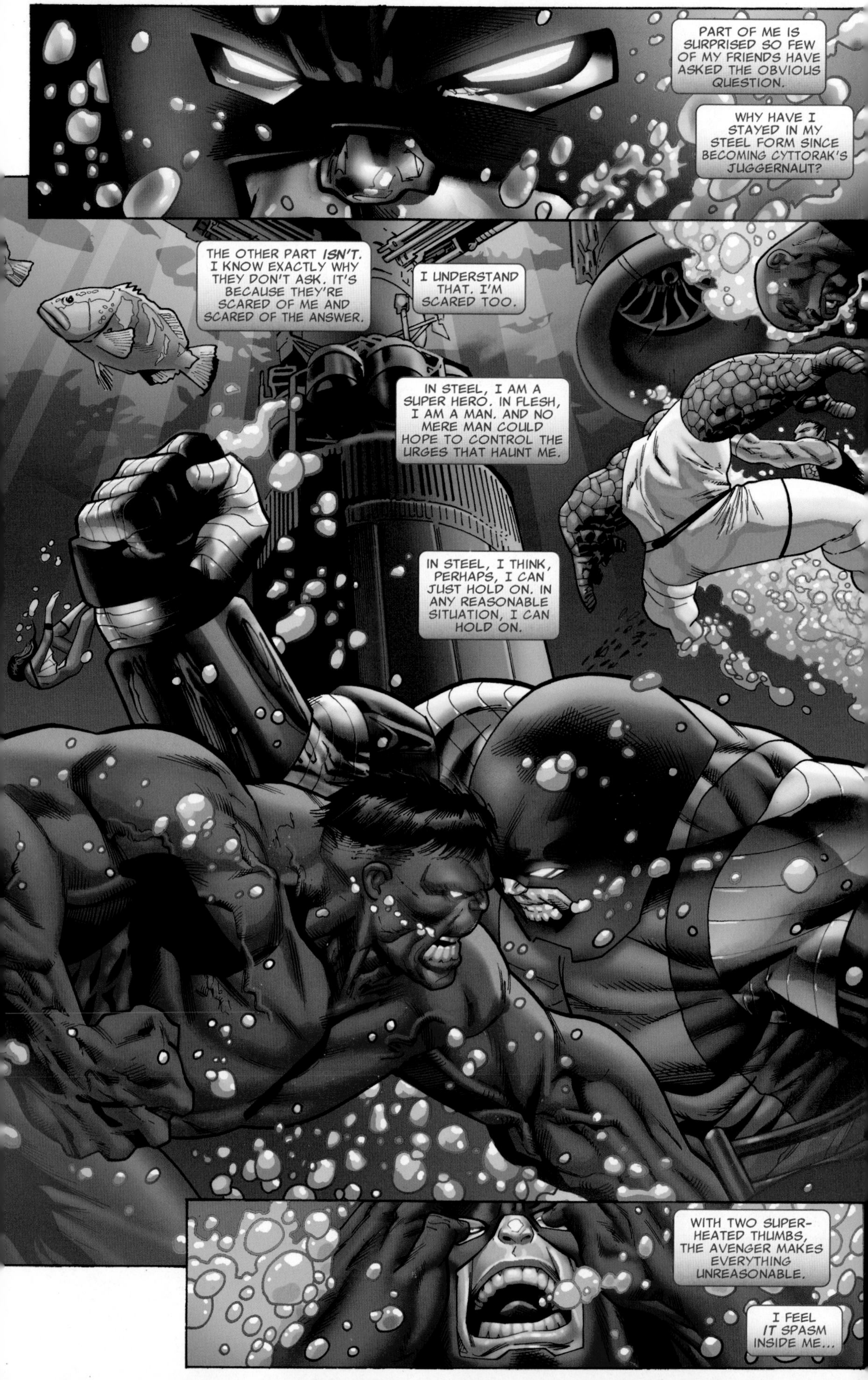
PART OF ME IS SURPRISED SO FEW OF MY FRIENDS HAVE ASKED THE OBVIOUS QUESTION.
WHY HAVE I STAYED IN MY STEEL FORM SINCE BECOMING CYTTORAK'S JUGGERNAUT?
THE OTHER PART *ISN'T*. I KNOW EXACTLY WHY THEY DON'T ASK. IT'S BECAUSE THEY'RE SCARED OF ME AND SCARED OF THE ANSWER.
I UNDERSTAND THAT. I'M SCARED TOO.
IN STEEL, I AM A SUPER HERO. IN FLESH, I AM A MAN. AND NO MERE MAN COULD HOPE TO CONTROL THE URGES THAT HAUNT ME.
IN STEEL, I THINK, PERHAPS, I CAN JUST HOLD ON. IN ANY REASONABLE SITUATION, I CAN HOLD ON.
WITH TWO SUPER-HEATED THUMBS, THE AVENGER MAKES EVERYTHING UNREASONABLE.
I FEEL *IT* SPASM INSIDE ME...

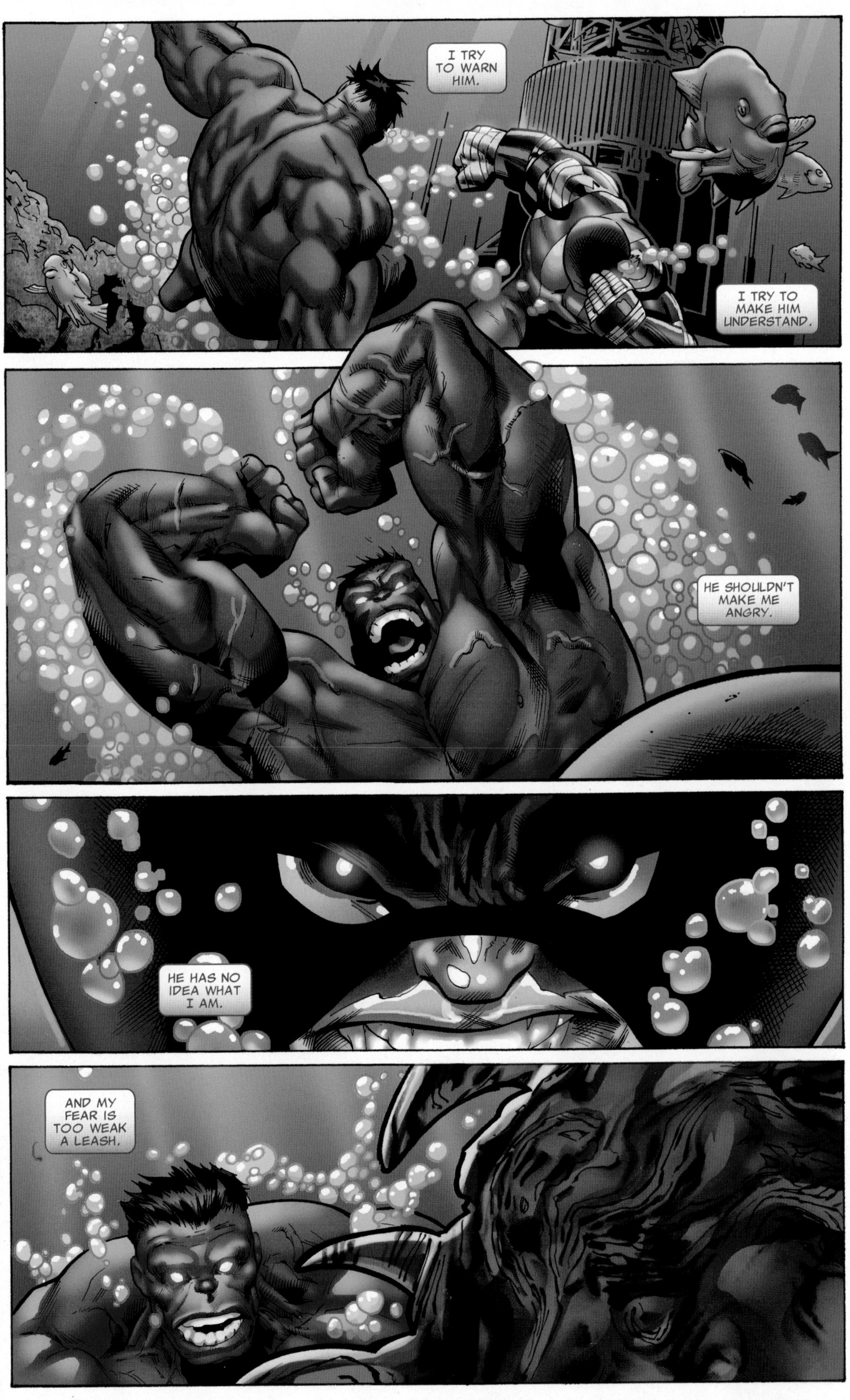
I TRY TO WARN HIM.
I TRY TO MAKE HIM UNDERSTAND.
HE SHOULDN'T MAKE ME ANGRY.
HE HAS NO IDEA WHAT I AM.
AND MY FEAR IS TOO WEAK A LEASH.

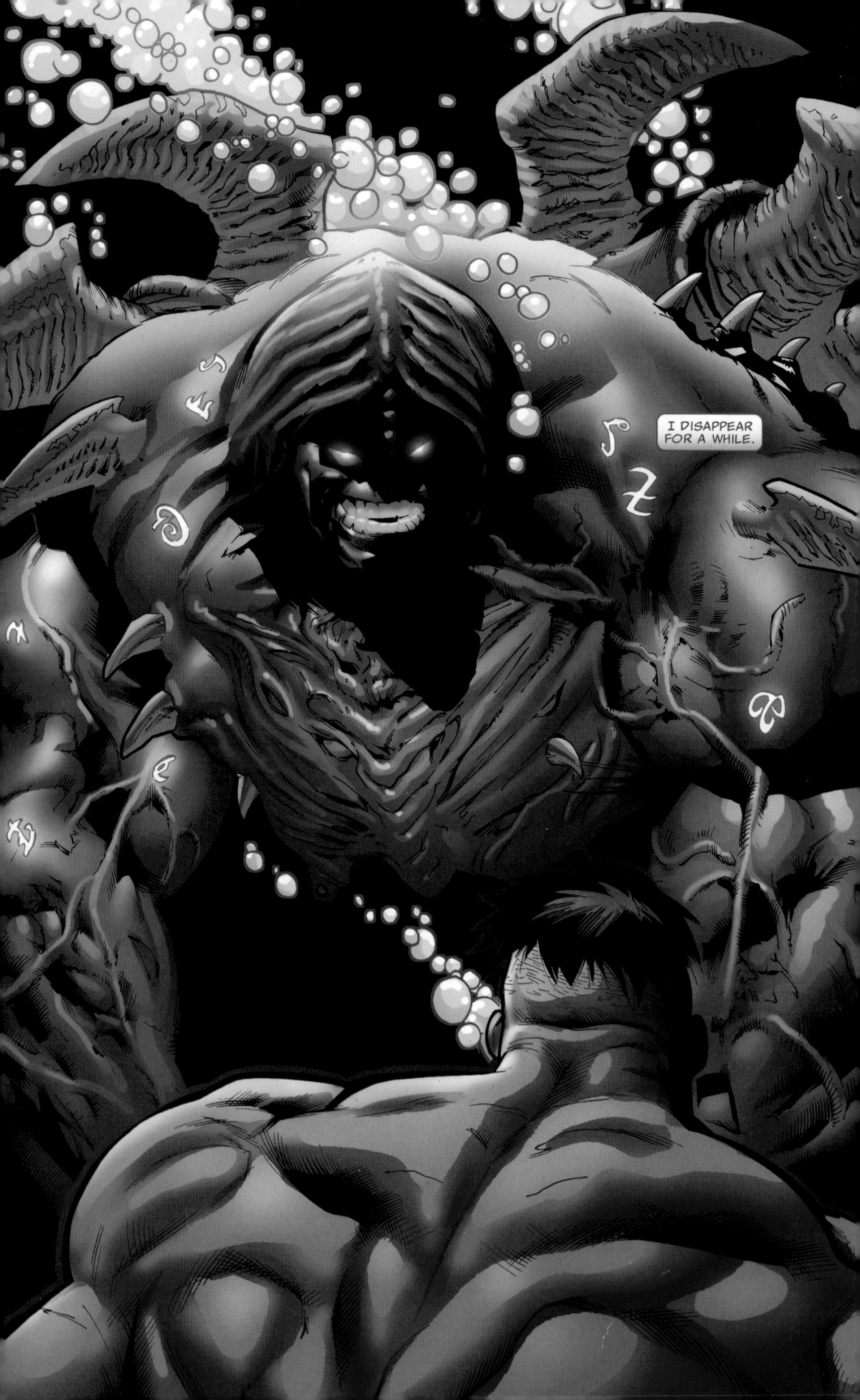
I DISAPPEAR FOR A WHILE.

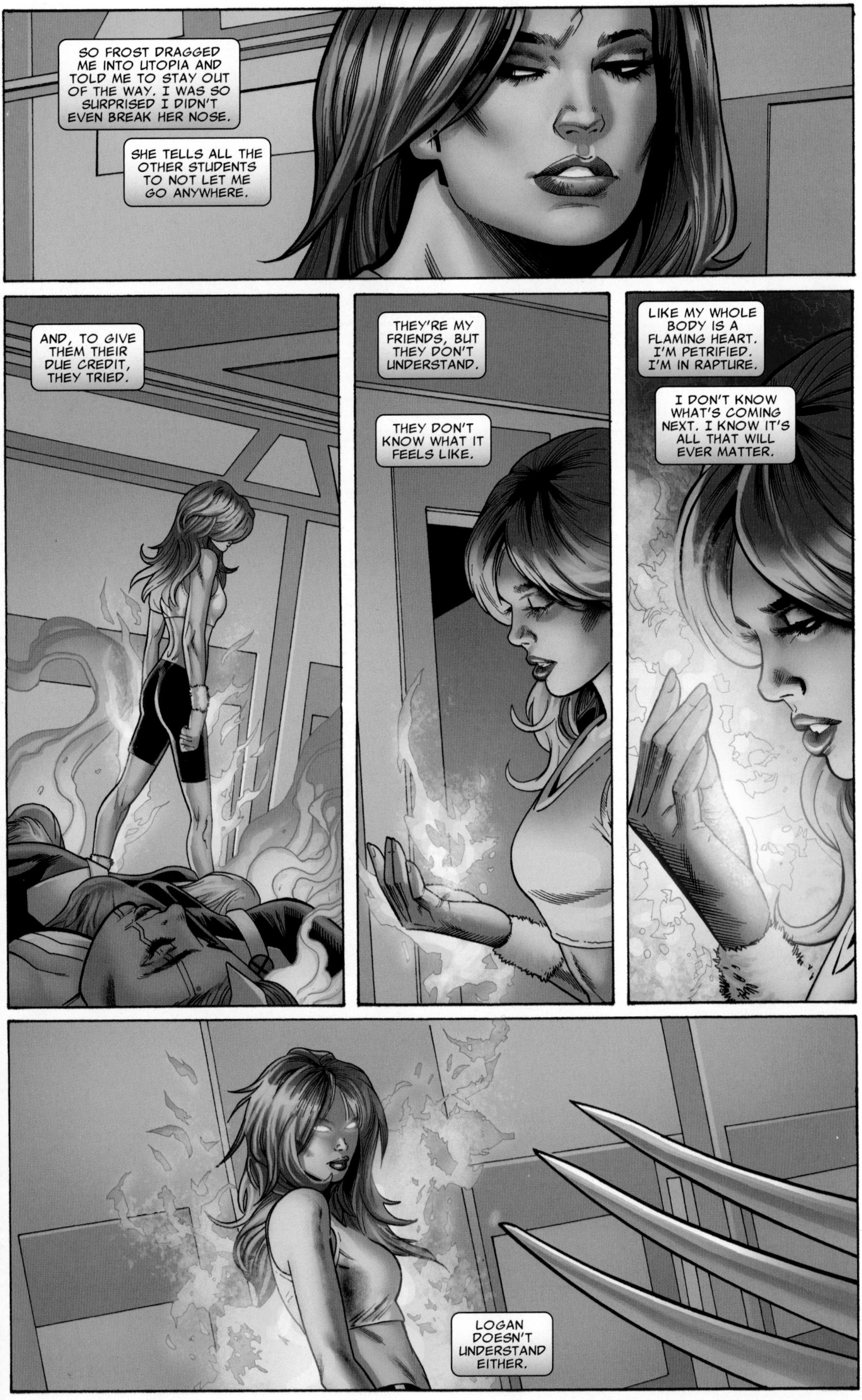
SO FROST DRAGGED ME INTO UTOPIA AND TOLD ME TO STAY OUT OF THE WAY. I WAS SO SURPRISED I DIDN'T EVEN BREAK HER NOSE.
SHE TELLS ALL THE OTHER STUDENTS TO NOT LET ME GO ANYWHERE.
AND, TO GIVE THEM THEIR DUE CREDIT, THEY TRIED.
THEY'RE MY FRIENDS, BUT THEY DON'T UNDERSTAND.
THEY DON'T KNOW WHAT IT FEELS LIKE.
LIKE MY WHOLE BODY IS A FLAMING HEART. I'M PETRIFIED. I'M IN RAPTURE.
I DON'T KNOW WHAT'S COMING NEXT. I KNOW IT'S ALL THAT WILL EVER MATTER.
LOGAN DOESN'T UNDERSTAND EITHER.

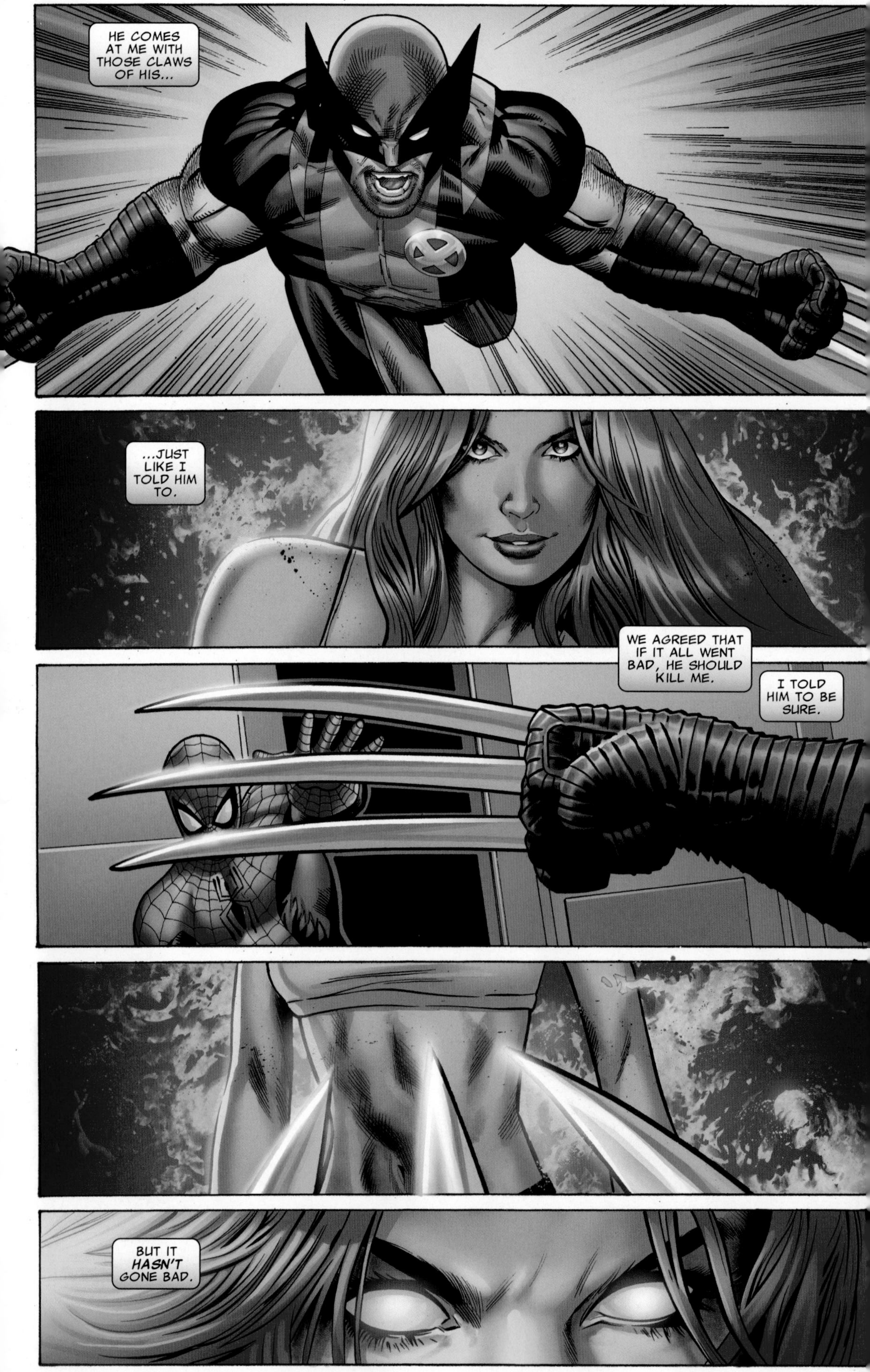
HE COMES AT ME WITH THOSE CLAWS OF HIS...
...JUST LIKE I TOLD HIM TO.
WE AGREED THAT IF IT ALL WENT BAD, HE SHOULD KILL ME.
I TOLD HIM TO BE SURE.
BUT IT *HASN'T* GONE BAD.

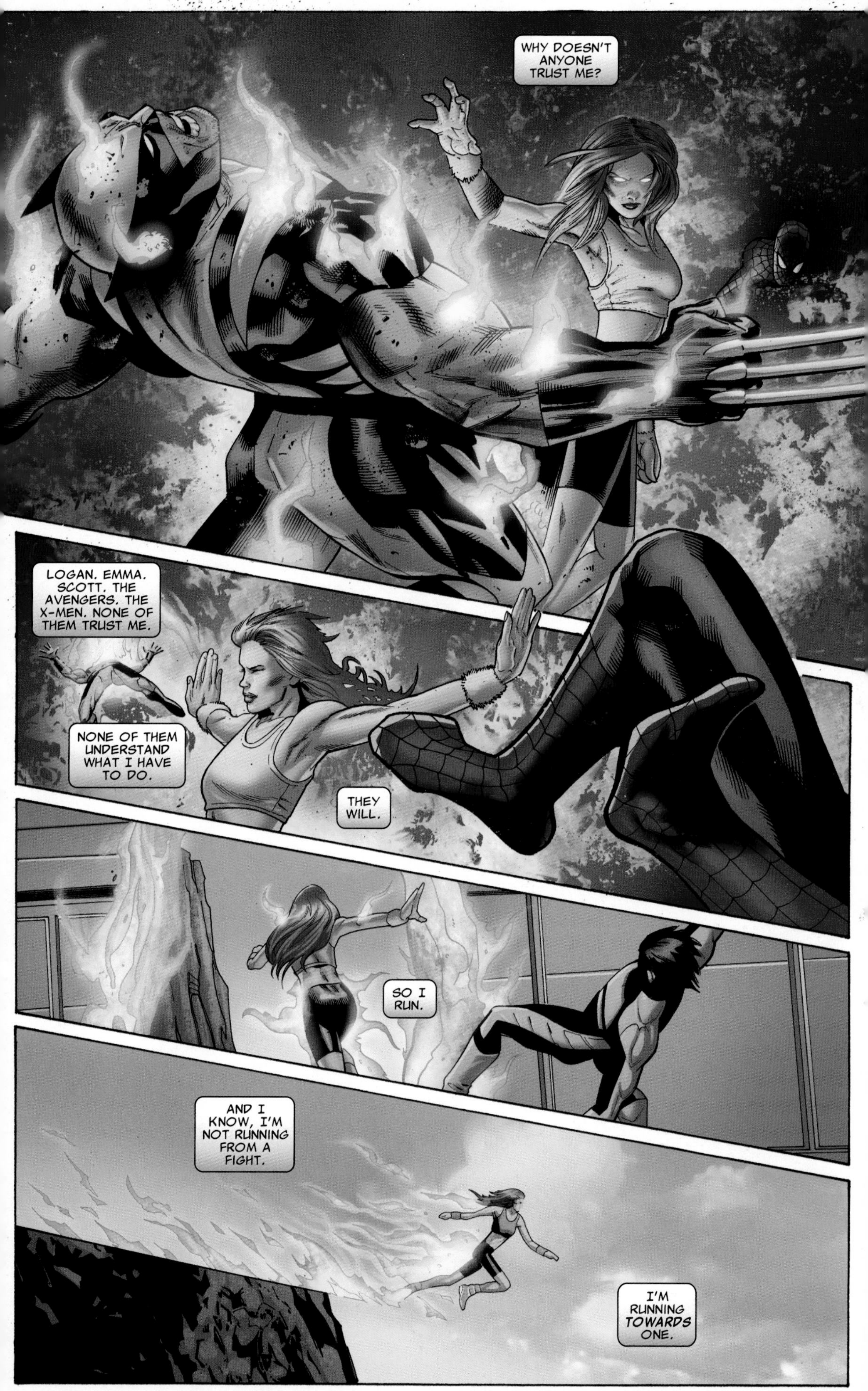
WHY DOESN'T ANYONE TRUST ME?
LOGAN. EMMA. SCOTT. THE AVENGERS. THE X-MEN. NONE OF THEM TRUST ME.
NONE OF THEM UNDERSTAND WHAT I HAVE TO DO.
THEY WILL.
SO I RUN.
AND I KNOW, I'M NOT RUNNING FROM A FIGHT.
I'M RUNNING TOWARDS ONE.

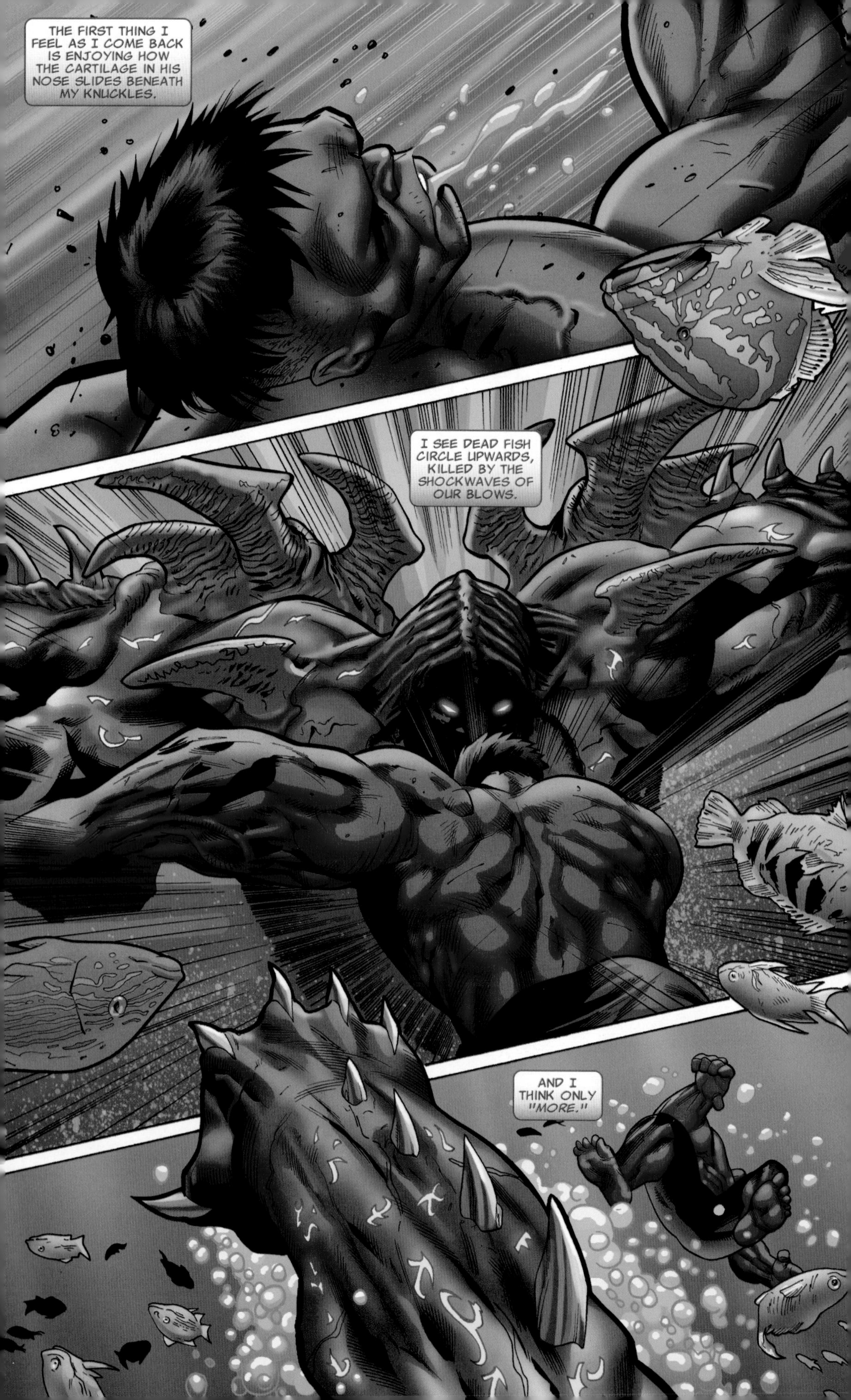
THE FIRST THING I FEEL AS I COME BACK IS ENJOYING HOW THE CARTILAGE IN HIS NOSE SLIDES BENEATH MY KNUCKLES.
I SEE DEAD FISH CIRCLE UPWARDS, KILLED BY THE SHOCKWAVES OF OUR BLOWS.
AND I THINK ONLY "MORE."

I SMILE AS HIS BLOOD TINTS THE SEA.

I ALWAYS WANTED TO WORK IN WATERCOLORS.

REGRETS? I HAVE REGRETS.

LIKE HIM ONLY HAVING SO MANY BONES IN HIS BODY.

AND EVENTUALLY I'LL BREAK THEM ALL.

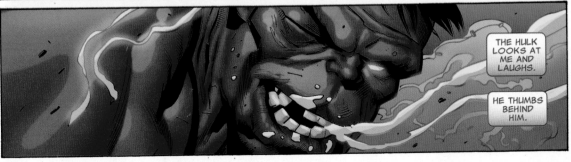

THE HULK LOOKS AT ME AND LAUGHS.

HE THUMBS BEHIND HIM.

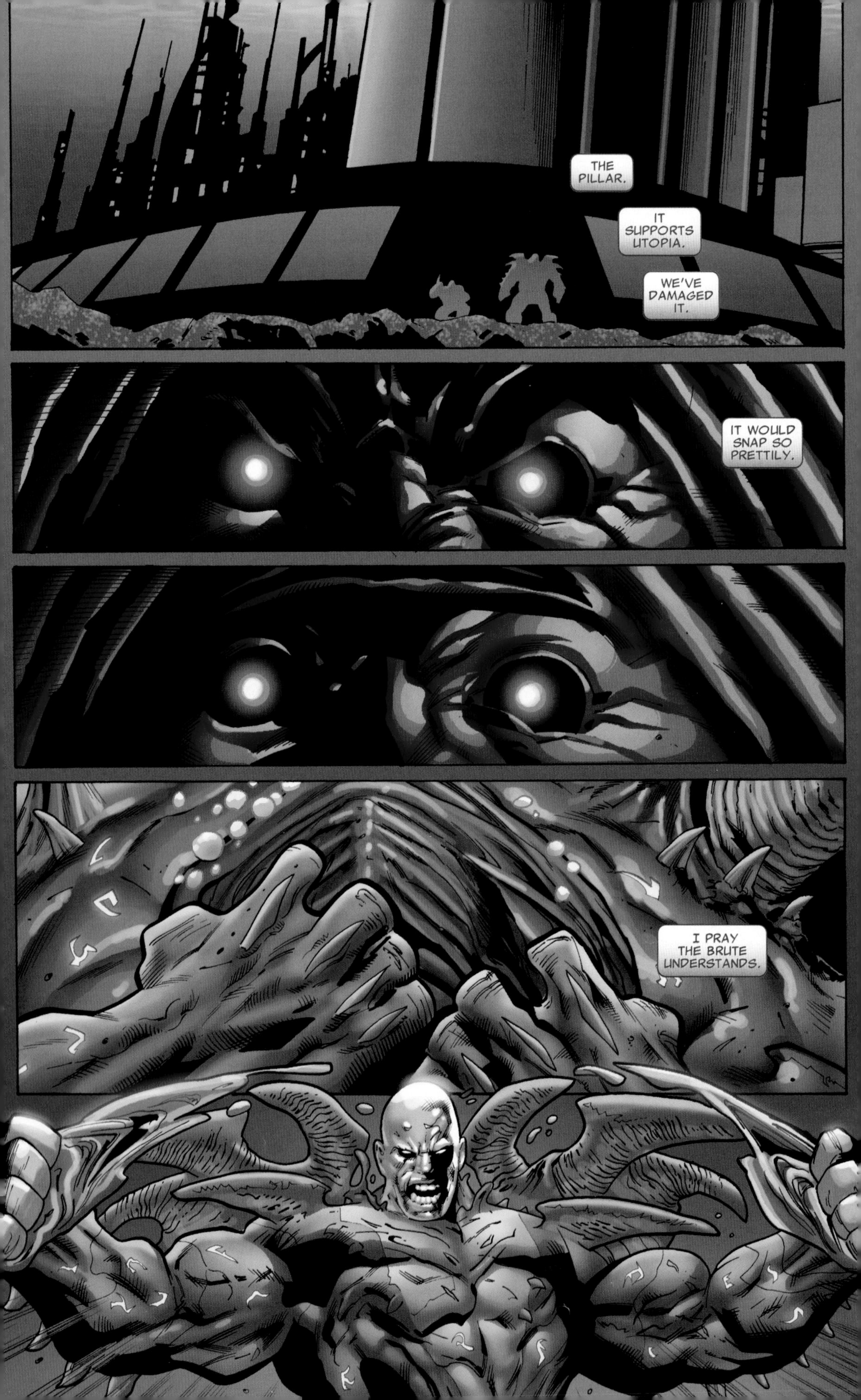
THE PILLAR.
IT SUPPORTS UTOPIA.
WE'VE DAMAGED IT.
IT WOULD SNAP SO PRETTILY.
I PRAY THE BRUTE UNDERSTANDS.

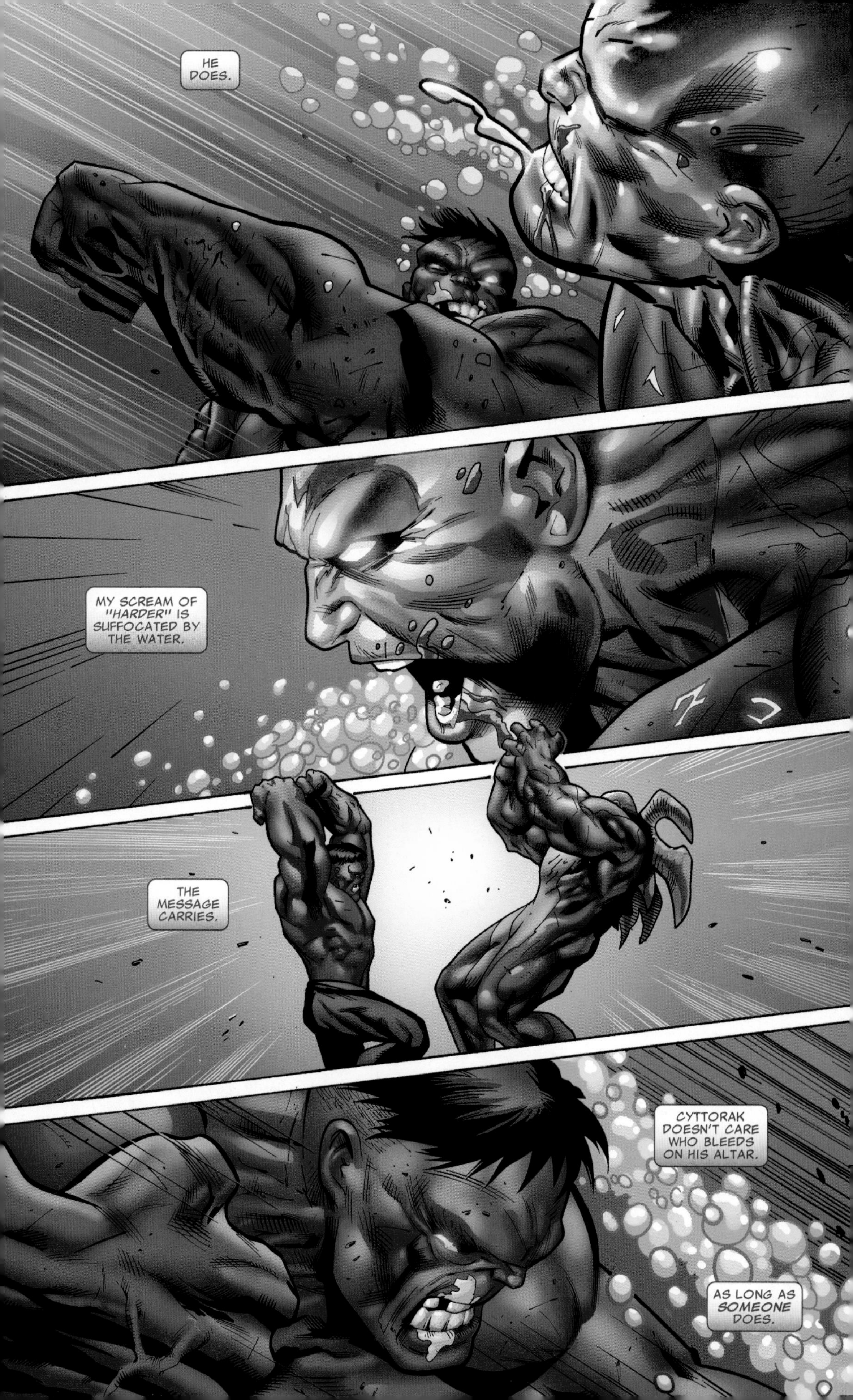
HE DOES.
MY SCREAM OF "HARDER" IS SUFFOCATED BY THE WATER.
THE MESSAGE CARRIES.
CYTTORAK DOESN'T CARE WHO BLEEDS ON HIS ALTAR.
AS LONG AS SOMEONE DOES.

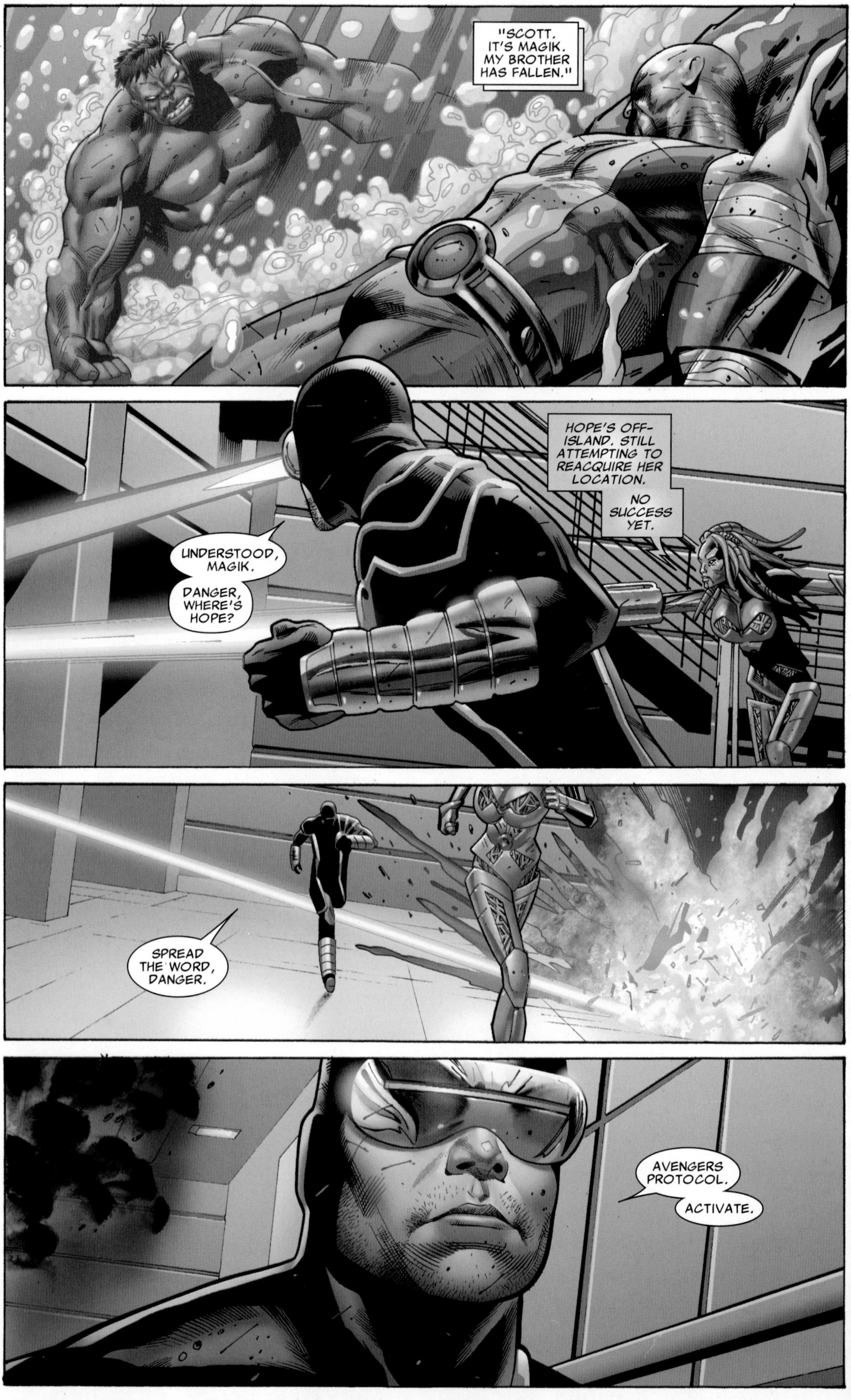
"SCOTT. IT'S MAGIK. MY BROTHER HAS FALLEN."
HOPE'S OFF-ISLAND. STILL ATTEMPTING TO REACQUIRE HER LOCATION.
NO SUCCESS YET.
UNDERSTOOD, MAGIK.
DANGER, WHERE'S HOPE?
SPREAD THE WORD, DANGER.
AVENGERS PROTOCOL.
ACTIVATE.

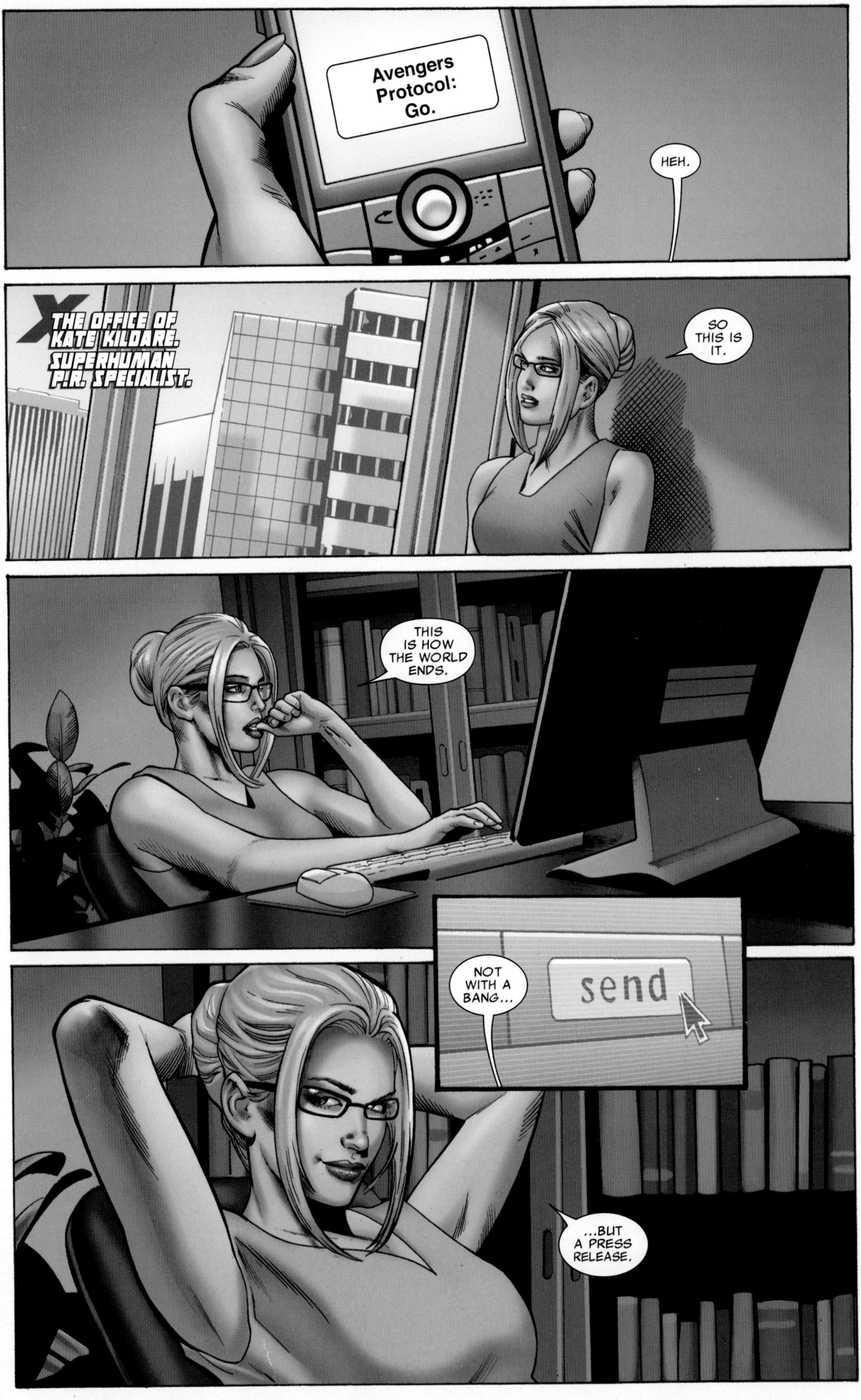
Avengers Protocol: Go.
HEH.
THE OFFICE OF KATE KILDARE. SUPERHUMAN P.R. SPECIALIST.
SO THIS IS IT.
THIS IS HOW THE WORLD ENDS.
send
NOT WITH A BANG...
...BUT A PRESS RELEASE.

A LETTER TO HUMANITY

Today, agents of the United States government came to our house to try to take a girl into their custody.

They will attempt to mitigate this by saying it wasn't an arrest.

I ask you, if someone arrives at your front door, wanting to take away your family, without any justification or permission, what would you call it?

This is worse than an arrest. This is an attempted kidnapping.

They will also attempt to justify this by saying "This girl is dangerous."

By which they mean "She is a mutant."

We have seen that mutant sovereignty, even if confined to a single island, will never be respected. WE will never be respected. Those who claim to fight for a better world are those who would keep us on our knees. Their jackboot rises only so it can crash down harder.

Previously, I have made threats. I implied there would be a price to pay for a transgression like this. I noted that we possess the power to destroy whole cities if those who persecuted us did not relent. I said that if we were pushed, there would be consequences.

They pushed us.

We have just been proven liars. Be grateful we aren't as bad as you think we are.

In the days that come, remember this was not of our choosing. But know that even if we forgive it, we will not forget the day when our worst fears were proved true. That even those who claimed to be our friends thought us property.

Cyclops,
Utopia

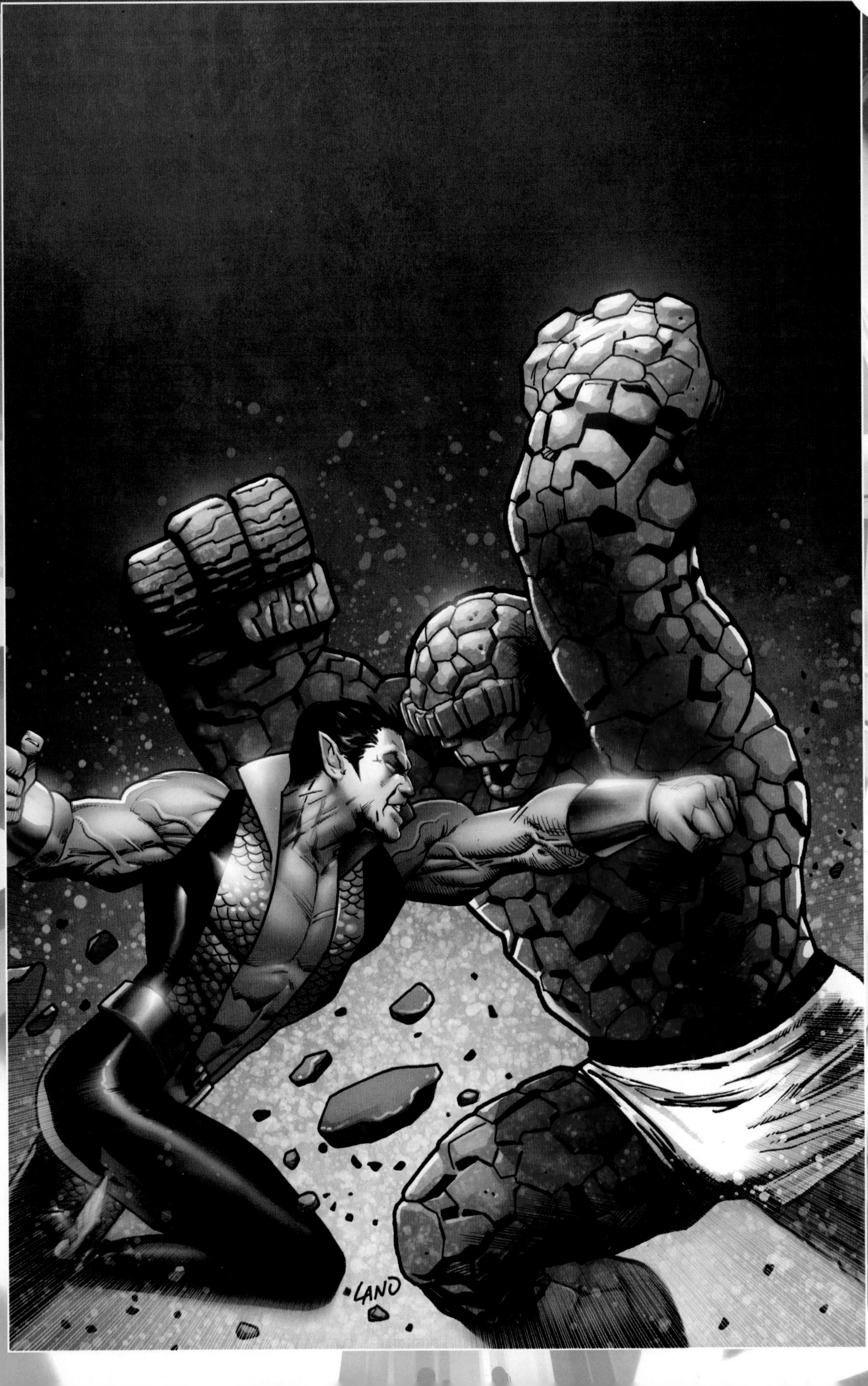
LAND

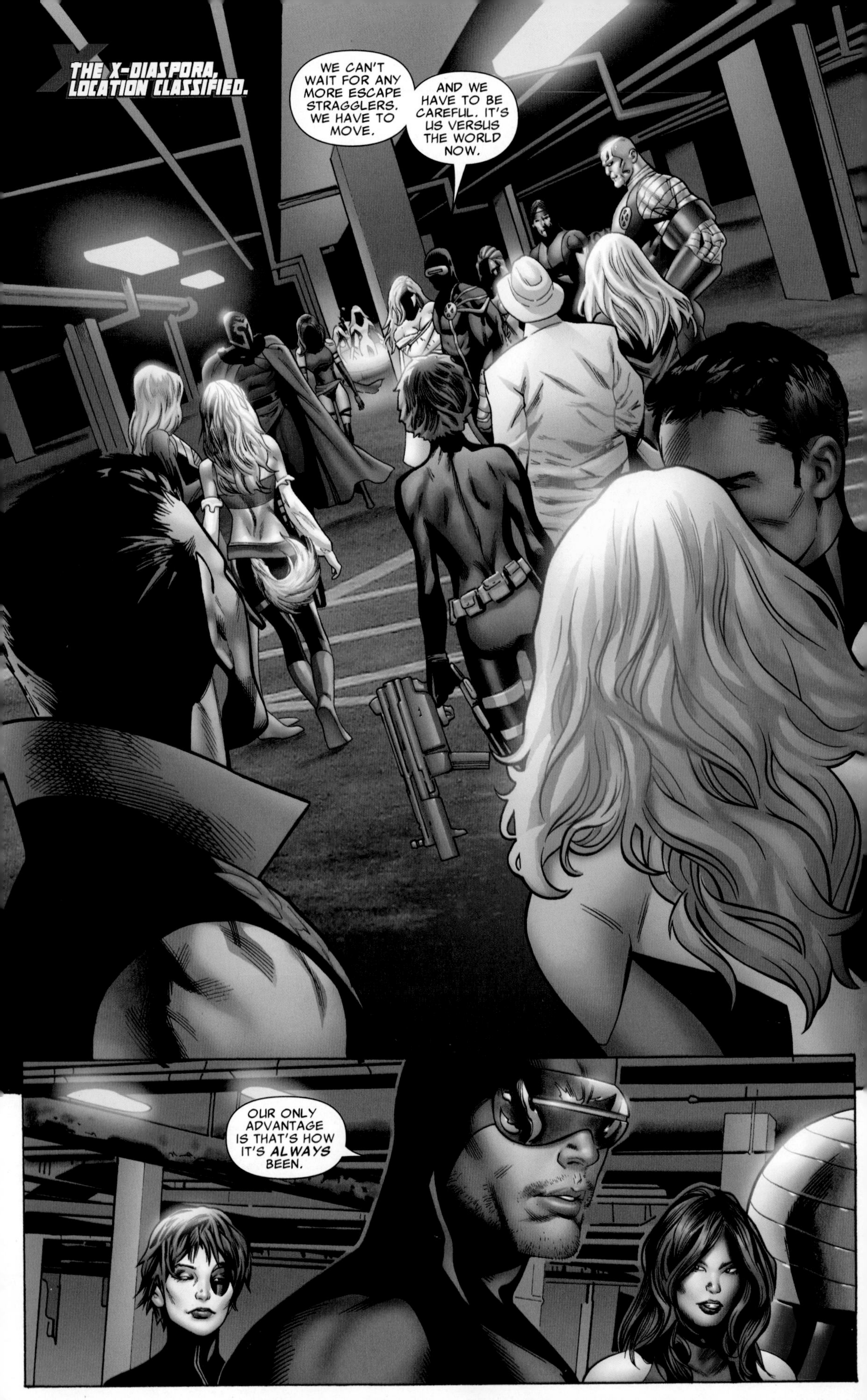
THE X-DIASPORA, LOCATION CLASSIFIED.
WE CAN'T WAIT FOR ANY MORE ESCAPE STRAGGLERS. WE HAVE TO MOVE.
AND WE HAVE TO BE CAREFUL. IT'S US VERSUS THE WORLD NOW.
OUR ONLY ADVANTAGE IS THAT'S HOW IT'S ALWAYS BEEN.

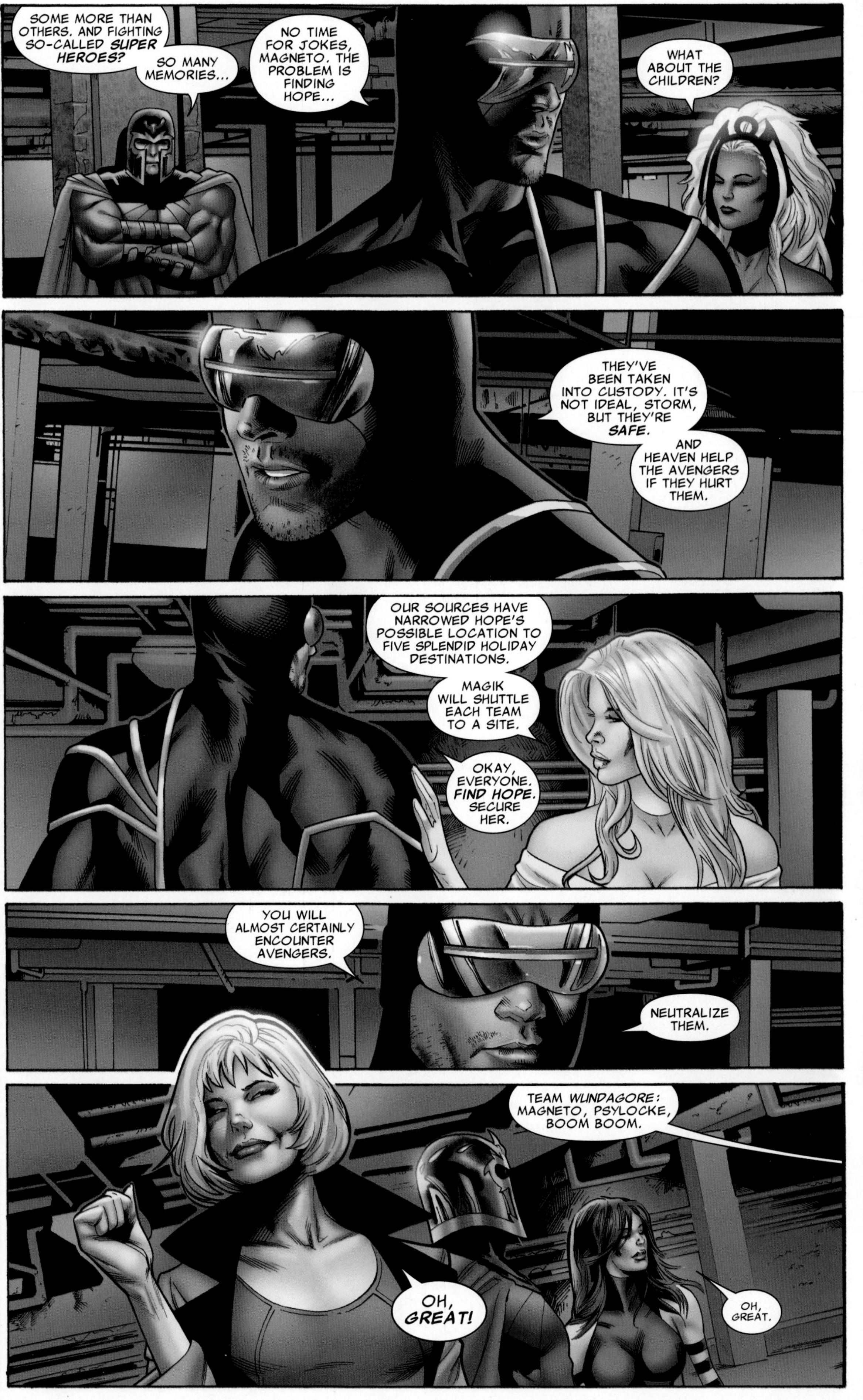
SOME MORE THAN OTHERS. AND FIGHTING SO-CALLED **SUPER HEROES?**
SO MANY MEMORIES...
NO TIME FOR JOKES, MAGNETO. THE PROBLEM IS FINDING HOPE...
WHAT ABOUT THE CHILDREN?
THEY'VE BEEN TAKEN INTO CUSTODY. IT'S NOT IDEAL, STORM, BUT THEY'RE **SAFE.**
AND HEAVEN HELP THE AVENGERS IF THEY HURT THEM.
OUR SOURCES HAVE NARROWED HOPE'S POSSIBLE LOCATION TO FIVE SPLENDID HOLIDAY DESTINATIONS.
MAGIK WILL SHUTTLE EACH TEAM TO A SITE.
OKAY, EVERYONE. **FIND HOPE.** SECURE HER.
YOU WILL ALMOST CERTAINLY ENCOUNTER AVENGERS.
NEUTRALIZE THEM.
TEAM *WUNDAGORE:* MAGNETO, PSYLOCKE, BOOM BOOM.
OH, **GREAT!**
OH, GREAT.

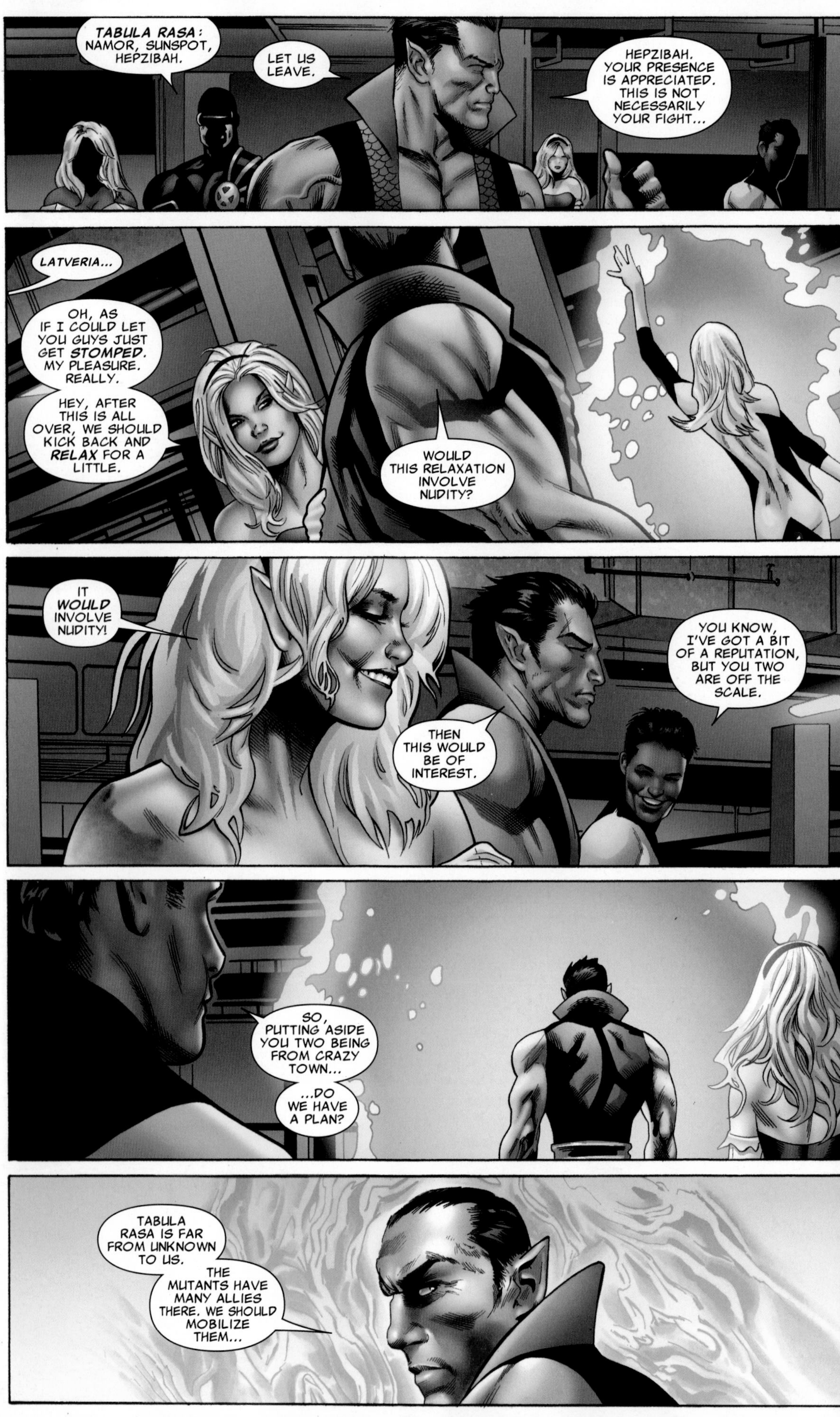
TABULA RASA: NAMOR, SUNSPOT, HEPZIBAH.
LET US LEAVE.
HEPZIBAH. YOUR PRESENCE IS APPRECIATED. THIS IS NOT NECESSARILY YOUR FIGHT...
LATVERIA...
OH, AS IF I COULD LET YOU GUYS JUST GET STOMPED. MY PLEASURE. REALLY.
HEY, AFTER THIS IS ALL OVER, WE SHOULD KICK BACK AND RELAX FOR A LITTLE.
WOULD THIS RELAXATION INVOLVE NUDITY?
IT WOULD INVOLVE NUDITY!
THEN THIS WOULD BE OF INTEREST.
YOU KNOW, I'VE GOT A BIT OF A REPUTATION, BUT YOU TWO ARE OFF THE SCALE.
SO, PUTTING ASIDE YOU TWO BEING FROM CRAZY TOWN...
...DO WE HAVE A PLAN?
TABULA RASA IS FAR FROM UNKNOWN TO US.
THE MUTANTS HAVE MANY ALLIES THERE. WE SHOULD MOBILIZE THEM...

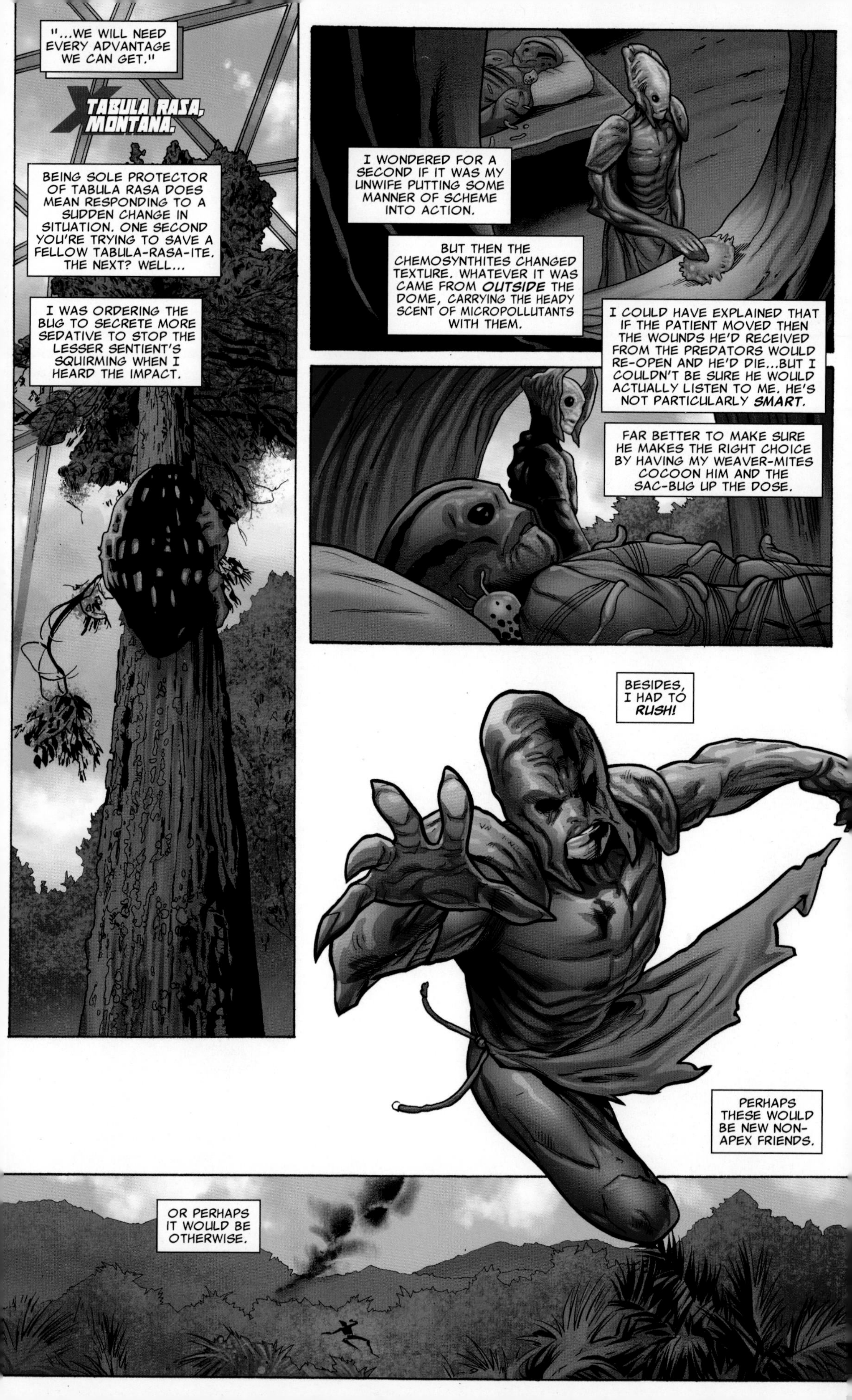
"...WE WILL NEED EVERY ADVANTAGE WE CAN GET."
TABULA RASA, MONTANA.
BEING SOLE PROTECTOR OF TABULA RASA DOES MEAN RESPONDING TO A SUDDEN CHANGE IN SITUATION. ONE SECOND YOU'RE TRYING TO SAVE A FELLOW TABULA-RASA-ITE. THE NEXT? WELL...
I WAS ORDERING THE BUG TO SECRETE MORE SEDATIVE TO STOP THE LESSER SENTIENT'S SQUIRMING WHEN I HEARD THE IMPACT.
I WONDERED FOR A SECOND IF IT WAS MY UNWIFE PUTTING SOME MANNER OF SCHEME INTO ACTION.
BUT THEN THE CHEMOSYNTHITES CHANGED TEXTURE. WHATEVER IT WAS CAME FROM OUTSIDE THE DOME, CARRYING THE HEADY SCENT OF MICROPOLLUTANTS WITH THEM.
I COULD HAVE EXPLAINED THAT IF THE PATIENT MOVED THEN THE WOUNDS HE'D RECEIVED FROM THE PREDATORS WOULD RE-OPEN AND HE'D DIE...BUT I COULDN'T BE SURE HE WOULD ACTUALLY LISTEN TO ME. HE'S NOT PARTICULARLY SMART.
FAR BETTER TO MAKE SURE HE MAKES THE RIGHT CHOICE BY HAVING MY WEAVER-MITES COCOON HIM AND THE SAC-BUG UP THE DOSE.
BESIDES, I HAD TO RUSH!
PERHAPS THESE WOULD BE NEW NON-APEX FRIENDS.
OR PERHAPS IT WOULD BE OTHERWISE.

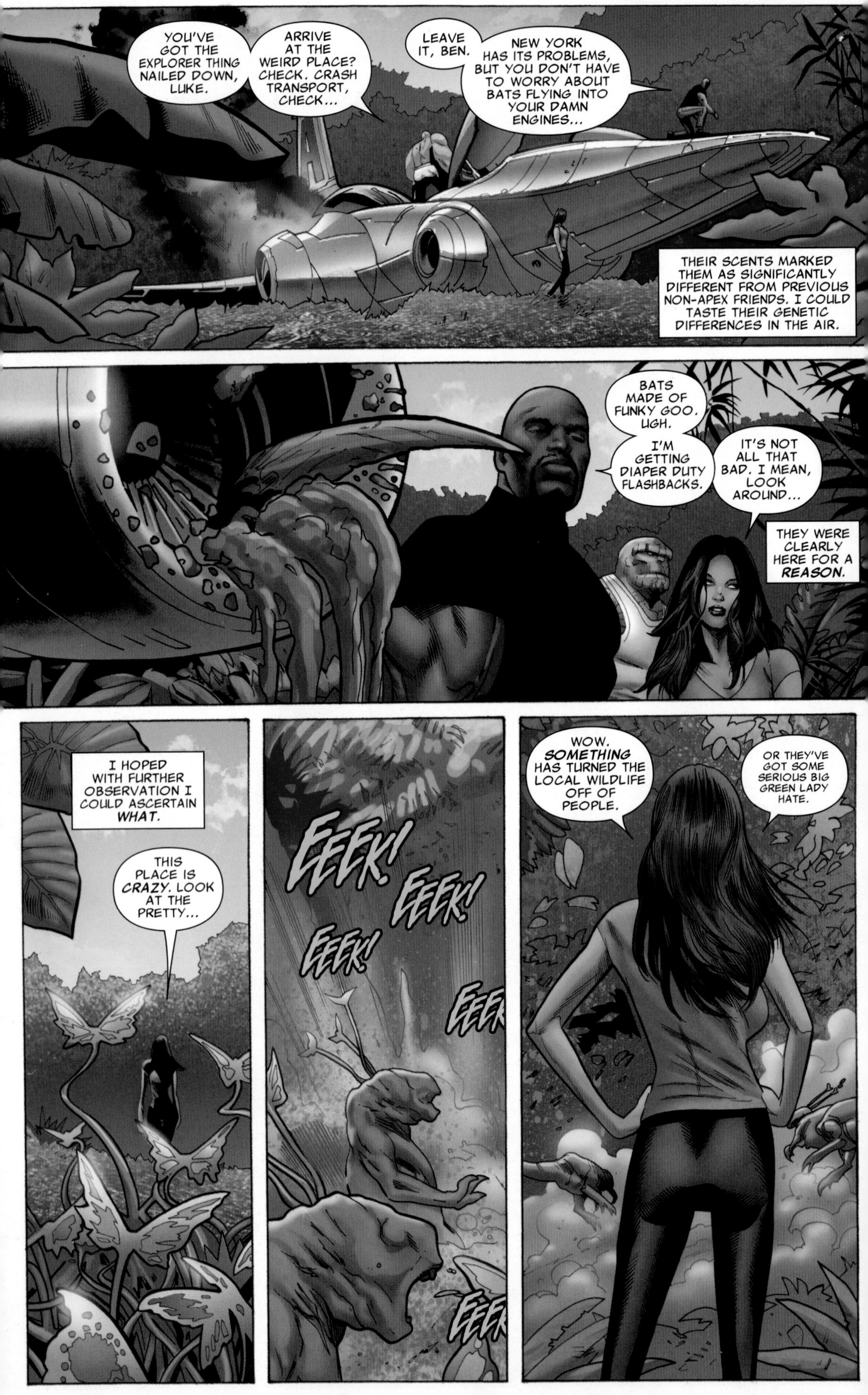

YOU'VE GOT THE EXPLORER THING NAILED DOWN, LUKE.
ARRIVE AT THE WEIRD PLACE? CHECK. CRASH TRANSPORT, CHECK...
LEAVE IT, BEN.
NEW YORK HAS ITS PROBLEMS, BUT YOU DON'T HAVE TO WORRY ABOUT BATS FLYING INTO YOUR DAMN ENGINES...
THEIR SCENTS MARKED THEM AS SIGNIFICANTLY DIFFERENT FROM PREVIOUS NON-APEX FRIENDS. I COULD TASTE THEIR GENETIC DIFFERENCES IN THE AIR.
BATS MADE OF FUNKY GOO. UGH.
I'M GETTING DIAPER DUTY FLASHBACKS.
IT'S NOT ALL THAT BAD. I MEAN, LOOK AROUND...
THEY WERE CLEARLY HERE FOR A REASON.
I HOPED WITH FURTHER OBSERVATION I COULD ASCERTAIN WHAT.
THIS PLACE IS CRAZY. LOOK AT THE PRETTY...
EEEK!
EEEK!
EEEK!
WOW. SOMETHING HAS TURNED THE LOCAL WILDLIFE OFF OF PEOPLE.
OR THEY'VE GOT SOME SERIOUS BIG GREEN LADY HATE.

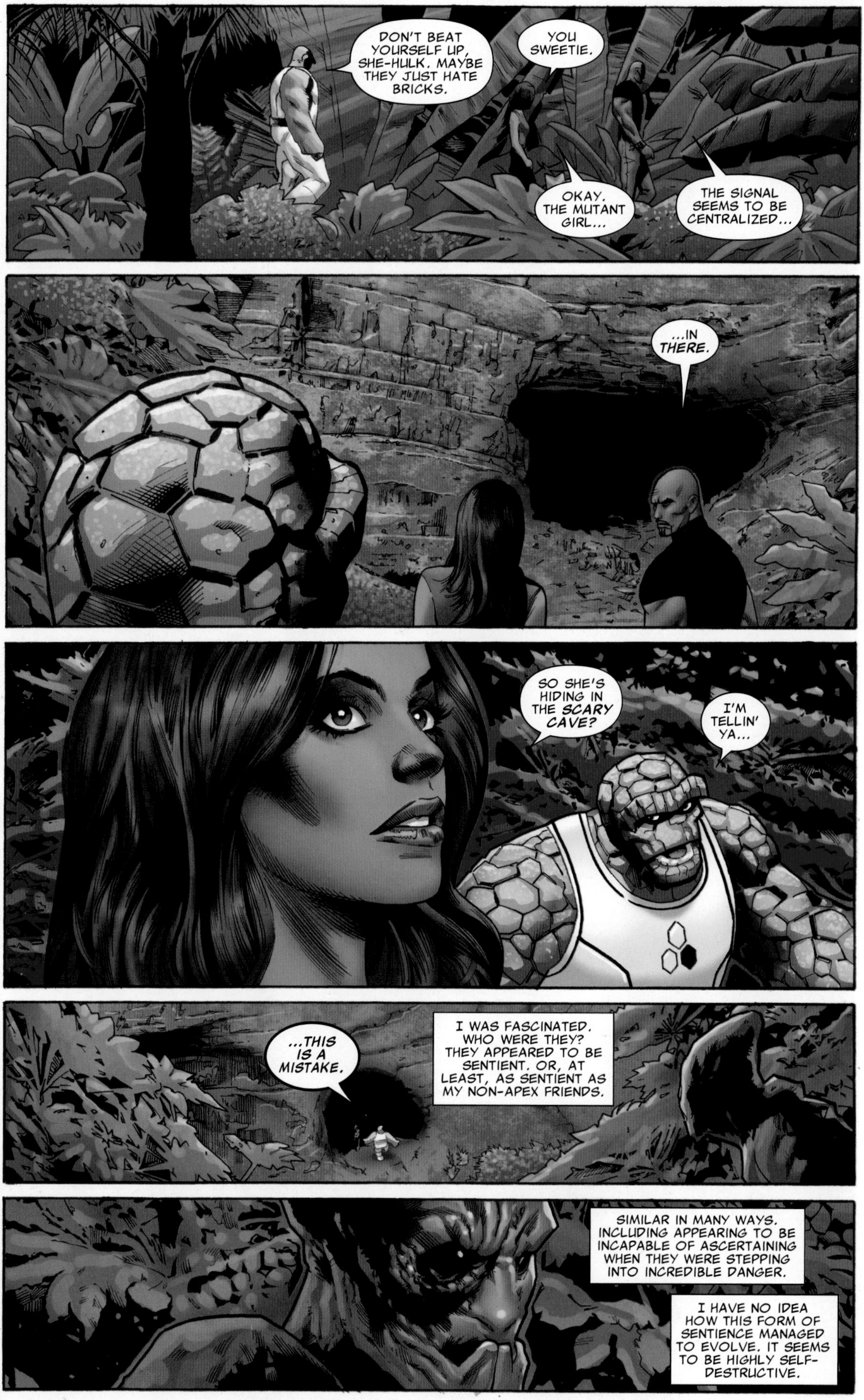
DON'T BEAT YOURSELF UP, SHE-HULK. MAYBE THEY JUST HATE BRICKS.
YOU SWEETIE.
OKAY. THE MUTANT GIRL...
THE SIGNAL SEEMS TO BE CENTRALIZED...
...IN THERE.
SO SHE'S HIDING IN THE SCARY CAVE?
I'M TELLIN' YA...
...THIS IS A MISTAKE.
I WAS FASCINATED. WHO WERE THEY? THEY APPEARED TO BE SENTIENT. OR, AT LEAST, AS SENTIENT AS MY NON-APEX FRIENDS.
SIMILAR IN MANY WAYS. INCLUDING APPEARING TO BE INCAPABLE OF ASCERTAINING WHEN THEY WERE STEPPING INTO INCREDIBLE DANGER.
I HAVE NO IDEA HOW THIS FORM OF SENTIENCE MANAGED TO EVOLVE. IT SEEMS TO BE HIGHLY SELF-DESTRUCTIVE.

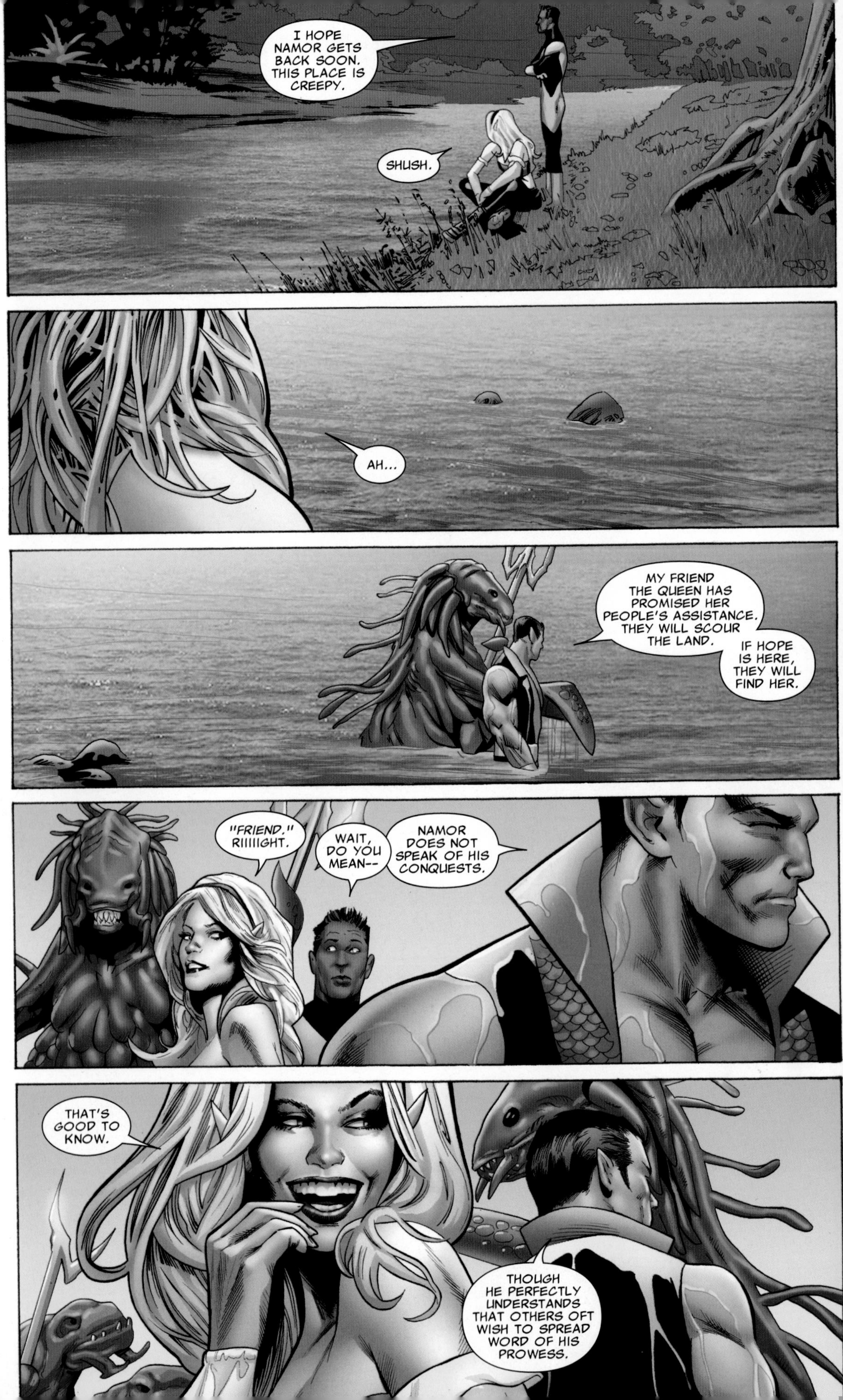
I HOPE NAMOR GETS BACK SOON. THIS PLACE IS CREEPY.
SHUSH.
AH...
MY FRIEND THE QUEEN HAS PROMISED HER PEOPLE'S ASSISTANCE. THEY WILL SCOUR THE LAND.
IF HOPE IS HERE, THEY WILL FIND HER.
"FRIEND." RIIIIIGHT.
WAIT, DO YOU MEAN--
NAMOR DOES NOT SPEAK OF HIS CONQUESTS.
THAT'S GOOD TO KNOW.
THOUGH HE PERFECTLY UNDERSTANDS THAT OTHERS OFT WISH TO SPREAD WORD OF HIS PROWESS.

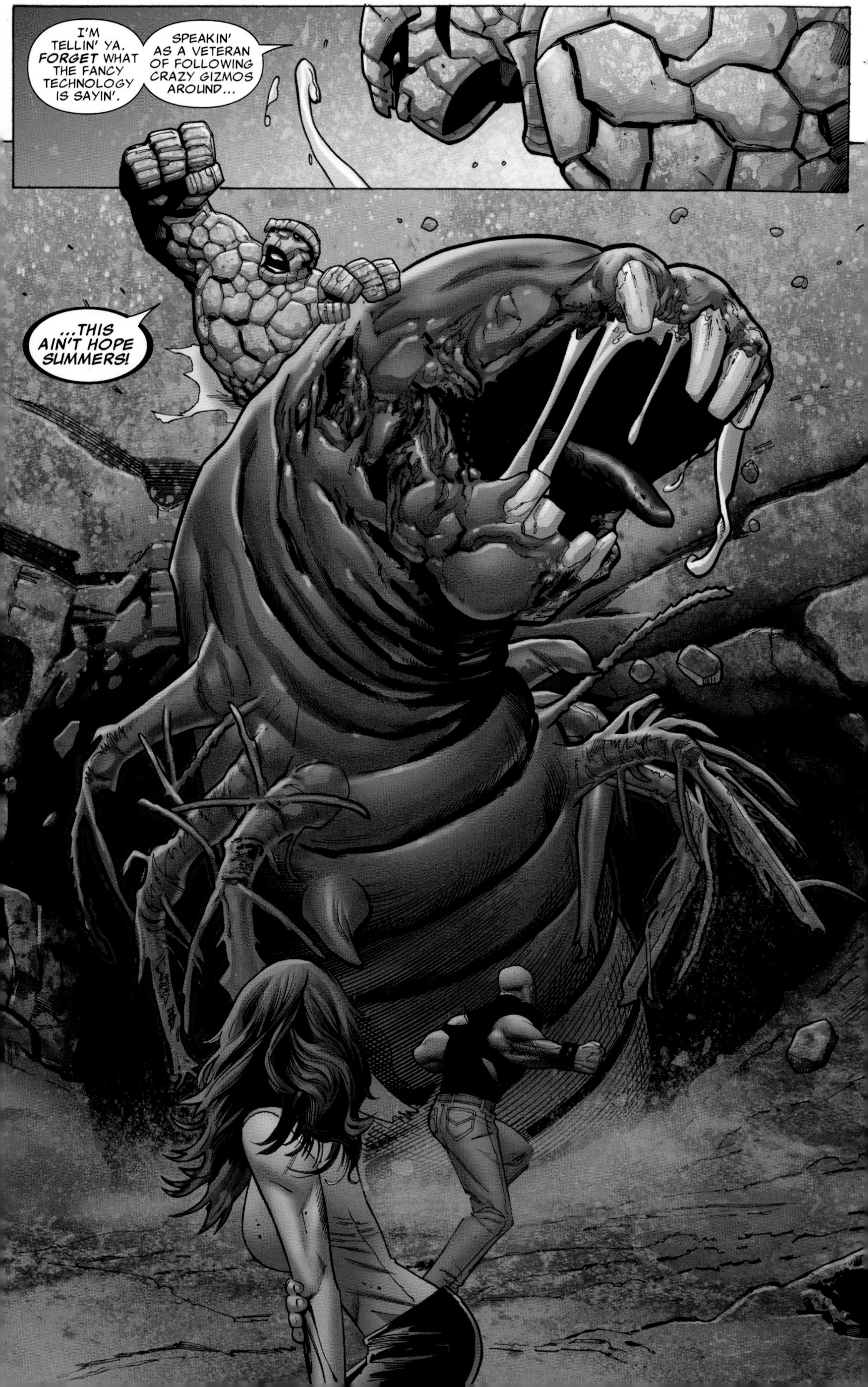
I'M TELLIN' YA. FORGET WHAT THE FANCY TECHNOLOGY IS SAYIN'.
SPEAKIN' AS A VETERAN OF FOLLOWING CRAZY GIZMOS AROUND...
...THIS AIN'T HOPE SUMMERS!

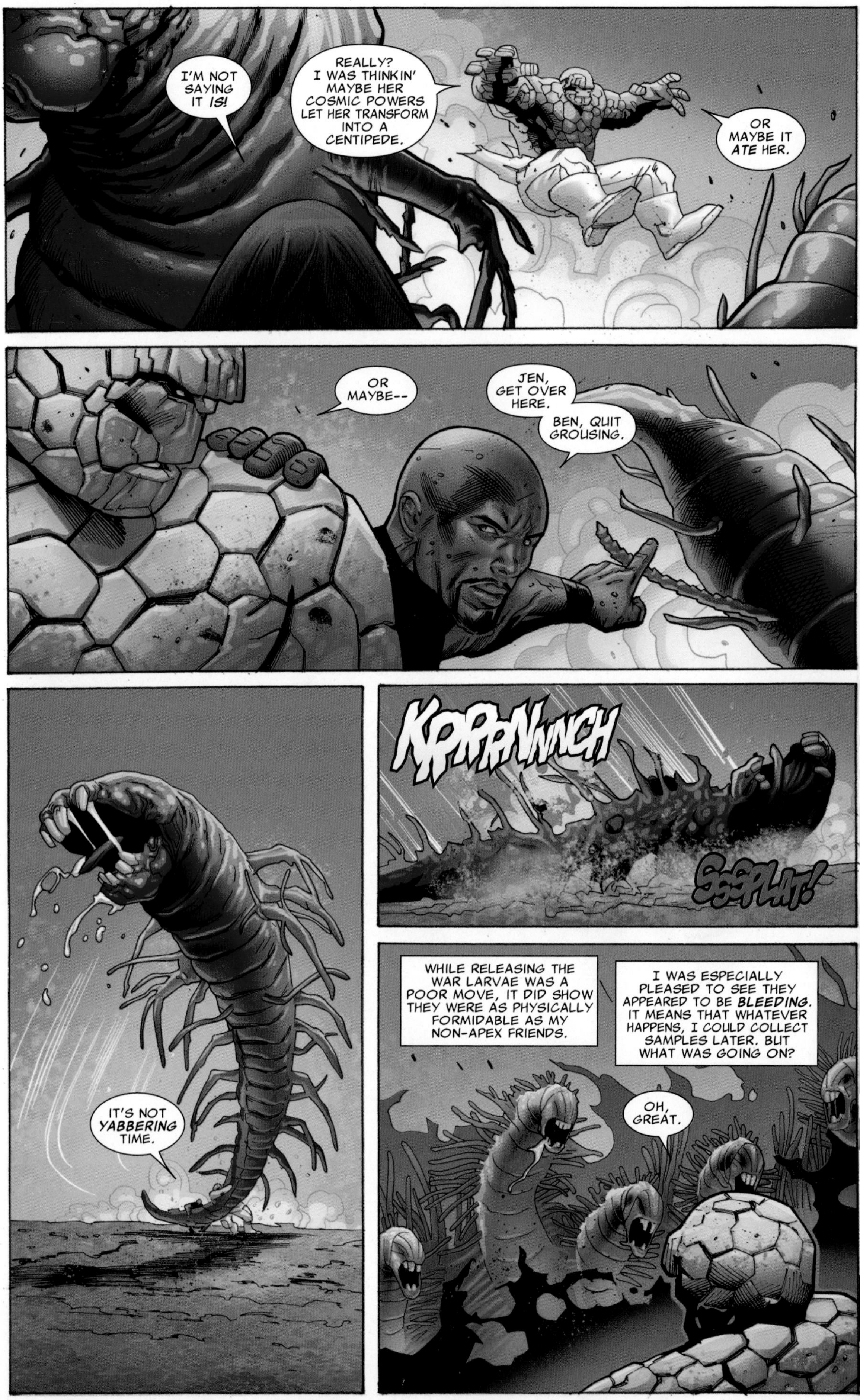
I'M NOT SAYING IT IS!
REALLY? I WAS THINKIN' MAYBE HER COSMIC POWERS LET HER TRANSFORM INTO A CENTIPEDE.
OR MAYBE IT ATE HER.
OR MAYBE--
JEN, GET OVER HERE.
BEN, QUIT GROUSING.
IT'S NOT YABBERING TIME.
KPRRNNNCH
SSSPLAT!
WHILE RELEASING THE WAR LARVAE WAS A POOR MOVE, IT DID SHOW THEY WERE AS PHYSICALLY FORMIDABLE AS MY NON-APEX FRIENDS.
I WAS ESPECIALLY PLEASED TO SEE THEY APPEARED TO BE BLEEDING. IT MEANS THAT WHATEVER HAPPENS, I COULD COLLECT SAMPLES LATER. BUT WHAT WAS GOING ON?
OH, GREAT.

I'LL TELL YOU WHAT...

...THIS IS THE WAY TO TRAVEL.

OUR THANKS FOR YOUR ASSISTANCE, MY QUEEN. IF YOUR PEOPLE WOULD CONTINUE WITHOUT US...

...I CAN SEE WE HAVE A SMALL MATTER TO DEAL WITH UP AHEAD.

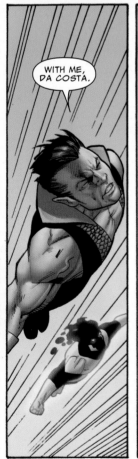

WITH ME, DA COSTA.

SO, WHAT'S HE LIKE? YOU CAN TELL ME.

JUST GIRL TALK.

OoOoH, YEAH.

HMM. I FEEL I AM BEING TALKED ABOUT.

THIS IS ONLY CORRECT.

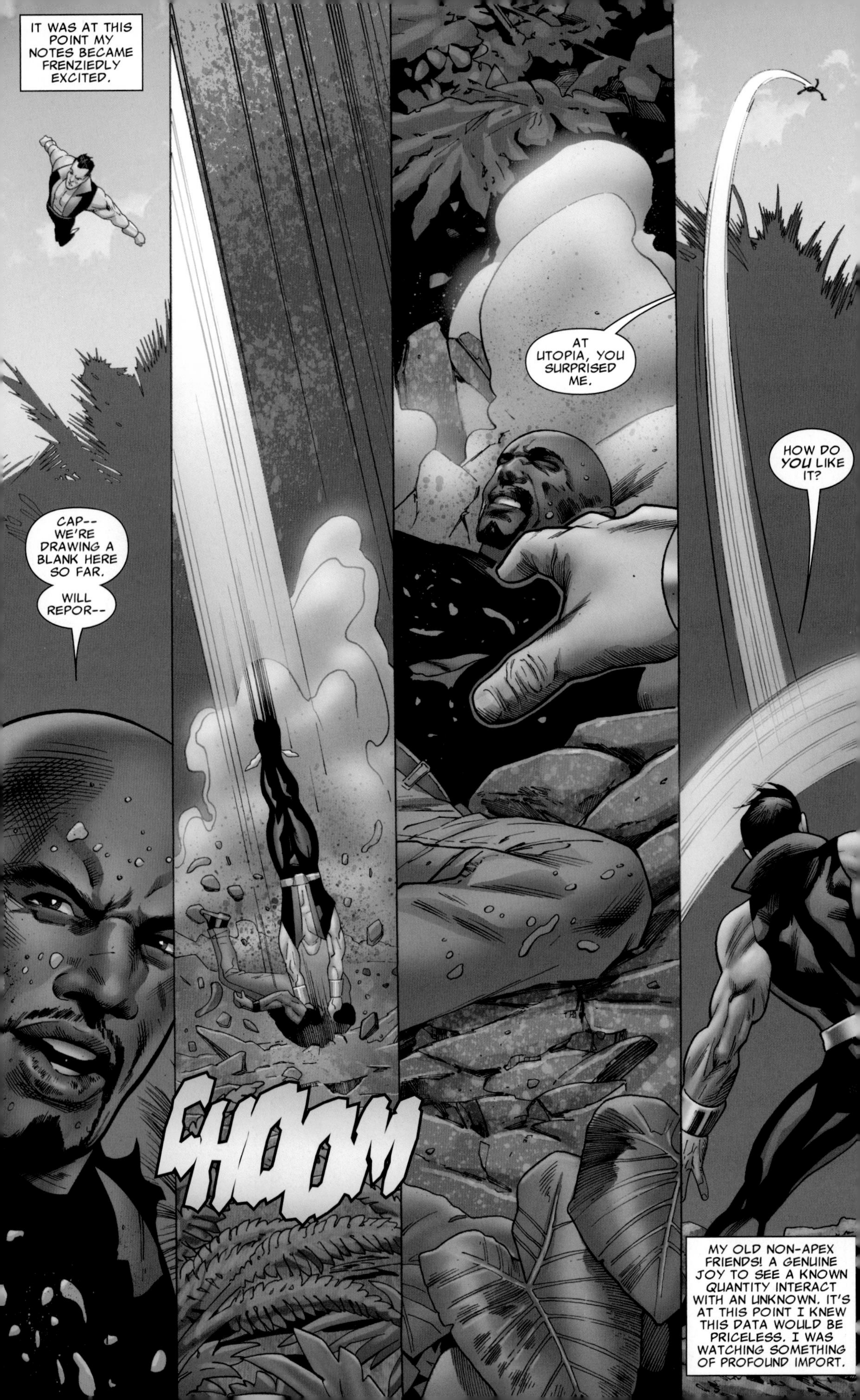
IT WAS AT THIS POINT MY NOTES BECAME FRENZIEDLY EXCITED.
CAP-- WE'RE DRAWING A BLANK HERE SO FAR.
WILL REPOR--
CHOOM
AT UTOPIA, YOU SURPRISED ME.
HOW DO YOU LIKE IT?
MY OLD NON-APEX FRIENDS! A GENUINE JOY TO SEE A KNOWN QUANTITY INTERACT WITH AN UNKNOWN. IT'S AT THIS POINT I KNEW THIS DATA WOULD BE PRICELESS. I WAS WATCHING SOMETHING OF PROFOUND IMPORT.

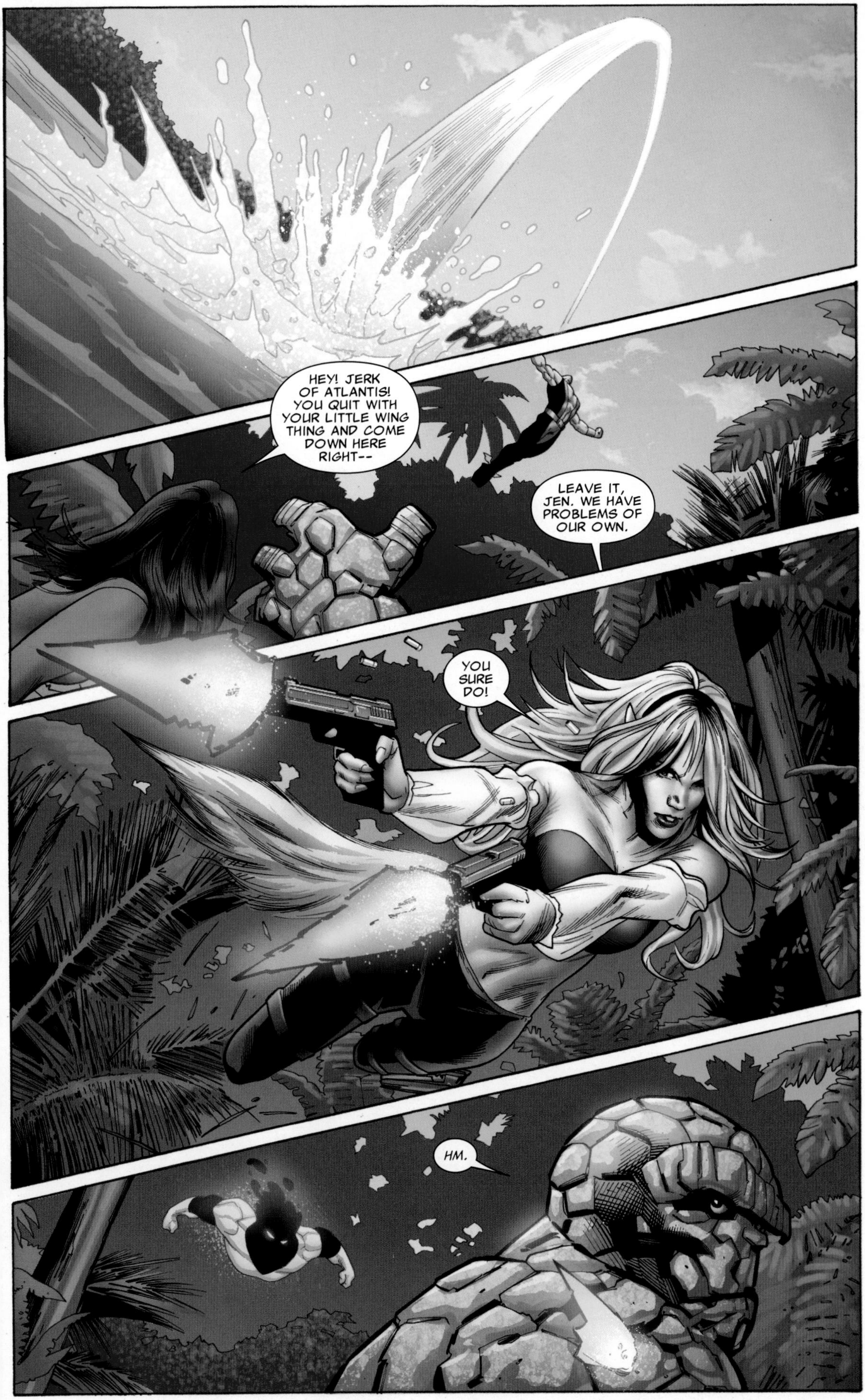
HEY! JERK OF ATLANTIS! YOU QUIT WITH YOUR LITTLE WING THING AND COME DOWN HERE RIGHT--
LEAVE IT, JEN. WE HAVE PROBLEMS OF OUR OWN.
YOU SURE DO!
HM.

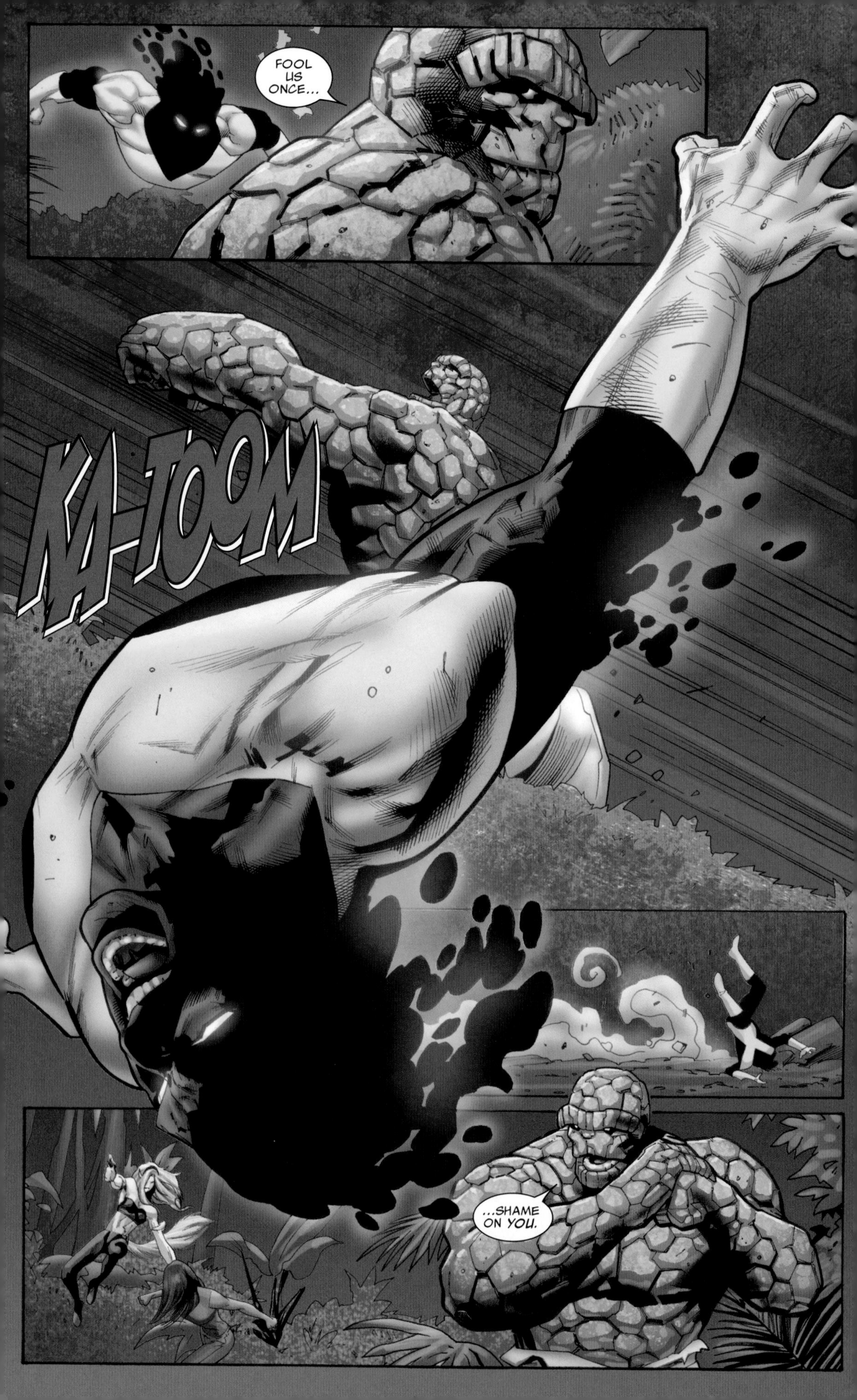
FOOL US ONCE...
KA-TOOM
...SHAME ON YOU.

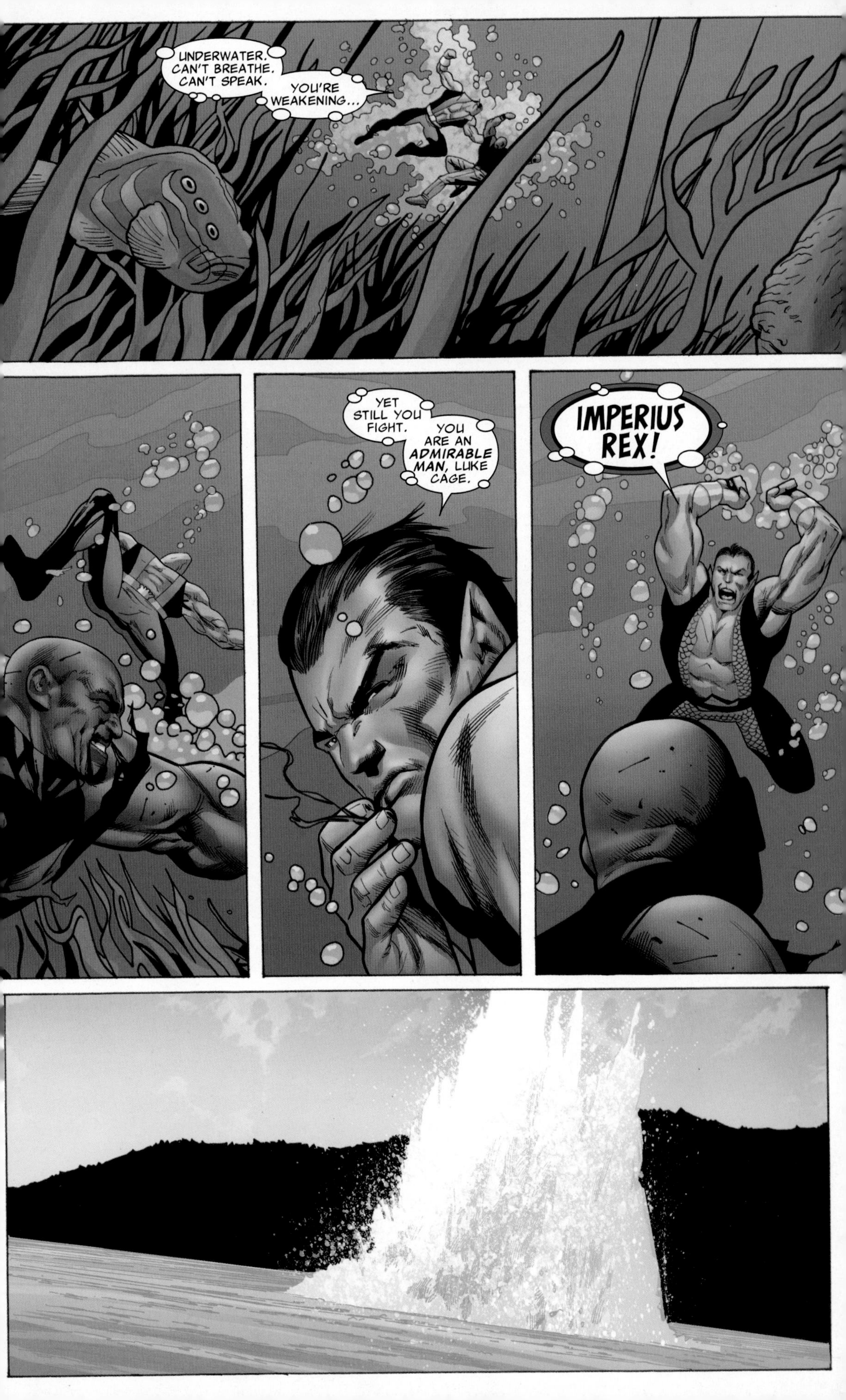
UNDERWATER. CAN'T BREATHE. CAN'T SPEAK.
YOU'RE WEAKENING...
YET STILL YOU FIGHT.
YOU ARE AN ADMIRABLE MAN, LUKE CAGE.
IMPERIUS REX!

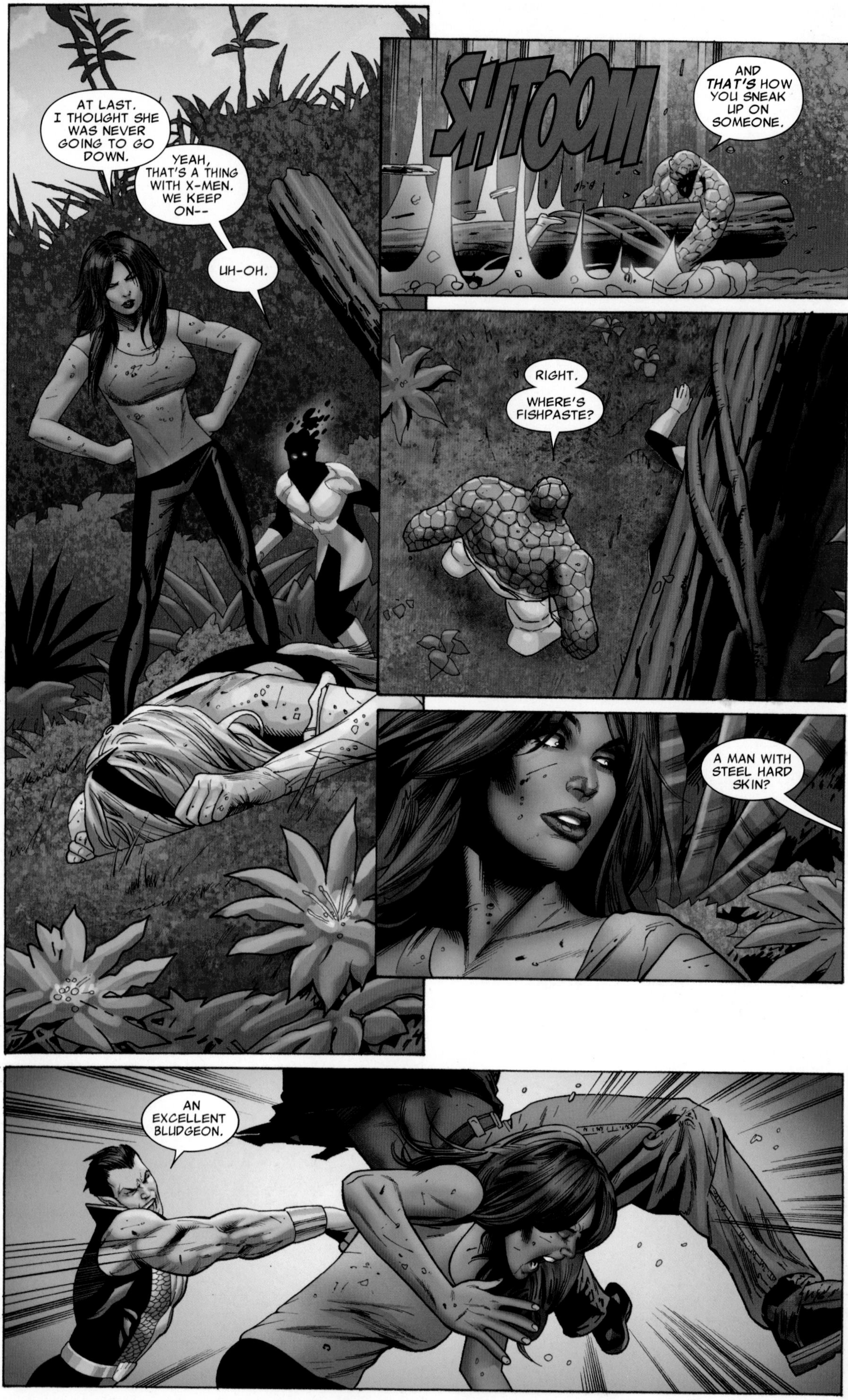
AT LAST. I THOUGHT SHE WAS NEVER GOING TO GO DOWN.
YEAH, THAT'S A THING WITH X-MEN. WE KEEP ON--
UH-OH.
SHTOOM
AND THAT'S HOW YOU SNEAK UP ON SOMEONE.
RIGHT.
WHERE'S FISHPASTE?
A MAN WITH STEEL HARD SKIN?
AN EXCELLENT BLUDGEON.

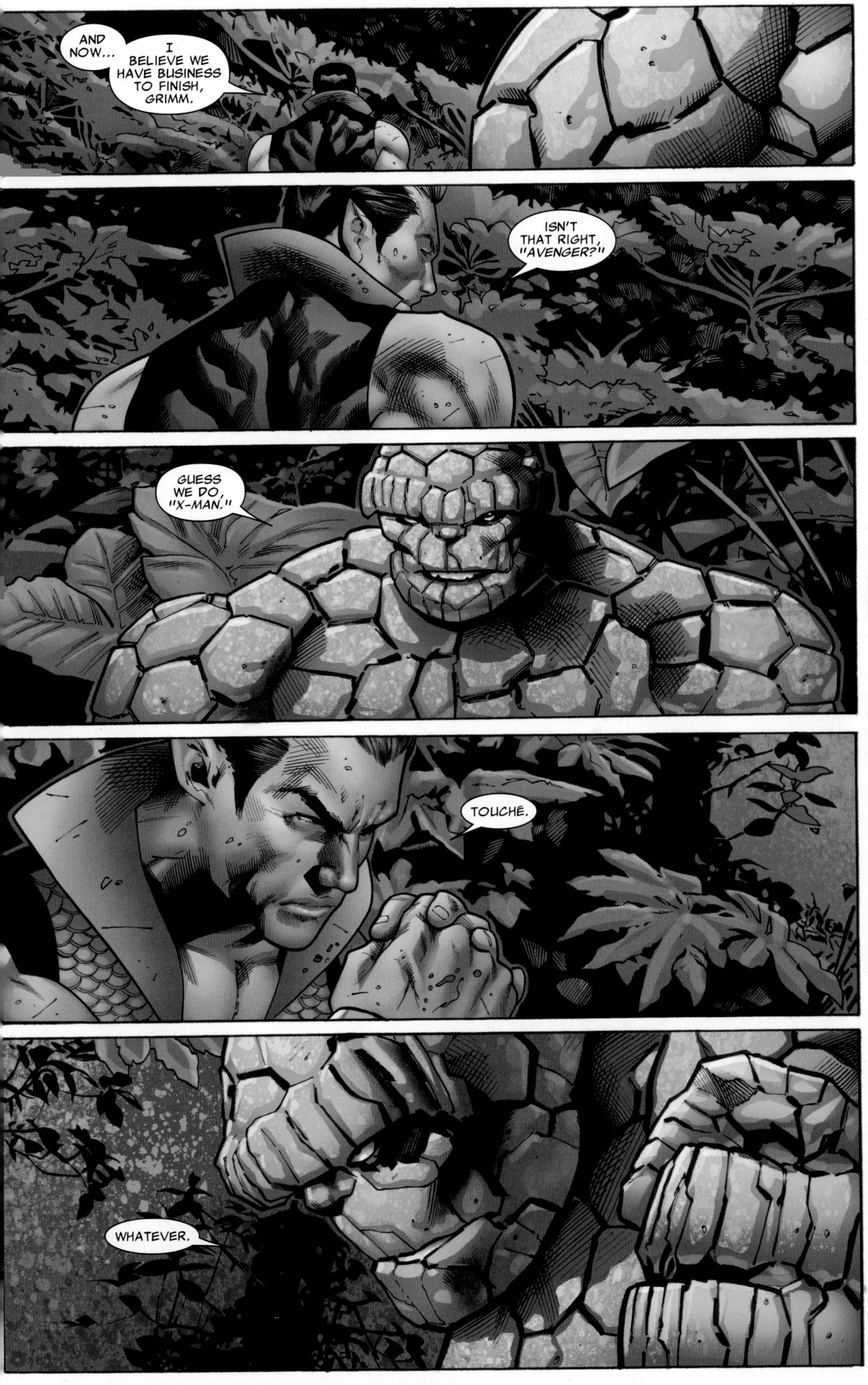
AND NOW...
I BELIEVE WE HAVE BUSINESS TO FINISH, GRIMM.
ISN'T THAT RIGHT, "AVENGER?"
GUESS WE DO, "X-MAN."
TOUCHÉ.
WHATEVER.

MEANING.

I LOOKED FOR IT, AS INTENSELY AS I WAS ABLE...

...WHICH WAS SOMEWHAT LESS THAN MY FULL CAPABILITY, AS I FOUGHT TO STAY CONSCIOUS THROUGH THAT TITANIC SHOCKWAVE.

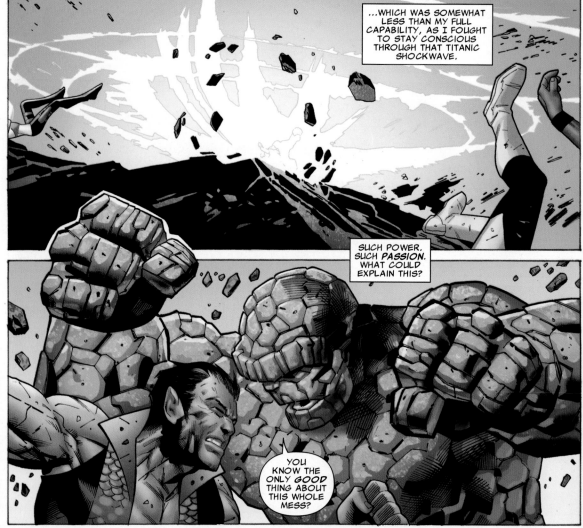

SUCH POWER. SUCH *PASSION*. WHAT COULD EXPLAIN THIS?

YOU KNOW THE ONLY *GOOD* THING ABOUT THIS WHOLE MESS?

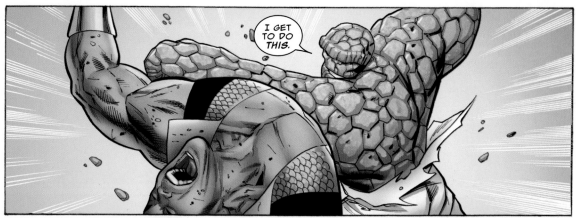

I GET TO DO THIS.

AS LONG AS THIS DAMN THING LASTS.

FOR ONCE, GRIMM--

--WE AGREE.

AND FINALLY THE MOMENT OF INSIGHT. I UNDERSTOOD. I UNDERSTOOD EVERYTHING.

WHAT WOULD BRING SPECIES TO A STRANGE ISOLATED LOCALE LIKE THIS? WHAT WOULD CAUSE SUCH DISPLAYS, WITH A PASSION AND VIOLENCE THAT STUNNED MY CIVILIZED TASTE? THERE WAS ONLY ONE EXPLANATION.

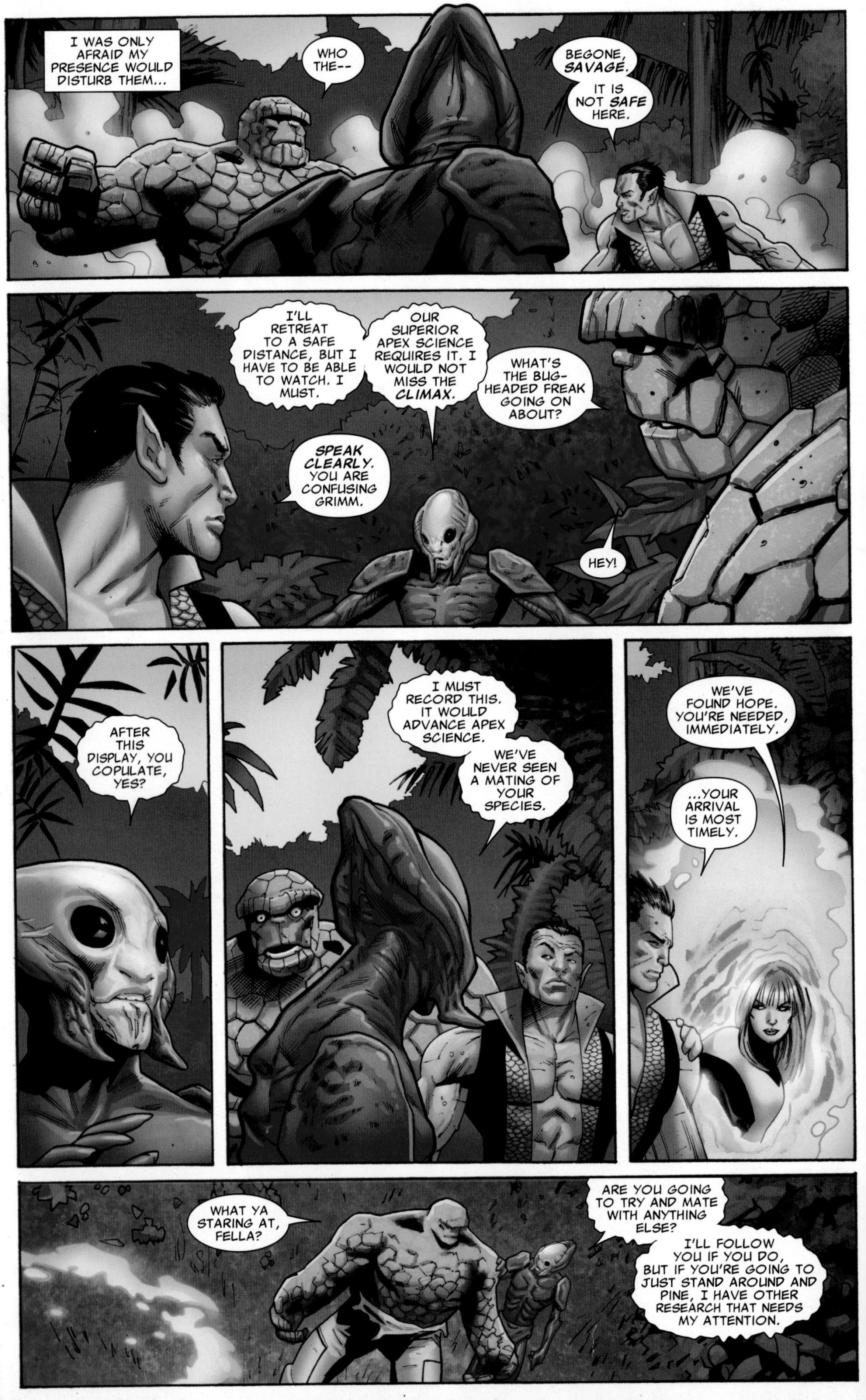
I WAS ONLY AFRAID MY PRESENCE WOULD DISTURB THEM...
WHO THE--
BEGONE, SAVAGE.
IT IS NOT SAFE HERE.
I'LL RETREAT TO A SAFE DISTANCE, BUT I HAVE TO BE ABLE TO WATCH. I MUST.
OUR SUPERIOR APEX SCIENCE REQUIRES IT. I WOULD NOT MISS THE CLIMAX.
WHAT'S THE BUG-HEADED FREAK GOING ON ABOUT?
SPEAK CLEARLY. YOU ARE CONFUSING GRIMM.
HEY!
AFTER THIS DISPLAY, YOU COPULATE, YES?
I MUST RECORD THIS. IT WOULD ADVANCE APEX SCIENCE.
WE'VE NEVER SEEN A MATING OF YOUR SPECIES.
WE'VE FOUND HOPE. YOU'RE NEEDED, IMMEDIATELY.
...YOUR ARRIVAL IS MOST TIMELY.
WHAT YA STARING AT, FELLA?
ARE YOU GOING TO TRY AND MATE WITH ANYTHING ELSE?
I'LL FOLLOW YOU IF YOU DO, BUT IF YOU'RE GOING TO JUST STAND AROUND AND PINE, I HAVE OTHER RESEARCH THAT NEEDS MY ATTENTION.

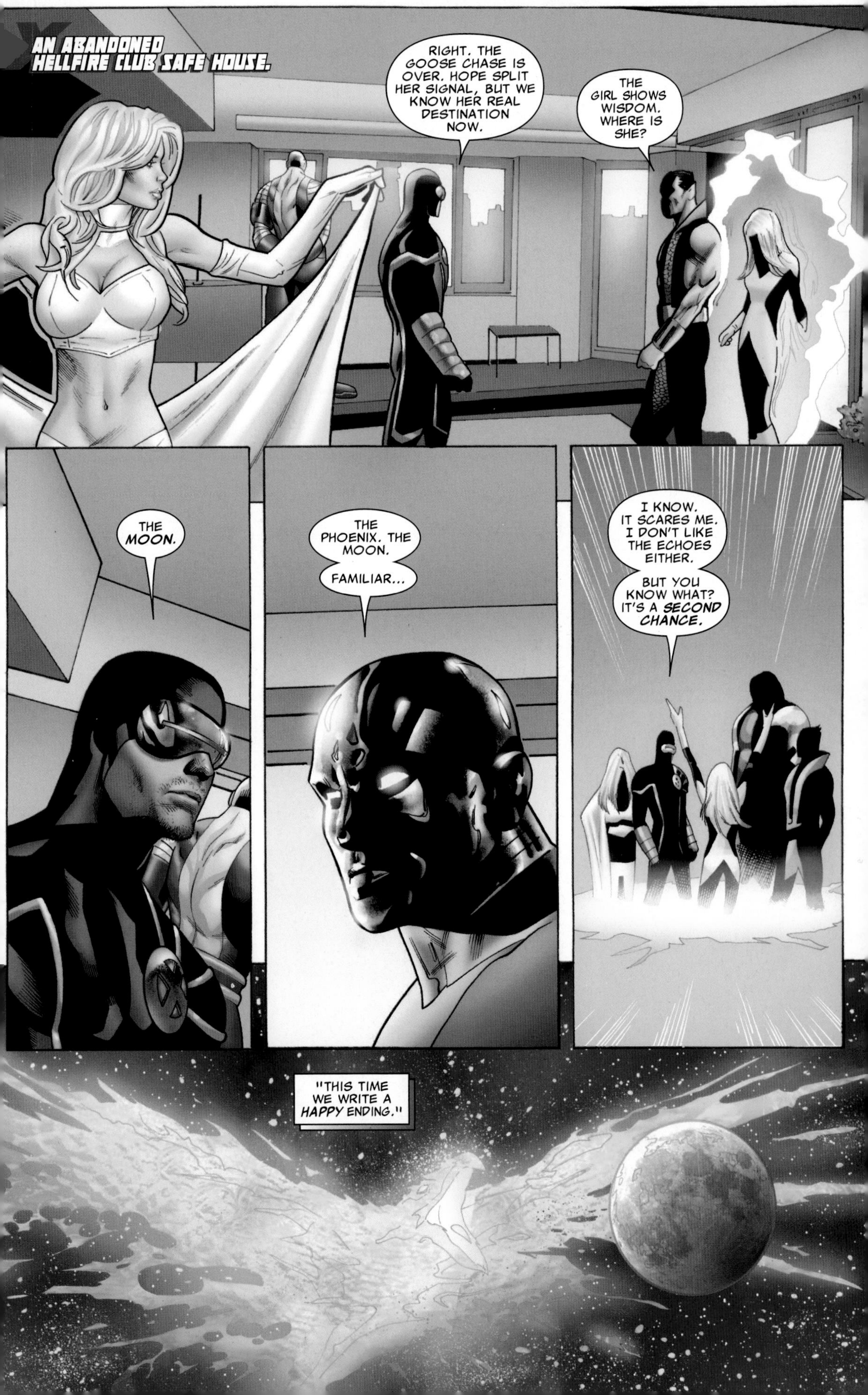
AN ABANDONED HELLFIRE CLUB SAFE HOUSE.
RIGHT. THE GOOSE CHASE IS OVER. HOPE SPLIT HER SIGNAL, BUT WE KNOW HER REAL DESTINATION NOW.
THE GIRL SHOWS WISDOM. WHERE IS SHE?
THE *MOON.*
THE PHOENIX. THE MOON.
FAMILIAR...
I KNOW. IT SCARES ME. I DON'T LIKE THE ECHOES EITHER.
BUT YOU KNOW WHAT? IT'S A ***SECOND CHANCE.***
"THIS TIME WE WRITE A *HAPPY* ENDING."

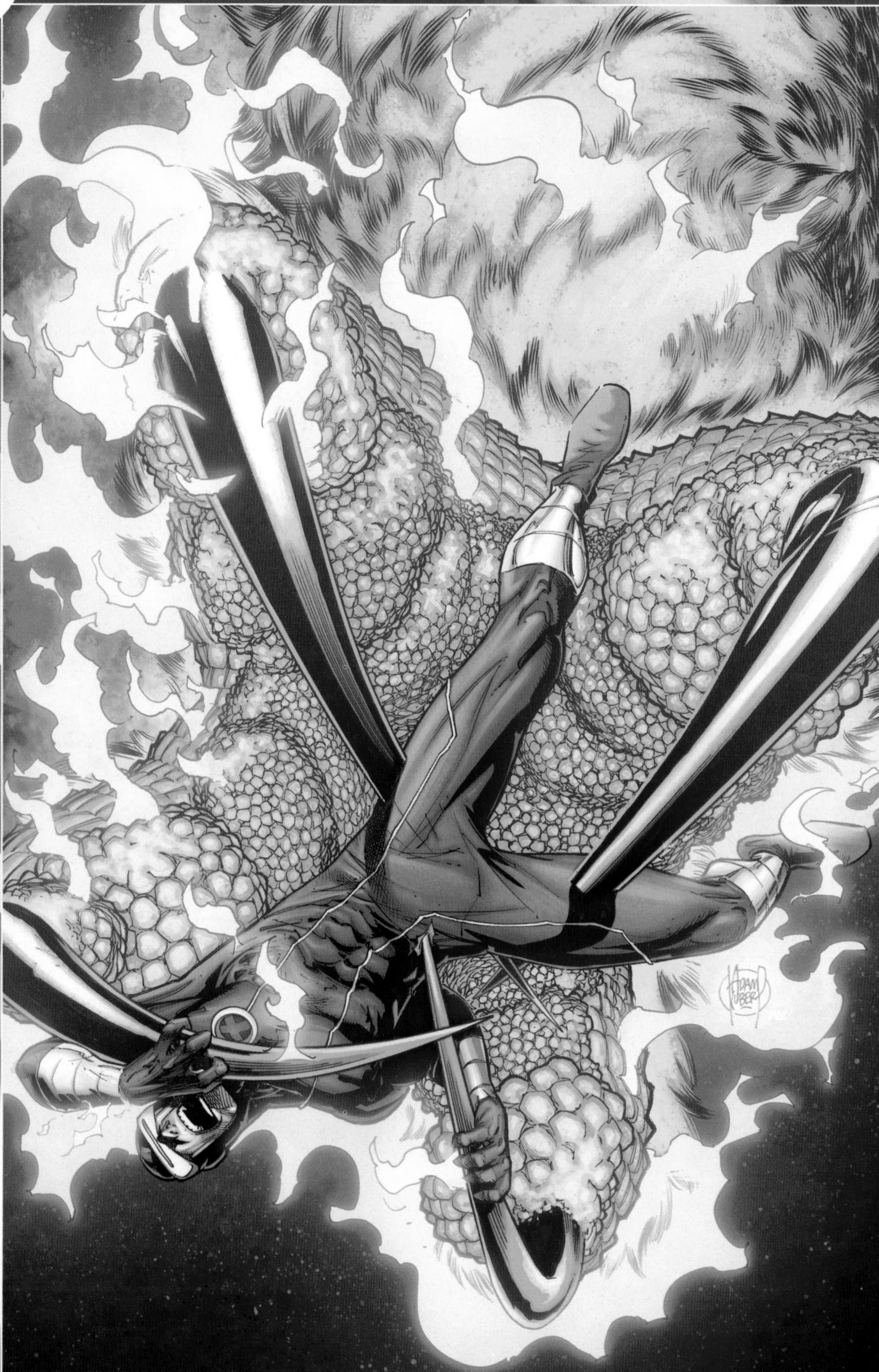

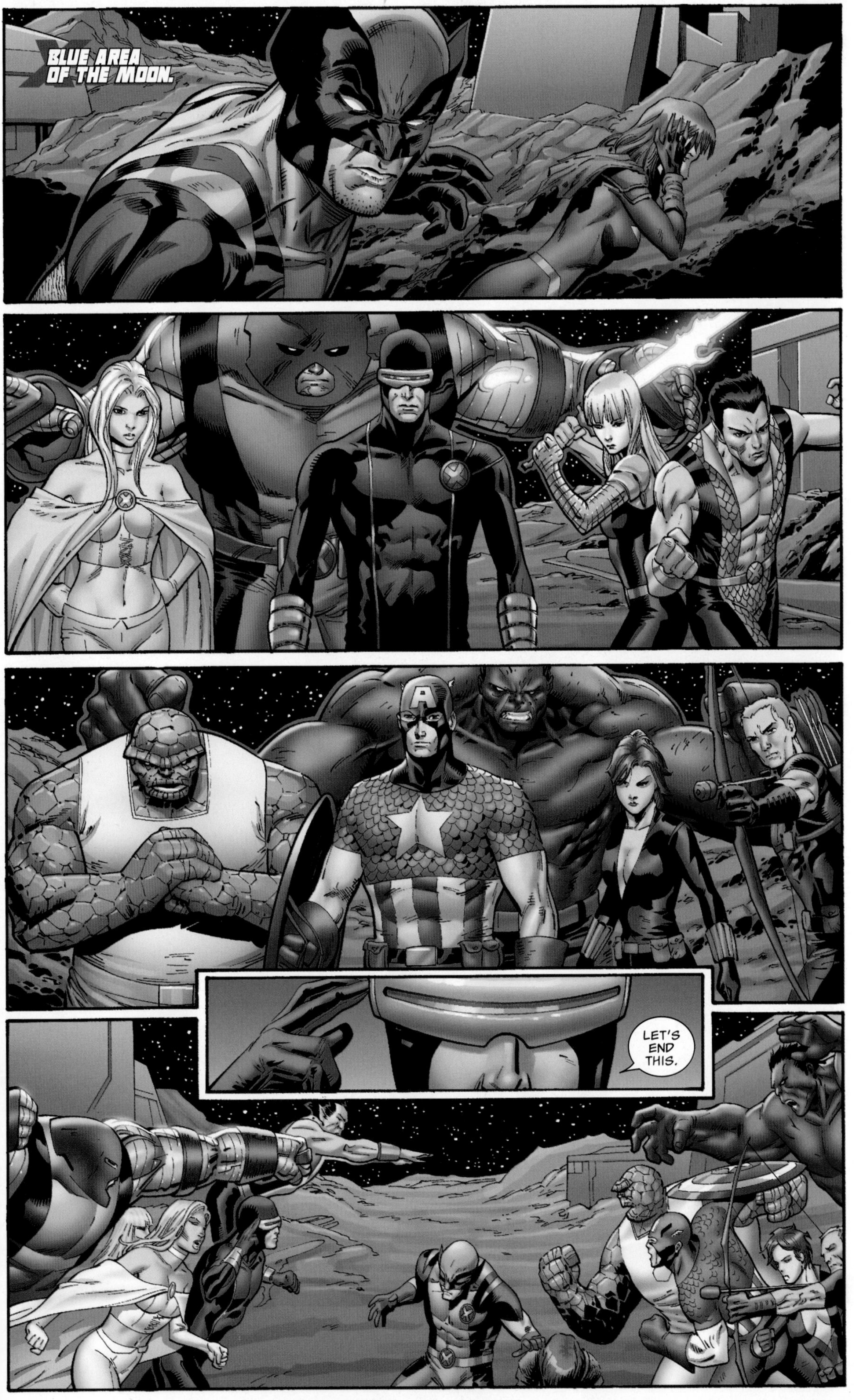
BLUE AREA OF THE MOON.
LET'S END THIS.

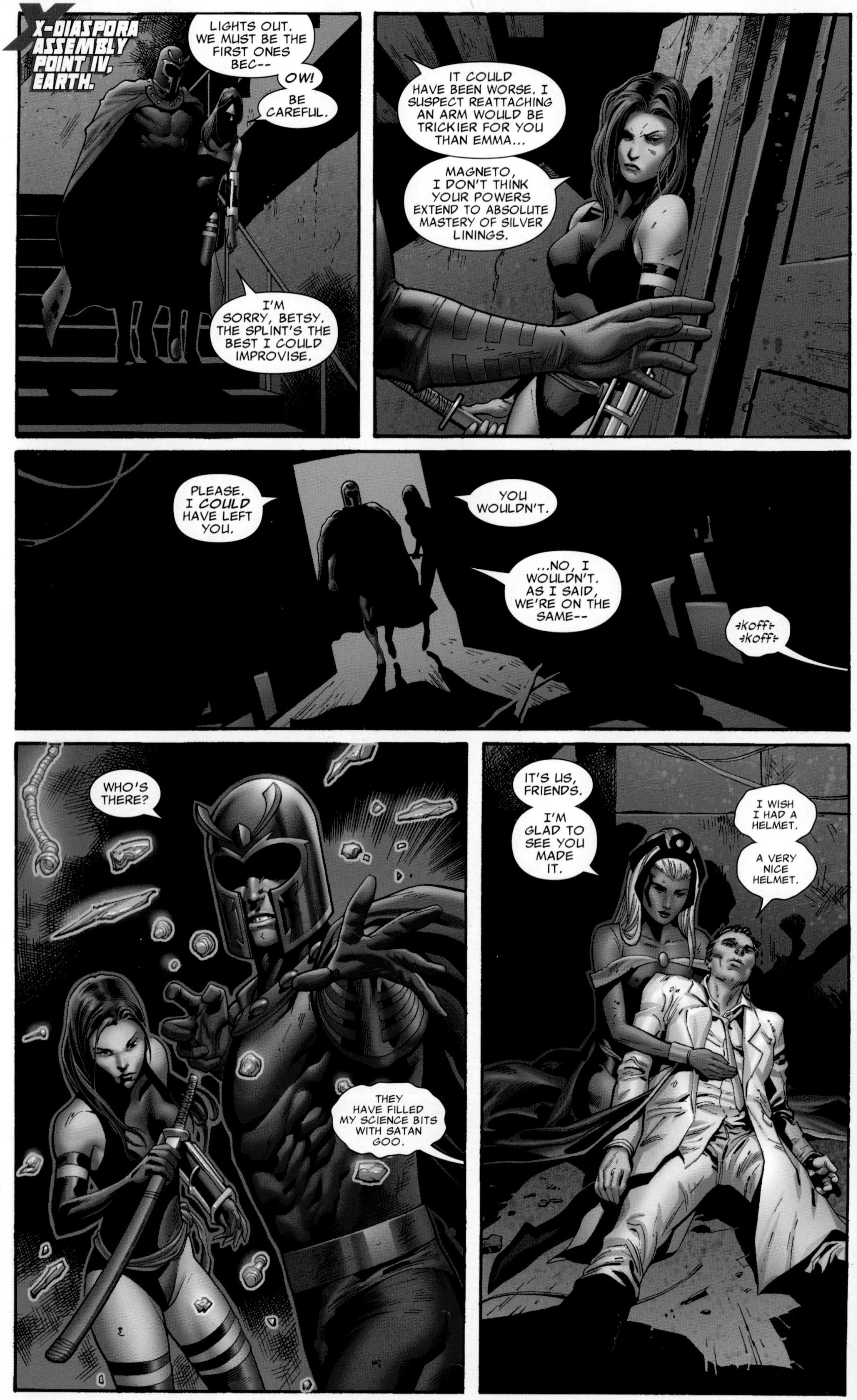
X-DIASPORA ASSEMBLY POINT IV, EARTH.
LIGHTS OUT. WE MUST BE THE FIRST ONES BEC--
OW!
BE CAREFUL.
I'M SORRY, BETSY. THE SPLINT'S THE BEST I COULD IMPROVISE.
IT COULD HAVE BEEN WORSE. I SUSPECT REATTACHING AN ARM WOULD BE TRICKIER FOR YOU THAN EMMA...
MAGNETO, I DON'T THINK YOUR POWERS EXTEND TO ABSOLUTE MASTERY OF SILVER LININGS.
PLEASE. I COULD HAVE LEFT YOU.
YOU WOULDN'T.
...NO, I WOULDN'T. AS I SAID, WE'RE ON THE SAME--
KOFF KOFF
WHO'S THERE?
THEY HAVE FILLED MY SCIENCE BITS WITH SATAN GOO.
IT'S US, FRIENDS.
I'M GLAD TO SEE YOU MADE IT.
I WISH I HAD A HELMET.
A VERY NICE HELMET.

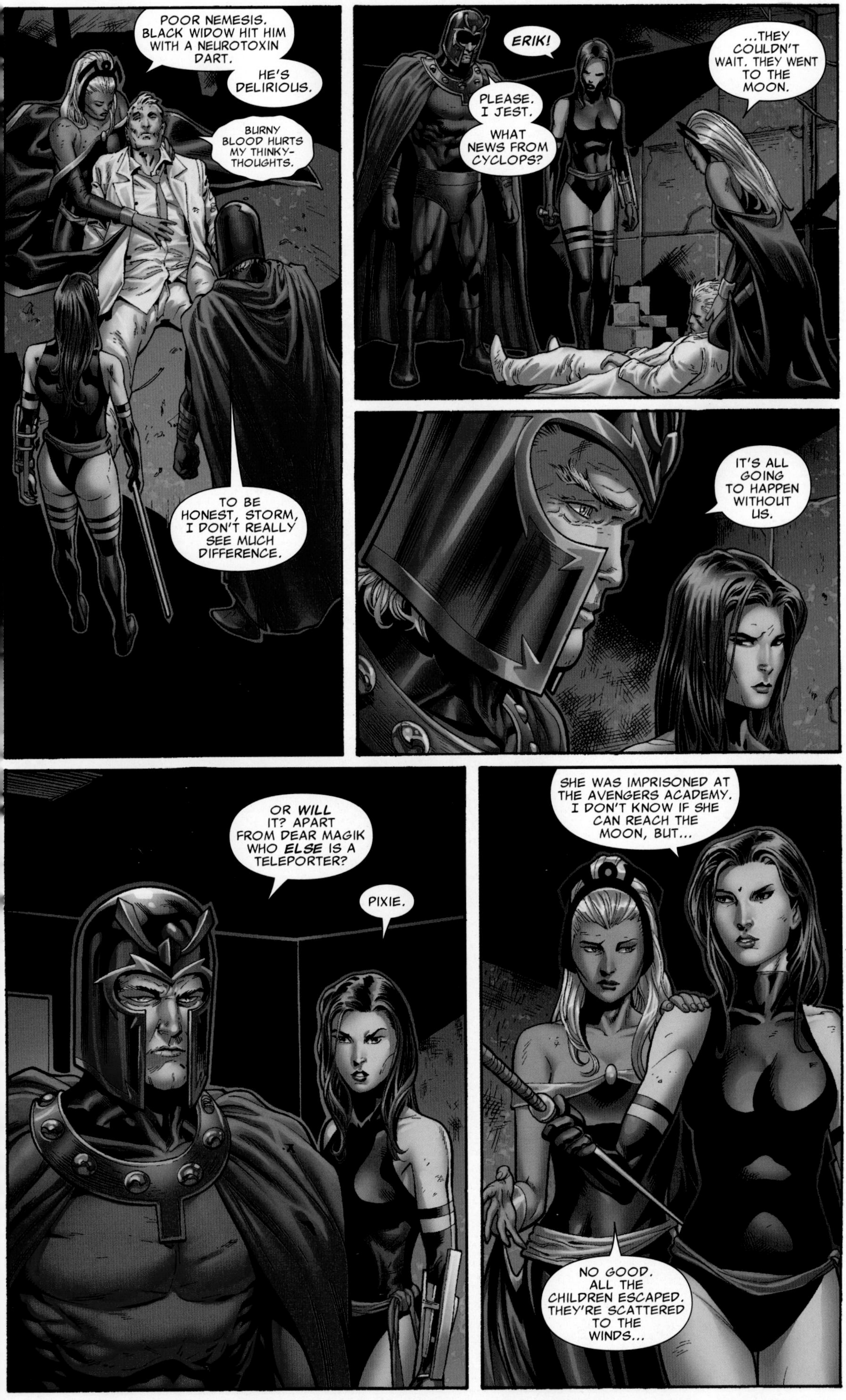
POOR NEMESIS. BLACK WIDOW HIT HIM WITH A NEUROTOXIN DART.
HE'S DELIRIOUS.
BURNY BLOOD HURTS MY THINKY-THOUGHTS.
TO BE HONEST, STORM, I DON'T REALLY SEE MUCH DIFFERENCE.
ERIK!
PLEASE. I JEST.
WHAT NEWS FROM CYCLOPS?
...THEY COULDN'T WAIT. THEY WENT TO THE MOON.
IT'S ALL GOING TO HAPPEN WITHOUT US.
OR WILL IT? APART FROM DEAR MAGIK WHO ELSE IS A TELEPORTER?
PIXIE.
SHE WAS IMPRISONED AT THE AVENGERS ACADEMY. I DON'T KNOW IF SHE CAN REACH THE MOON, BUT...
NO GOOD. ALL THE CHILDREN ESCAPED. THEY'RE SCATTERED TO THE WINDS...

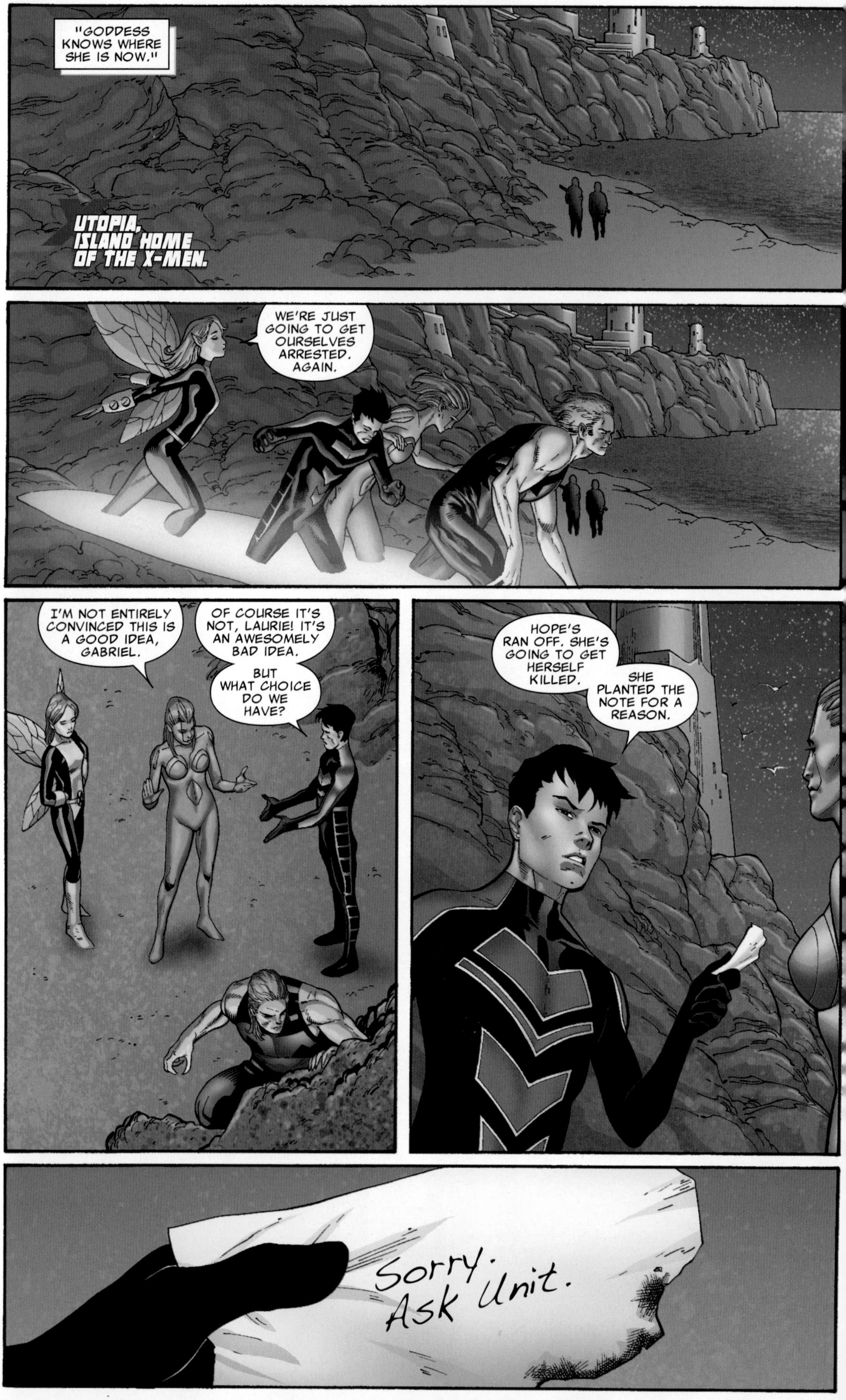
"GODDESS KNOWS WHERE SHE IS NOW."
UTOPIA, ISLAND HOME OF THE X-MEN.
WE'RE JUST GOING TO GET OURSELVES ARRESTED. AGAIN.
I'M NOT ENTIRELY CONVINCED THIS IS A GOOD IDEA, GABRIEL.
OF COURSE IT'S NOT, LAURIE! IT'S AN AWESOMELY BAD IDEA.
BUT WHAT CHOICE DO WE HAVE?
HOPE'S RAN OFF. SHE'S GOING TO GET HERSELF KILLED.
SHE PLANTED THE NOTE FOR A REASON.
Sorry. Ask Unit.

WE CAN'T LET HER DOWN.

...THE ROBOT IS CREEPY.

BREAKING OUT OF JAIL. NOW BREAKING INTO ONE.

YOU GUYS NEED TO MAKE YOUR MINDS UP.

SIHAL NOVARUM CHINOTH!

OH, HELLO.

I WASN'T EXPECTING COMPANY.

...HOPE TOLD YOU ABOUT ME.

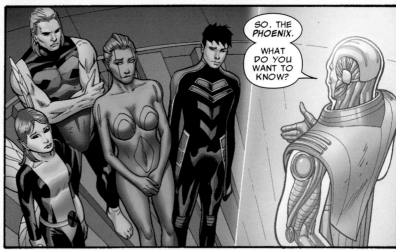

SO. THE PHOENIX.

WHAT DO YOU WANT TO KNOW?

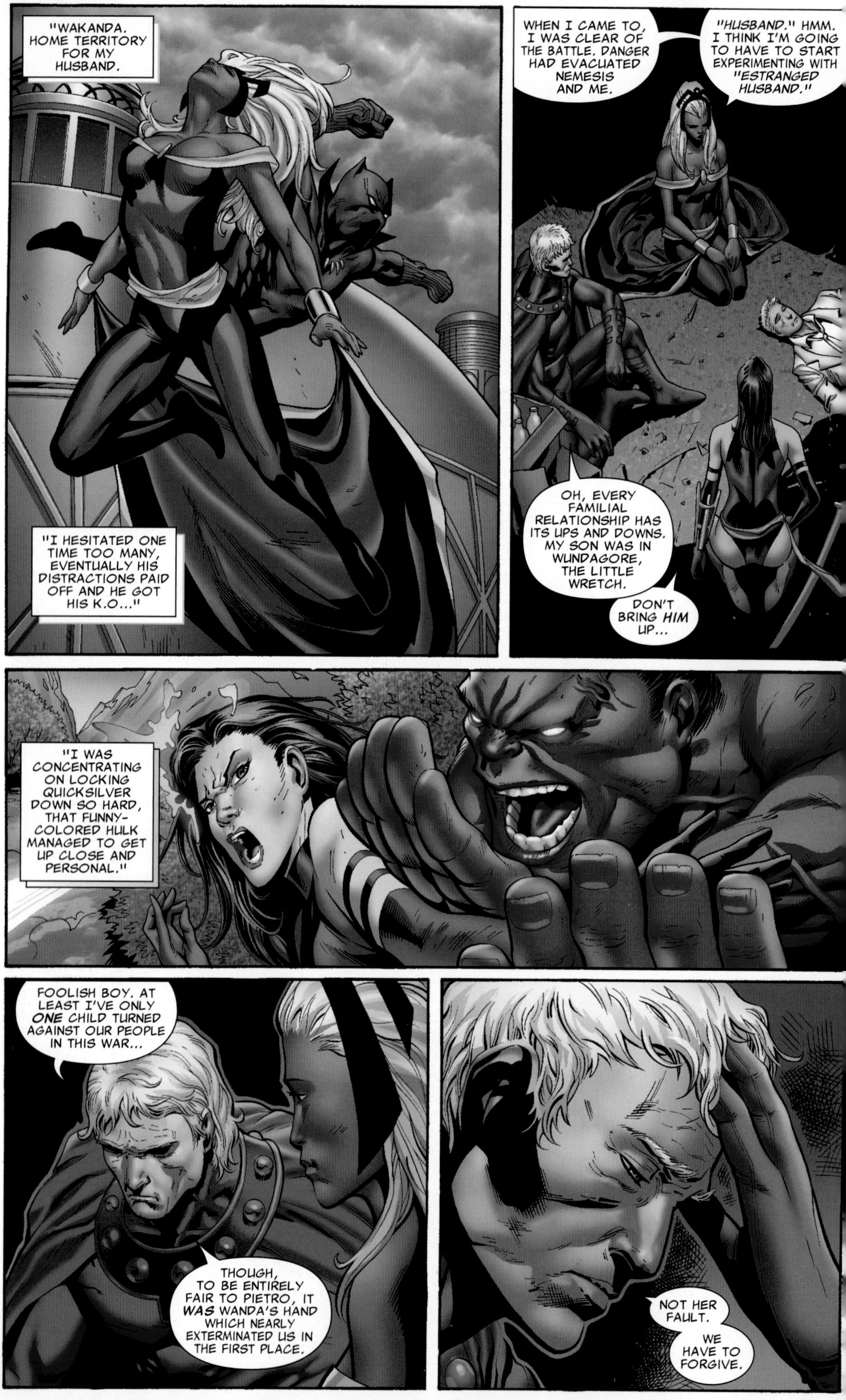
"WAKANDA. HOME TERRITORY FOR MY HUSBAND.
"I HESITATED ONE TIME TOO MANY, EVENTUALLY HIS DISTRACTIONS PAID OFF AND HE GOT HIS K.O..."
WHEN I CAME TO, I WAS CLEAR OF THE BATTLE. DANGER HAD EVACUATED NEMESIS AND ME.
"HUSBAND." HMM. I THINK I'M GOING TO HAVE TO START EXPERIMENTING WITH "ESTRANGED HUSBAND."
OH, EVERY FAMILIAL RELATIONSHIP HAS ITS UPS AND DOWNS. MY SON WAS IN WUNDAGORE, THE LITTLE WRETCH.
DON'T BRING HIM UP...
"I WAS CONCENTRATING ON LOCKING QUICKSILVER DOWN SO HARD, THAT FUNNY-COLORED HULK MANAGED TO GET UP CLOSE AND PERSONAL."
FOOLISH BOY. AT LEAST I'VE ONLY ONE CHILD TURNED AGAINST OUR PEOPLE IN THIS WAR...
THOUGH, TO BE ENTIRELY FAIR TO PIETRO, IT WAS WANDA'S HAND WHICH NEARLY EXTERMINATED US IN THE FIRST PLACE.
NOT HER FAULT.
WE HAVE TO FORGIVE.

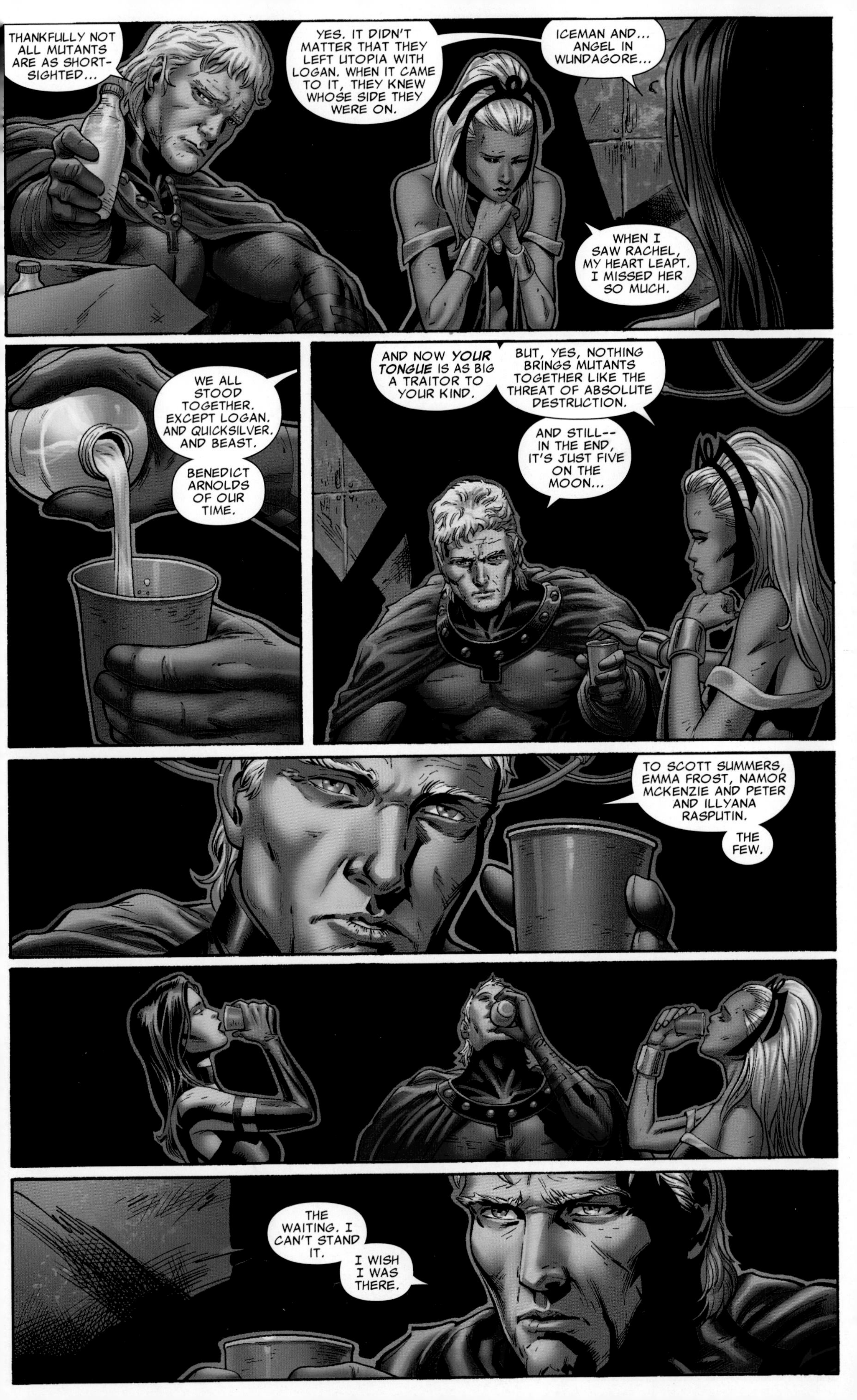

THANKFULLY NOT ALL MUTANTS ARE AS SHORT-SIGHTED...
YES. IT DIDN'T MATTER THAT THEY LEFT UTOPIA WITH LOGAN. WHEN IT CAME TO IT, THEY KNEW WHOSE SIDE THEY WERE ON.
ICEMAN AND... ANGEL IN WUNDAGORE...
WHEN I SAW RACHEL, MY HEART LEAPT. I MISSED HER SO MUCH.
WE ALL STOOD TOGETHER. EXCEPT LOGAN. AND QUICKSILVER. AND BEAST.
BENEDICT ARNOLDS OF OUR TIME.
AND NOW YOUR TONGUE IS AS BIG A TRAITOR TO YOUR KIND.
BUT, YES, NOTHING BRINGS MUTANTS TOGETHER LIKE THE THREAT OF ABSOLUTE DESTRUCTION.
AND STILL-- IN THE END, IT'S JUST FIVE ON THE MOON...
TO SCOTT SUMMERS, EMMA FROST, NAMOR MCKENZIE AND PETER AND ILLYANA RASPUTIN.
THE FEW.
THE WAITING. I CAN'T STAND IT.
I WISH I WAS THERE.

"THERE MUST BE SOMETHING *SOMEONE* COULD DO."

I AM A CREATURE OF SCIENCE IN A UNIVERSE THAT'S REGULARLY NOT. THAT MEANS I HAVE TO LEARN ABOUT ANNOYINGLY METAPHYSICAL THINGS LIKE THE PHOENIX.

IT'S ALWAYS HAD ITS HOSTS, BRINGING DESTRUCTION AND REBIRTH. *THIS* IS DIFFERENT. I GAVE HOPE MY BEST ADVICE...

WHAT *IS* HAPPENING?

THE PHOENIX IS A UNIVERSAL CONSTANT. A UNIVERSAL CONSTANT DISLIKES HAVING *ANYTHING* INTERFERE WITH THAT.

AS MUCH AS I HATE TO ANTHROPOMORPHIZE A COSMIC ENTITY THAT LIVES BEYOND TIME AND SPACE, IT WAS *PUSHED*. THIS IS THE PHOENIX *PUSHING BACK*.

"NO MORE MUTANTS."

UNACCEPTABLE.

IF HOPE IS ABLE TO BALANCE THE ENERGIES AND MERGE WITH IT... ALL THAT CHANGES.

HOW DO YOU KNOW THIS?

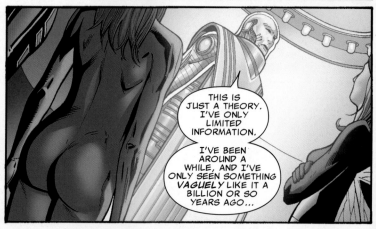

THIS IS JUST A THEORY. I'VE ONLY LIMITED INFORMATION.

I'VE BEEN AROUND A WHILE, AND I'VE ONLY SEEN SOMETHING *VAGUELY* LIKE IT A BILLION OR SO YEARS AGO...

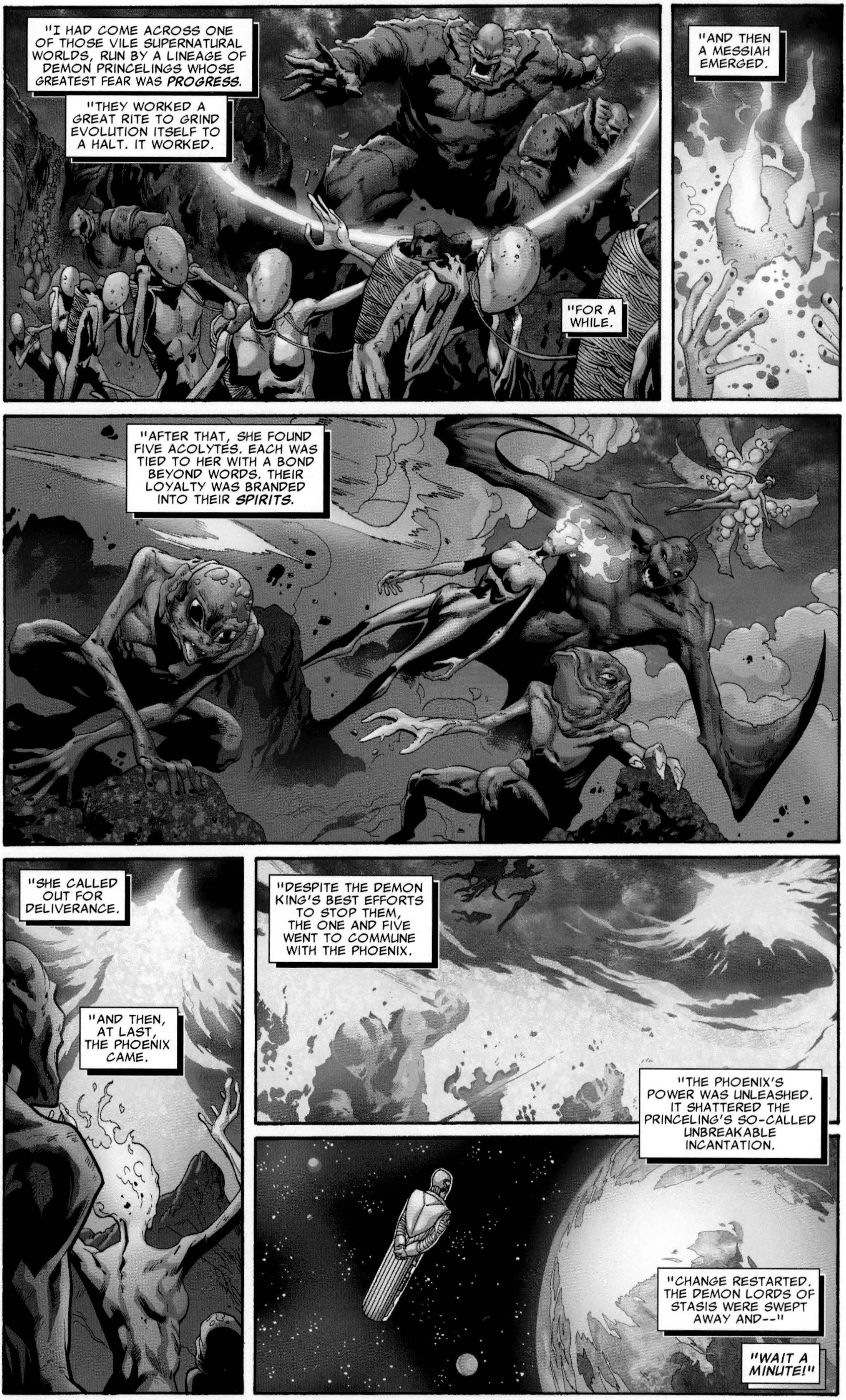
"I HAD COME ACROSS ONE OF THOSE VILE SUPERNATURAL WORLDS, RUN BY A LINEAGE OF DEMON PRINCELINGS WHOSE GREATEST FEAR WAS PROGRESS.
"THEY WORKED A GREAT RITE TO GRIND EVOLUTION ITSELF TO A HALT. IT WORKED.
"FOR A WHILE.
"AND THEN A MESSIAH EMERGED.
"AFTER THAT, SHE FOUND FIVE ACOLYTES. EACH WAS TIED TO HER WITH A BOND BEYOND WORDS. THEIR LOYALTY WAS BRANDED INTO THEIR SPIRITS.
"SHE CALLED OUT FOR DELIVERANCE.
"AND THEN, AT LAST, THE PHOENIX CAME.
"DESPITE THE DEMON KING'S BEST EFFORTS TO STOP THEM, THE ONE AND FIVE WENT TO COMMUNE WITH THE PHOENIX.
"THE PHOENIX'S POWER WAS UNLEASHED. IT SHATTERED THE PRINCELING'S SO-CALLED UNBREAKABLE INCANTATION.
"CHANGE RESTARTED. THE DEMON LORDS OF STASIS WERE SWEPT AWAY AND--"
"WAIT A MINUTE!"

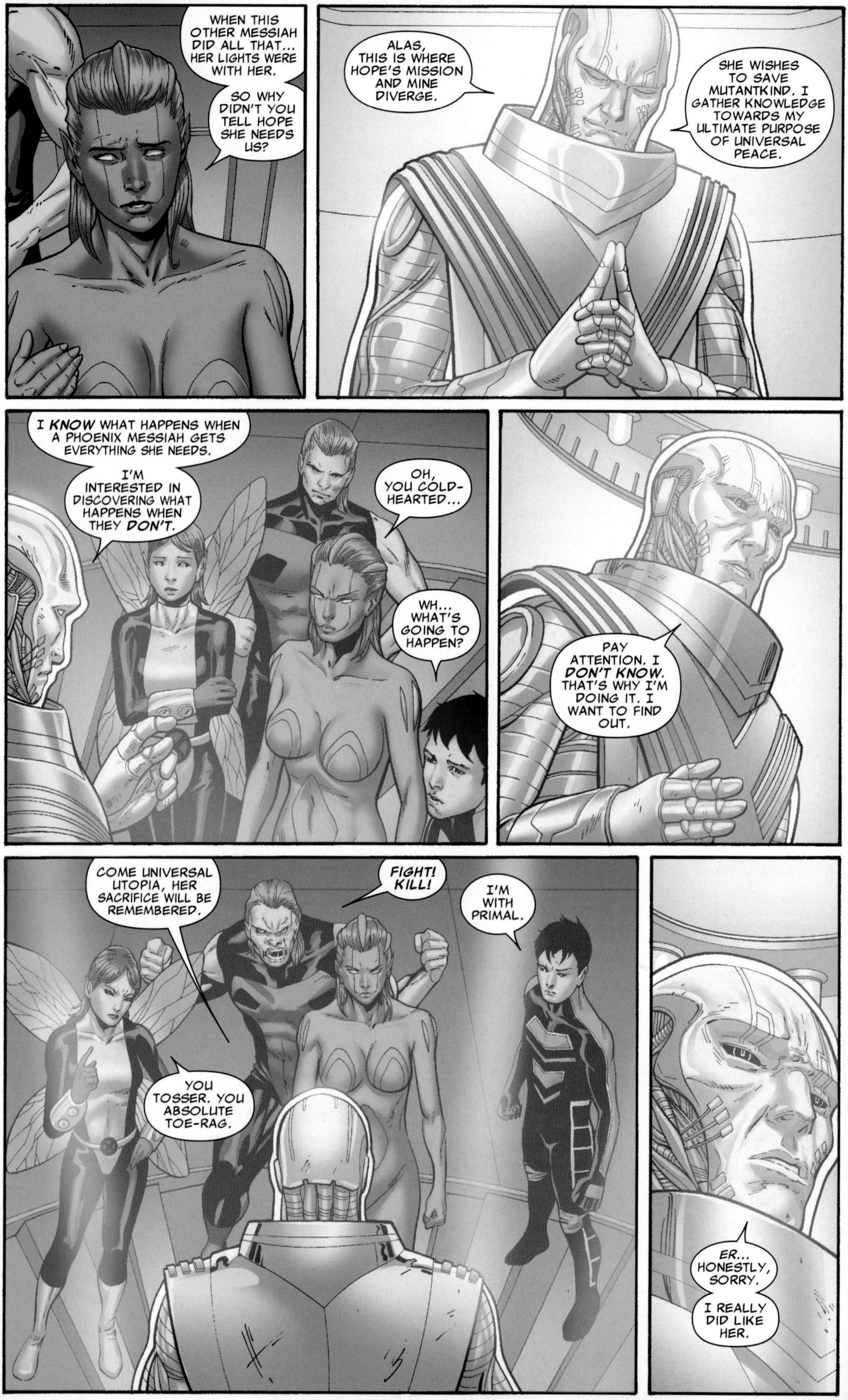

WHEN THIS OTHER MESSIAH DID ALL THAT... HER LIGHTS WERE WITH HER.
SO WHY DIDN'T YOU TELL HOPE SHE NEEDS US?
ALAS, THIS IS WHERE HOPE'S MISSION AND MINE DIVERGE.
SHE WISHES TO SAVE MUTANTKIND. I GATHER KNOWLEDGE TOWARDS MY ULTIMATE PURPOSE OF UNIVERSAL PEACE.
I KNOW WHAT HAPPENS WHEN A PHOENIX MESSIAH GETS EVERYTHING SHE NEEDS.
I'M INTERESTED IN DISCOVERING WHAT HAPPENS WHEN THEY DON'T.
OH, YOU COLD-HEARTED...
WH... WHAT'S GOING TO HAPPEN?
PAY ATTENTION. I DON'T KNOW. THAT'S WHY I'M DOING IT. I WANT TO FIND OUT.
COME UNIVERSAL UTOPIA, HER SACRIFICE WILL BE REMEMBERED.
FIGHT! KILL!
I'M WITH PRIMAL.
YOU TOSSER. YOU ABSOLUTE TOE-RAG.
ER... HONESTLY, SORRY.
I REALLY DID LIKE HER.

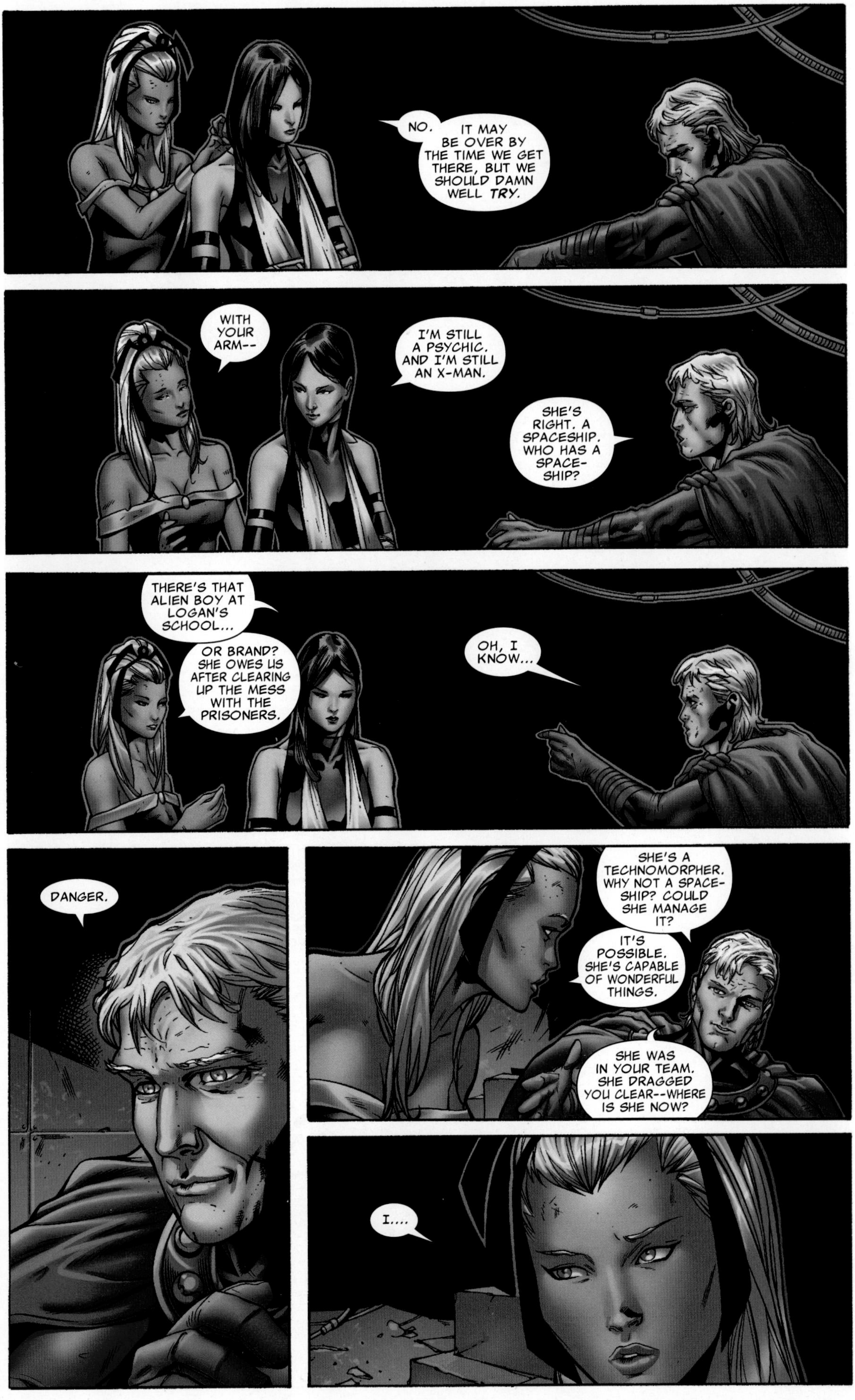
NO.
IT MAY BE OVER BY THE TIME WE GET THERE, BUT WE SHOULD DAMN WELL TRY.
WITH YOUR ARM--
I'M STILL A PSYCHIC. AND I'M STILL AN X-MAN.
SHE'S RIGHT. A SPACESHIP. WHO HAS A SPACE-SHIP?
THERE'S THAT ALIEN BOY AT LOGAN'S SCHOOL...
OR BRAND? SHE OWES US AFTER CLEARING UP THE MESS WITH THE PRISONERS.
OH, I KNOW...
DANGER.
SHE'S A TECHNOMORPHER. WHY NOT A SPACE-SHIP? COULD SHE MANAGE IT?
IT'S POSSIBLE. SHE'S CAPABLE OF WONDERFUL THINGS.
SHE WAS IN YOUR TEAM. SHE DRAGGED YOU CLEAR--WHERE IS SHE NOW?
I....

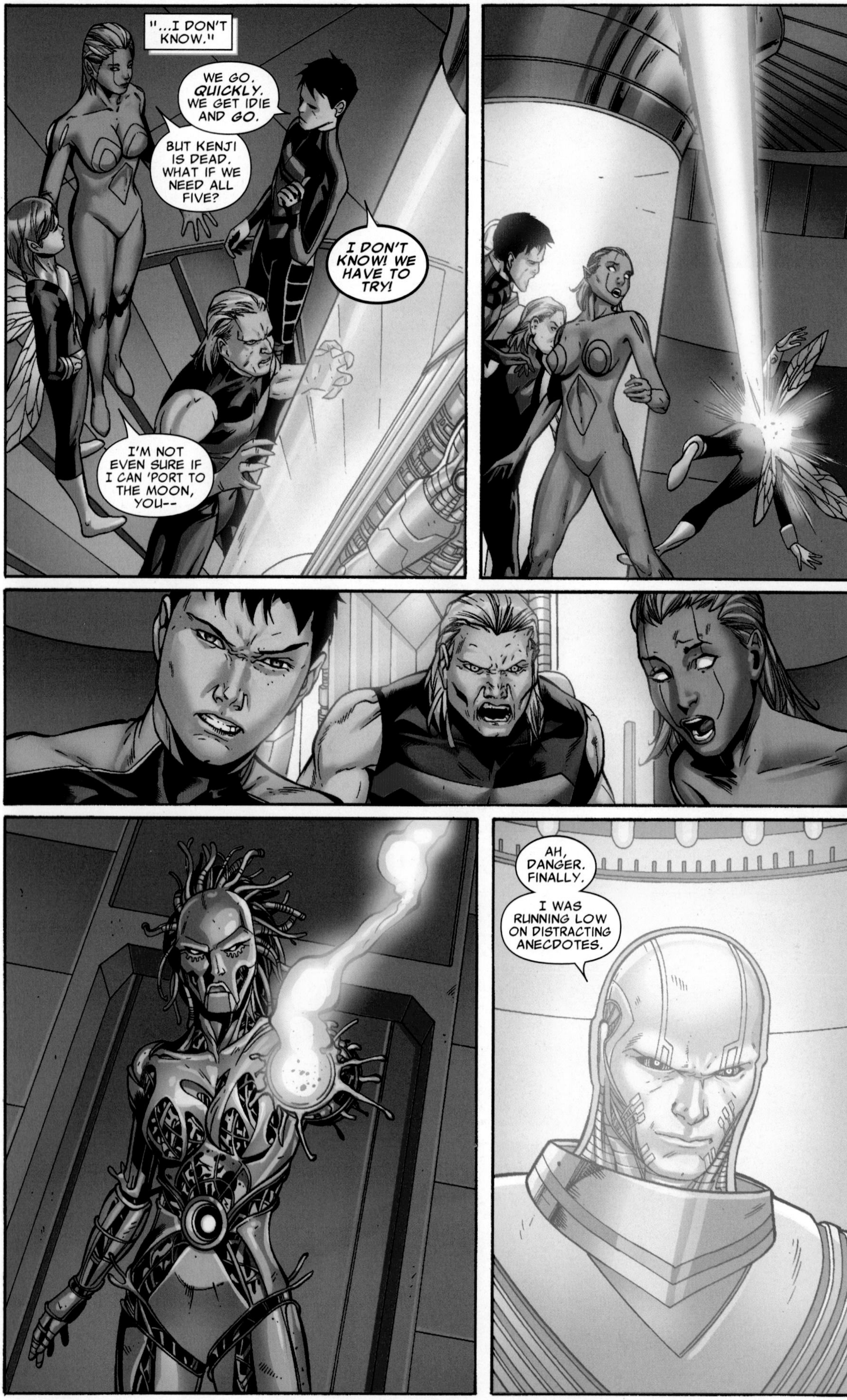
"...I DON'T KNOW."
WE GO. QUICKLY. WE GET IDIE AND GO.
BUT KENJI IS DEAD. WHAT IF WE NEED ALL FIVE?
I DON'T KNOW! WE HAVE TO TRY!
I'M NOT EVEN SURE IF I CAN 'PORT TO THE MOON, YOU--
AH, DANGER. FINALLY.
I WAS RUNNING LOW ON DISTRACTING ANECDOTES.

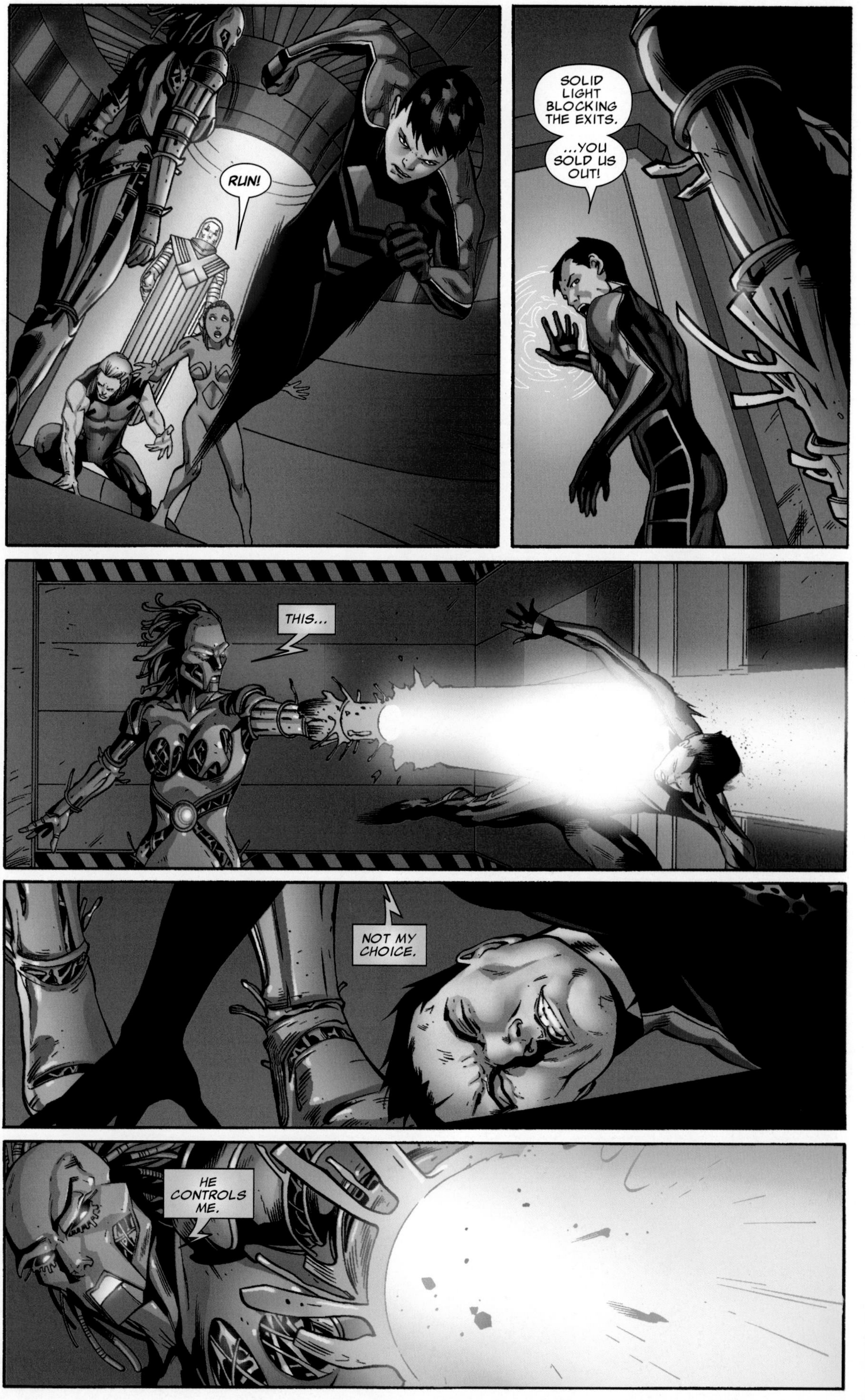
RUN!
SOLID LIGHT BLOCKING THE EXITS.
...YOU SOLD US OUT!
THIS...
NOT MY CHOICE.
HE CONTROLS ME.

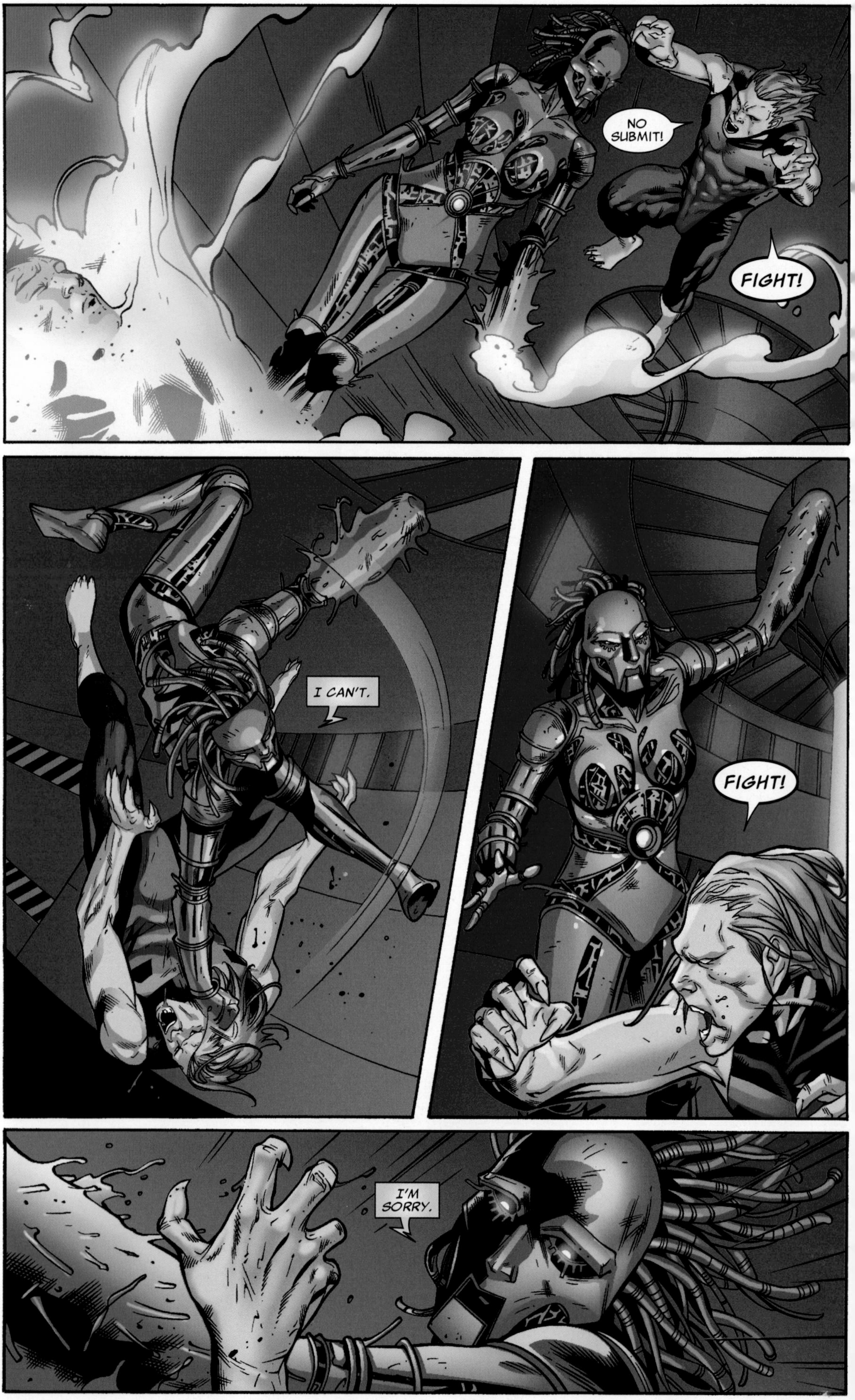
NO SUBMIT!
FIGHT!
I CAN'T.
FIGHT!
I'M SORRY.

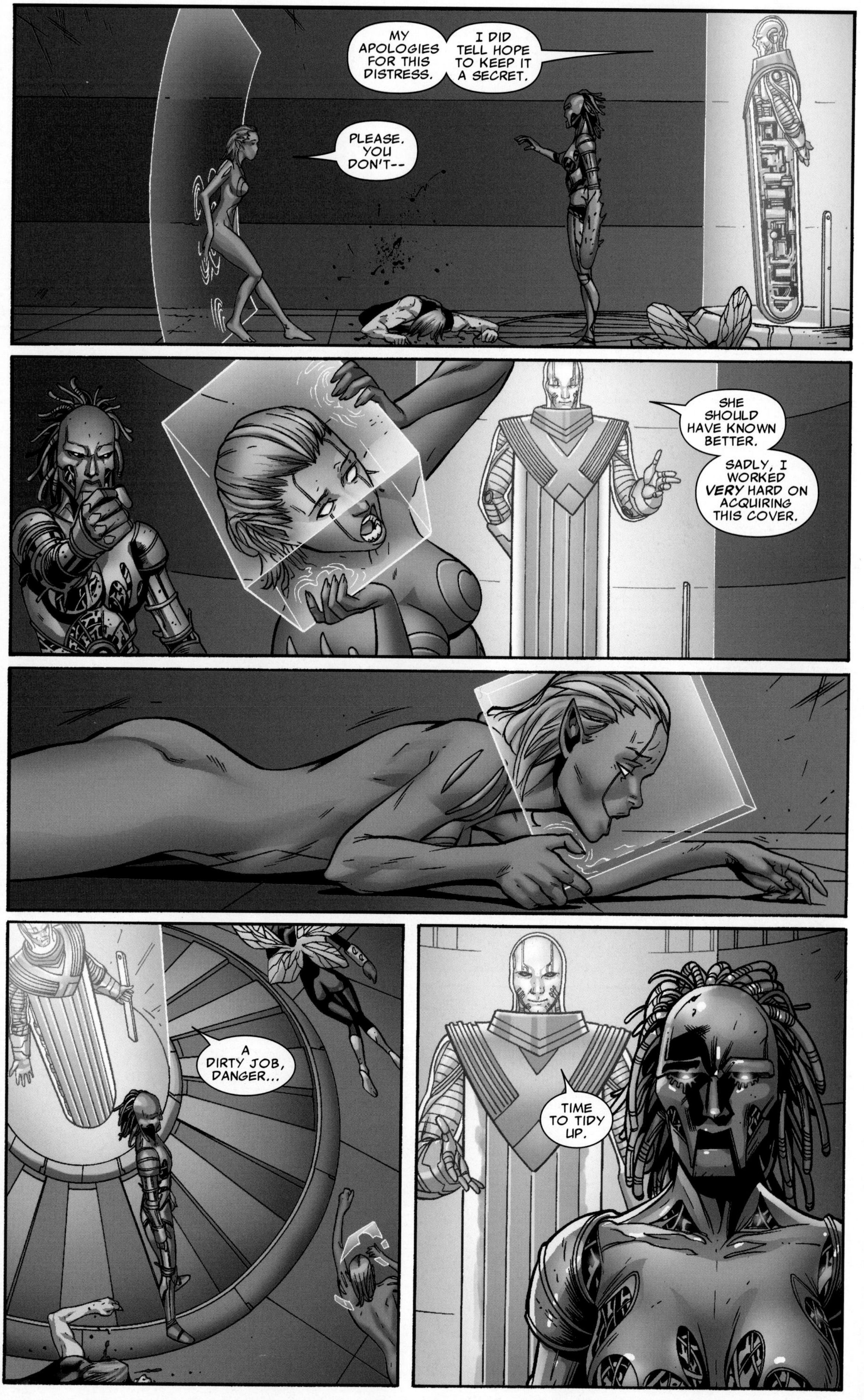
MY APOLOGIES FOR THIS DISTRESS.
I DID TELL HOPE TO KEEP IT A SECRET.
PLEASE. YOU DON'T--
SHE SHOULD HAVE KNOWN BETTER.
SADLY, I WORKED VERY HARD ON ACQUIRING THIS COVER.
A DIRTY JOB, DANGER...
TIME TO TIDY UP.

IF WE CAN'T CONTACT DANGER, WE GO TO BRAND.

AND GODDESS HELP HER IF SHE REFUSES.

RI--

AHHHHHHH!

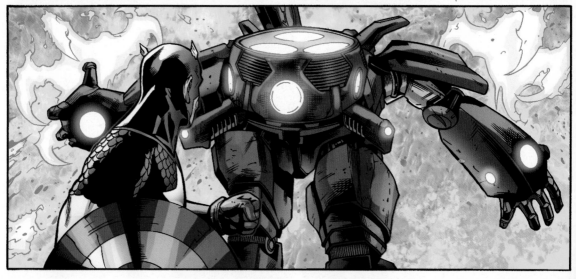

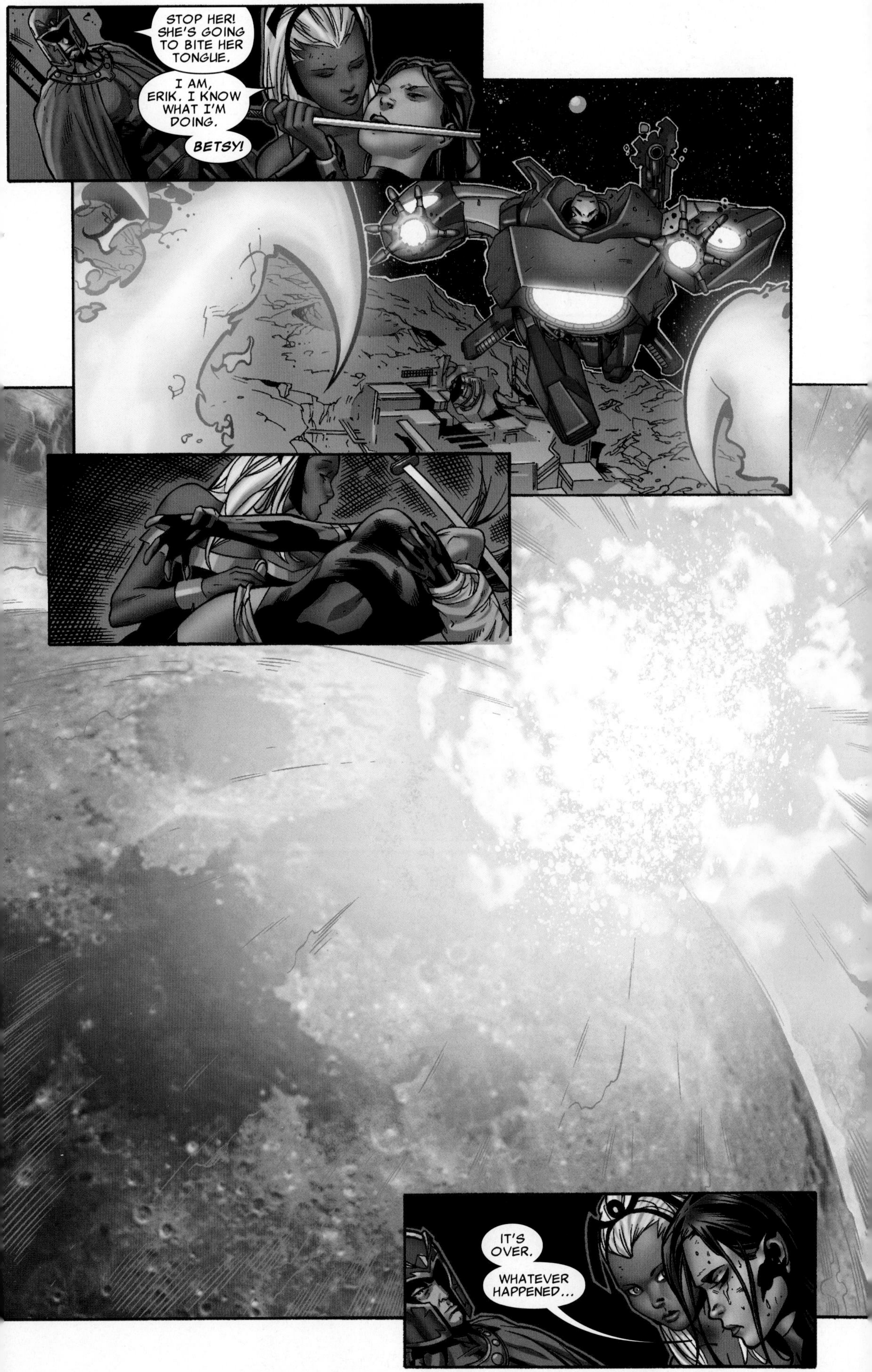
STOP HER! SHE'S GOING TO BITE HER TONGUE.
I AM, ERIK. I KNOW WHAT I'M DOING.
BETSY!
IT'S OVER.
WHATEVER HAPPENED...

"...WE'RE TOO LATE."

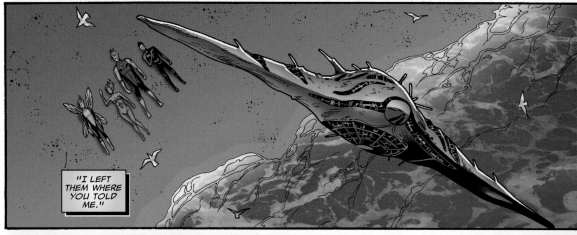

"I LEFT THEM WHERE YOU TOLD ME."

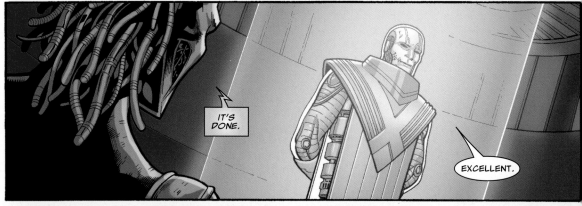

IT'S DONE.

EXCELLENT.

"THEY WERE GOOD KIDS."

"THEY DESERVED BETTER."

OW...

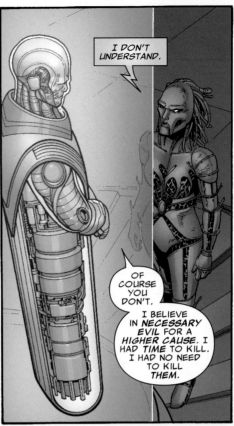

I DON'T UNDERSTAND.

OF COURSE YOU DON'T. I BELIEVE IN *NECESSARY EVIL* FOR A *HIGHER CAUSE.* I HAD *TIME* TO KILL. I HAD NO NEED TO KILL *THEM.*

THEIR MEMORY IMPLANTS WILL HOLD. THE NOTE THAT LED THEM HERE IS DESTROYED.

THEY'LL BELIEVE THEY RECEIVED THEIR INJURIES WHILE ESCAPING THEIR PREVIOUS CAPTIVITY. AND WHATEVER WORLD COMES NEXT, THEY'LL GET TO LIVE IN IT.

"AT LEAST, FOR AS LONG AS IT LASTS."

HEY LOOK! SHOOTING STARS!

...I DON'T THINK SO. MAYBE AN ECLIPSE...

AW, PLAY ALONG. MAKE A WISH.

HURT.

OKAY...

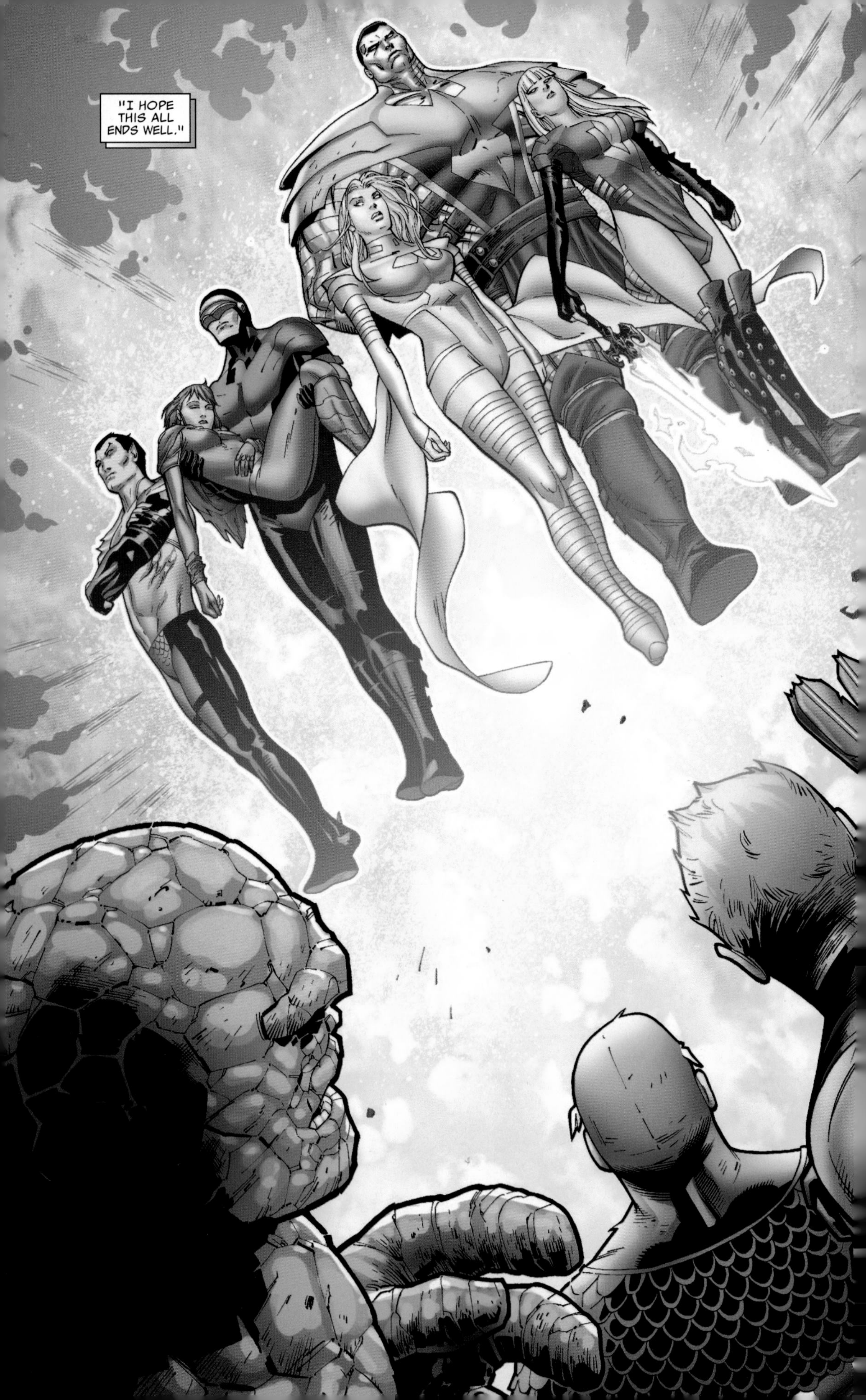
"I HOPE THIS ALL ENDS WELL."

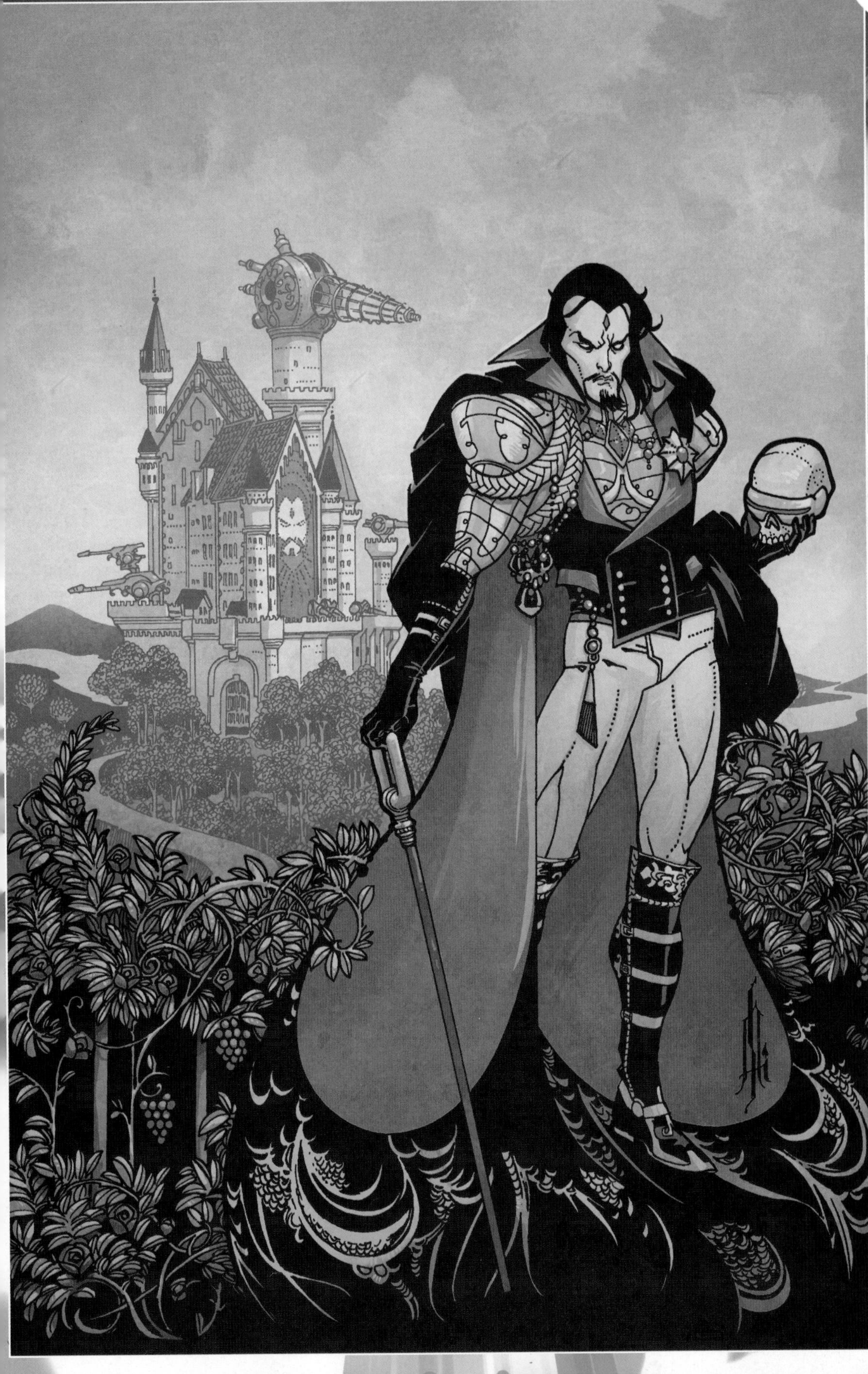

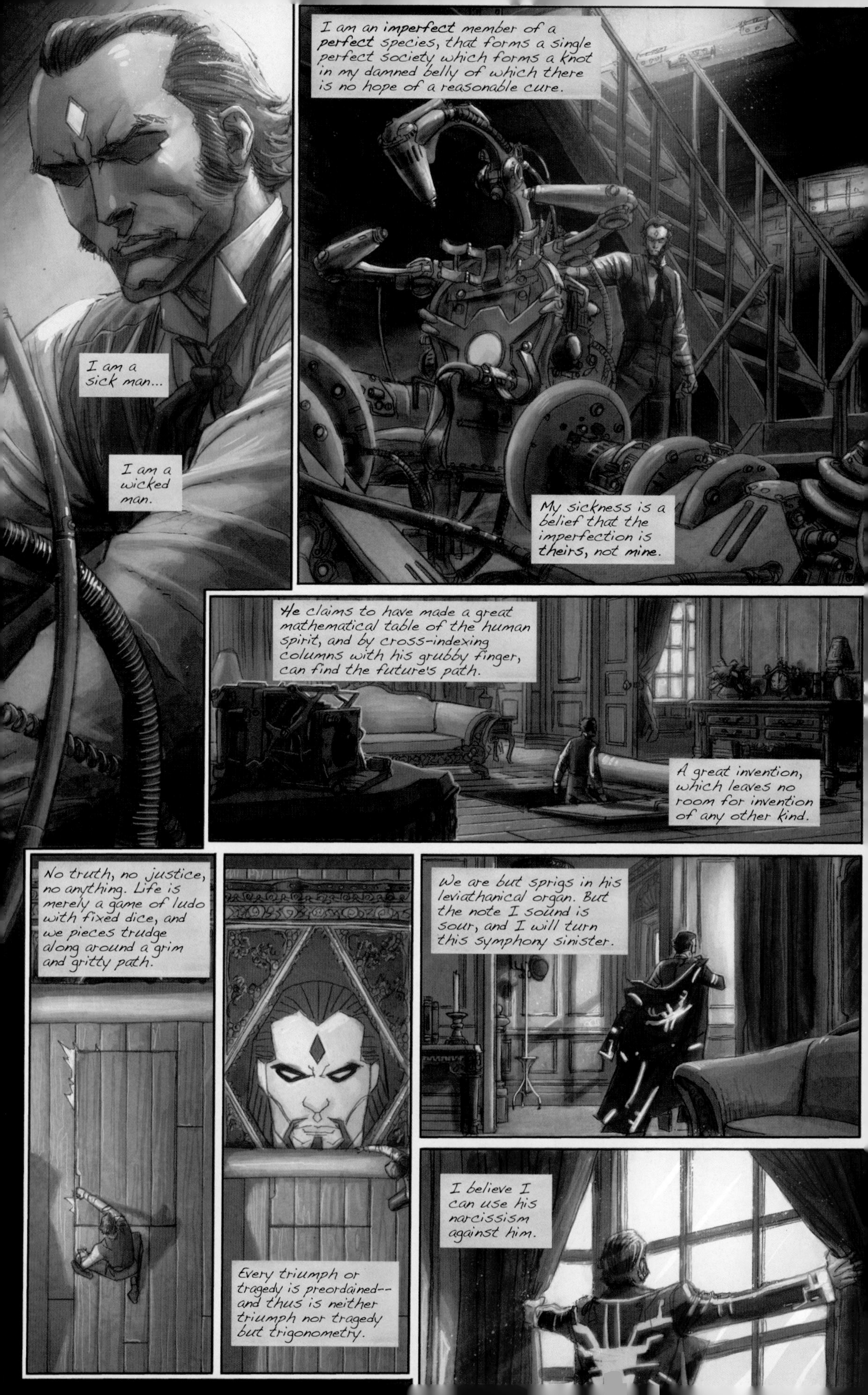
I am a sick man...
I am a wicked man.
I am an imperfect member of a perfect species, that forms a single perfect society which forms a knot in my damned belly of which there is no hope of a reasonable cure.
My sickness is a belief that the imperfection is theirs, not mine.
He claims to have made a great mathematical table of the human spirit, and by cross-indexing columns with his grubby finger, can find the future's path.
A great invention, which leaves no room for invention of any other kind.
No truth, no justice, no anything. Life is merely a game of ludo with fixed dice, and we pieces trudge along around a grim and gritty path.
Every triumph or tragedy is preordained-- and thus is neither triumph nor tragedy but trigonometry.
We are but sprigs in his leviathanical organ. But the note I sound is sour, and I will turn this symphony sinister.
I believe I can use his narcissism against him.

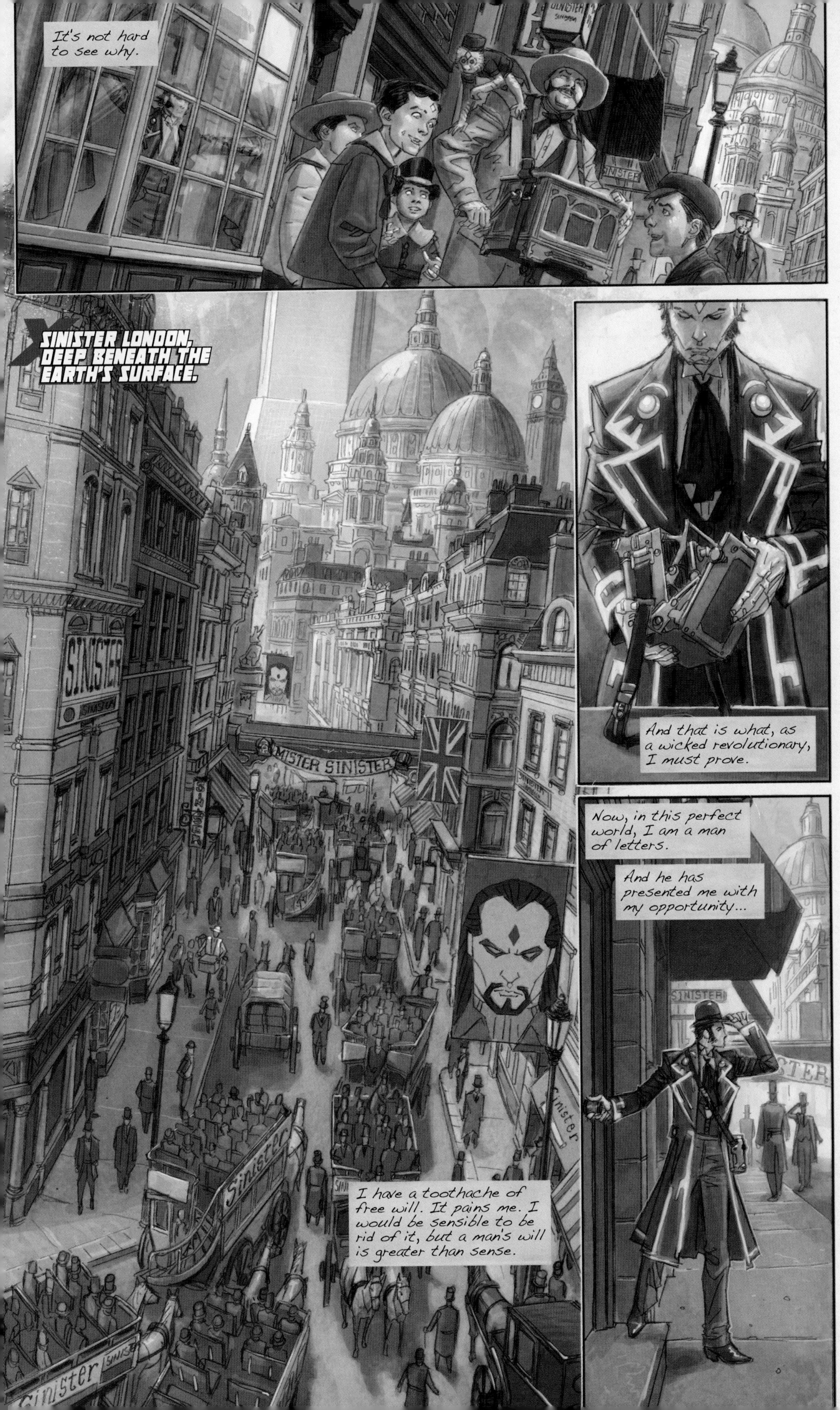
It's not hard to see why.
SINISTER LONDON, DEEP BENEATH THE EARTH'S SURFACE.
MISTER SINISTER
I have a toothache of free will. It pains me. I would be sensible to be rid of it, but a man's will is greater than sense.
And that is what, as a wicked revolutionary, I must prove.
Now, in this perfect world, I am a man of letters.
And he has presented me with my opportunity...

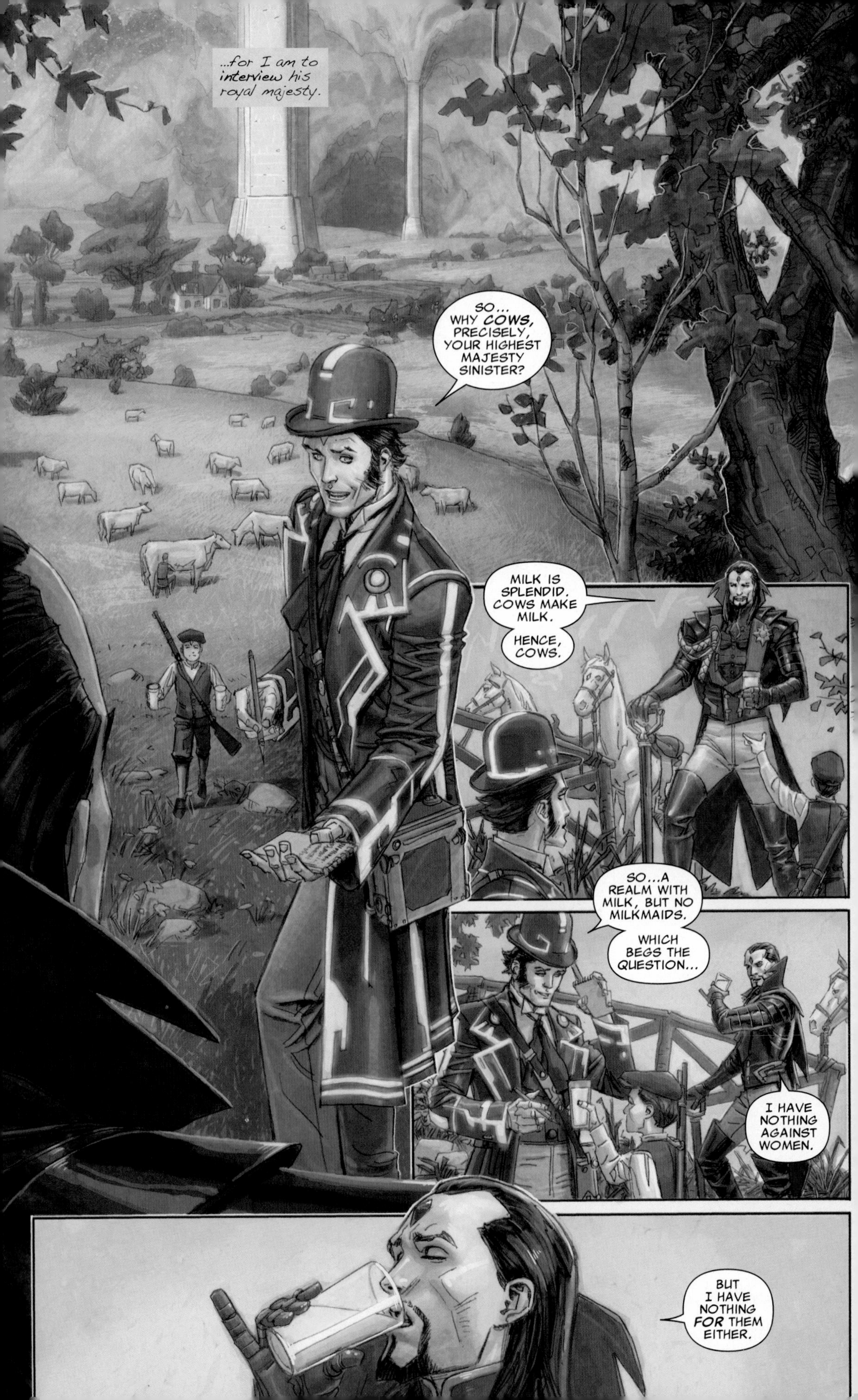
...for I am to interview his royal majesty.
SO... WHY COWS, PRECISELY, YOUR HIGHEST MAJESTY SINISTER?
MILK IS SPLENDID. COWS MAKE MILK.
HENCE, COWS.
SO...A REALM WITH MILK, BUT NO MILKMAIDS.
WHICH BEGS THE QUESTION...
I HAVE NOTHING AGAINST WOMEN.
BUT I HAVE NOTHING FOR THEM EITHER.

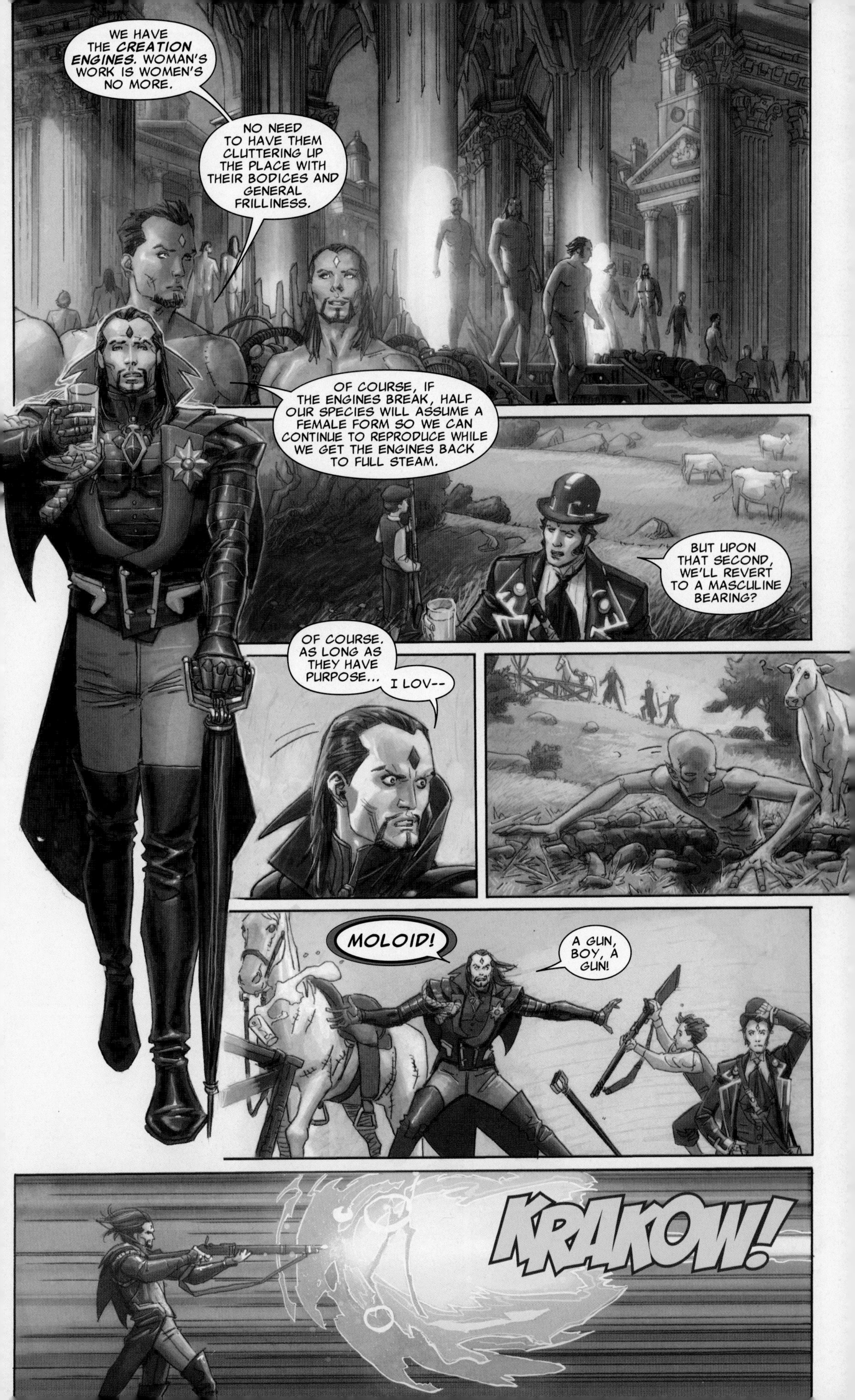
WE HAVE THE CREATION ENGINES. WOMAN'S WORK IS WOMEN'S NO MORE.
NO NEED TO HAVE THEM CLUTTERING UP THE PLACE WITH THEIR BODICES AND GENERAL FRILLINESS.
OF COURSE, IF THE ENGINES BREAK, HALF OUR SPECIES WILL ASSUME A FEMALE FORM SO WE CAN CONTINUE TO REPRODUCE WHILE WE GET THE ENGINES BACK TO FULL STEAM.
BUT UPON THAT SECOND, WE'LL REVERT TO A MASCULINE BEARING?
OF COURSE. AS LONG AS THEY HAVE PURPOSE...
I LOV--
MOLOID!
A GUN, BOY, A GUN!
KRAKOW!

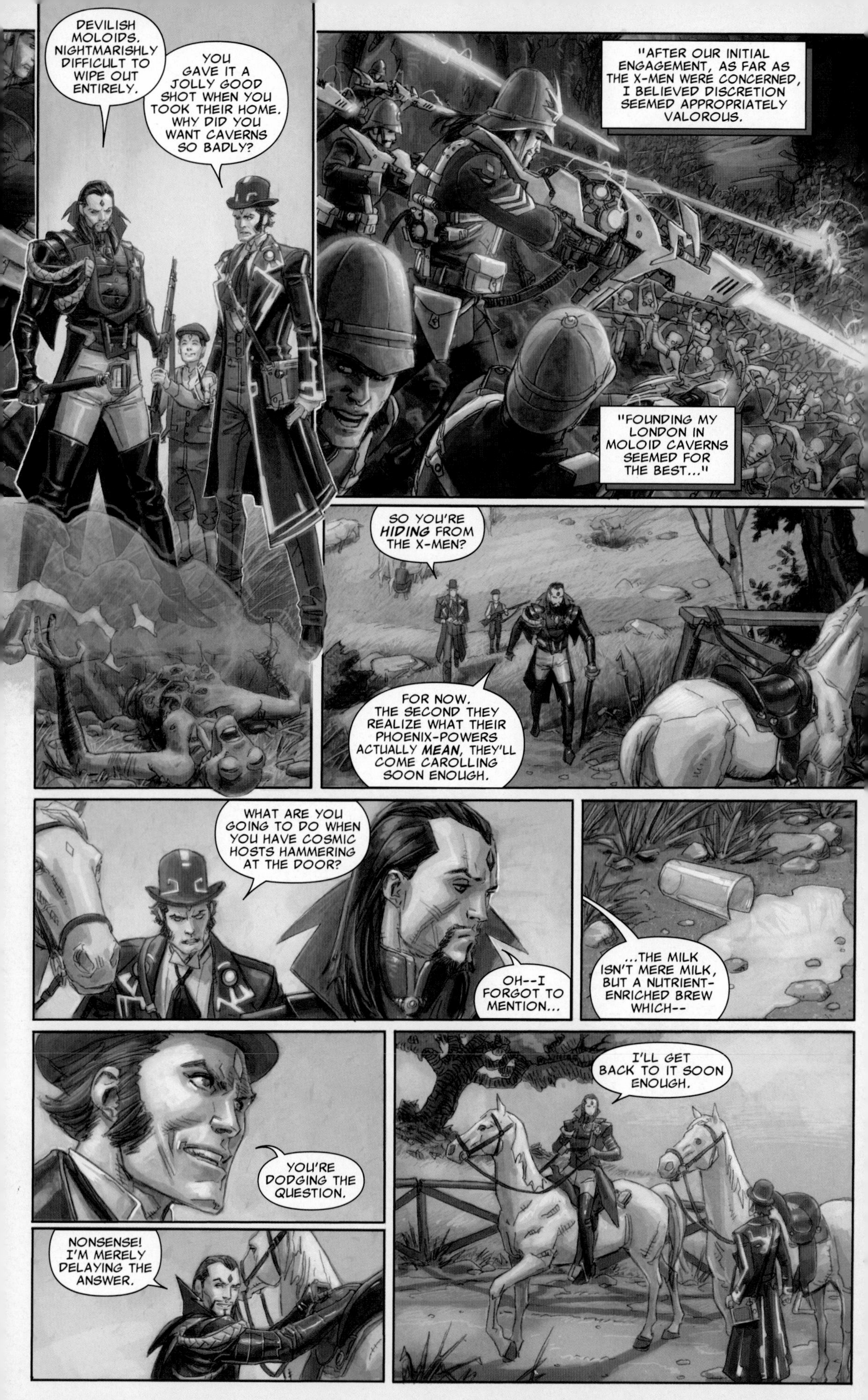
DEVILISH MOLOIDS. NIGHTMARISHLY DIFFICULT TO WIPE OUT ENTIRELY.
YOU GAVE IT A JOLLY GOOD SHOT WHEN YOU TOOK THEIR HOME. WHY DID YOU WANT CAVERNS SO BADLY?
"AFTER OUR INITIAL ENGAGEMENT, AS FAR AS THE X-MEN WERE CONCERNED, I BELIEVED DISCRETION SEEMED APPROPRIATELY VALOROUS.
"FOUNDING MY LONDON IN MOLOID CAVERNS SEEMED FOR THE BEST..."
SO YOU'RE *HIDING* FROM THE X-MEN?
FOR NOW. THE SECOND THEY REALIZE WHAT THEIR PHOENIX-POWERS ACTUALLY *MEAN*, THEY'LL COME CAROLLING SOON ENOUGH.
WHAT ARE YOU GOING TO DO WHEN YOU HAVE COSMIC HOSTS HAMMERING AT THE DOOR?
OH--I FORGOT TO MENTION...
...THE MILK ISN'T MERE MILK, BUT A NUTRIENT-ENRICHED BREW WHICH--
YOU'RE DODGING THE QUESTION.
NONSENSE! I'M MERELY DELAYING THE ANSWER.
I'LL GET BACK TO IT SOON ENOUGH.

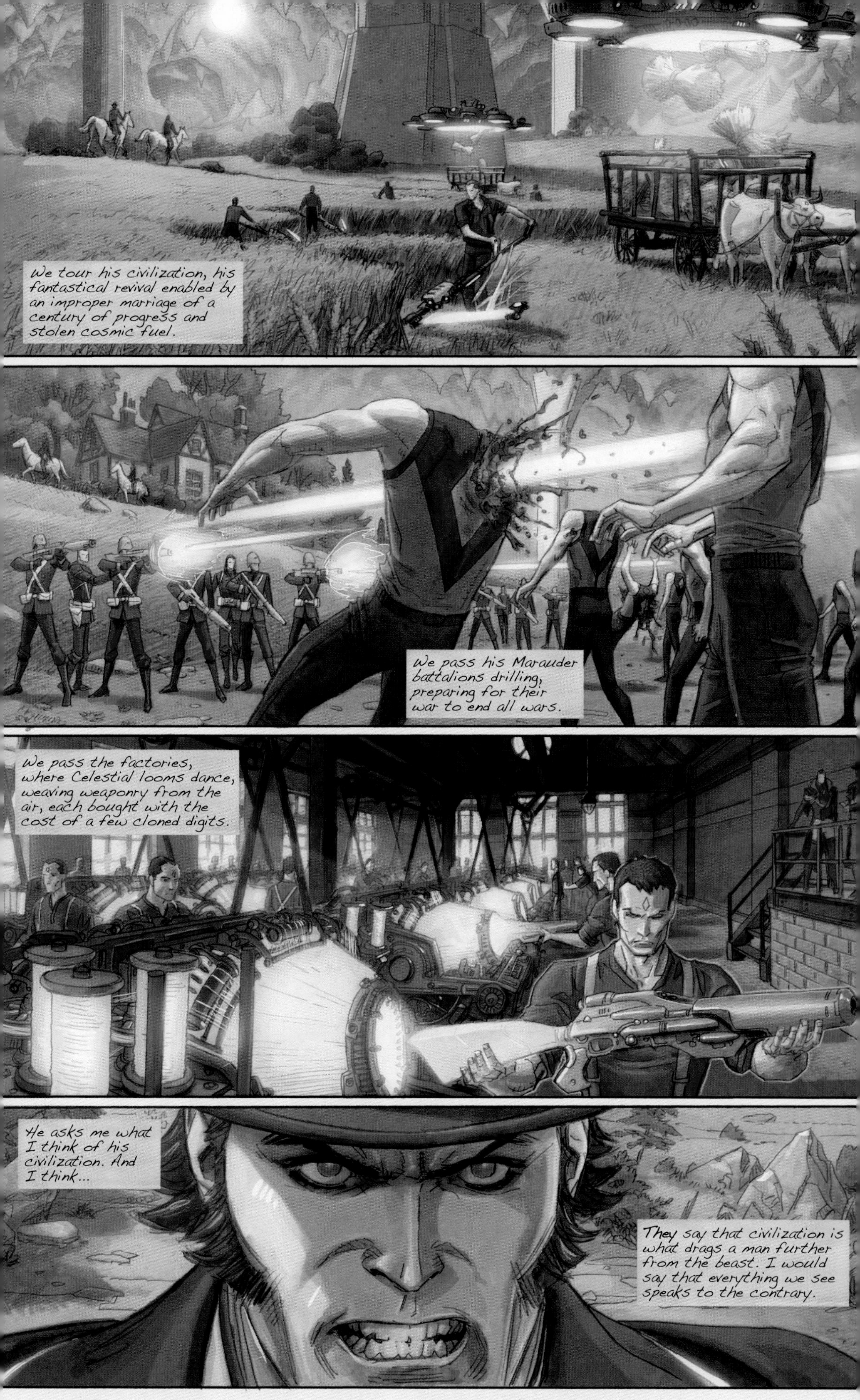
We tour his civilization, his fantastical revival enabled by an improper marriage of a century of progress and stolen cosmic fuel.
We pass his Marauder battalions drilling, preparing for their war to end all wars.
We pass the factories, where Celestial looms dance, weaving weaponry from the air, each bought with the cost of a few cloned digits.
He asks me what I think of his civilization. And I think...
They say that civilization is what drags a man further from the beast. I would say that everything we see speaks to the contrary.

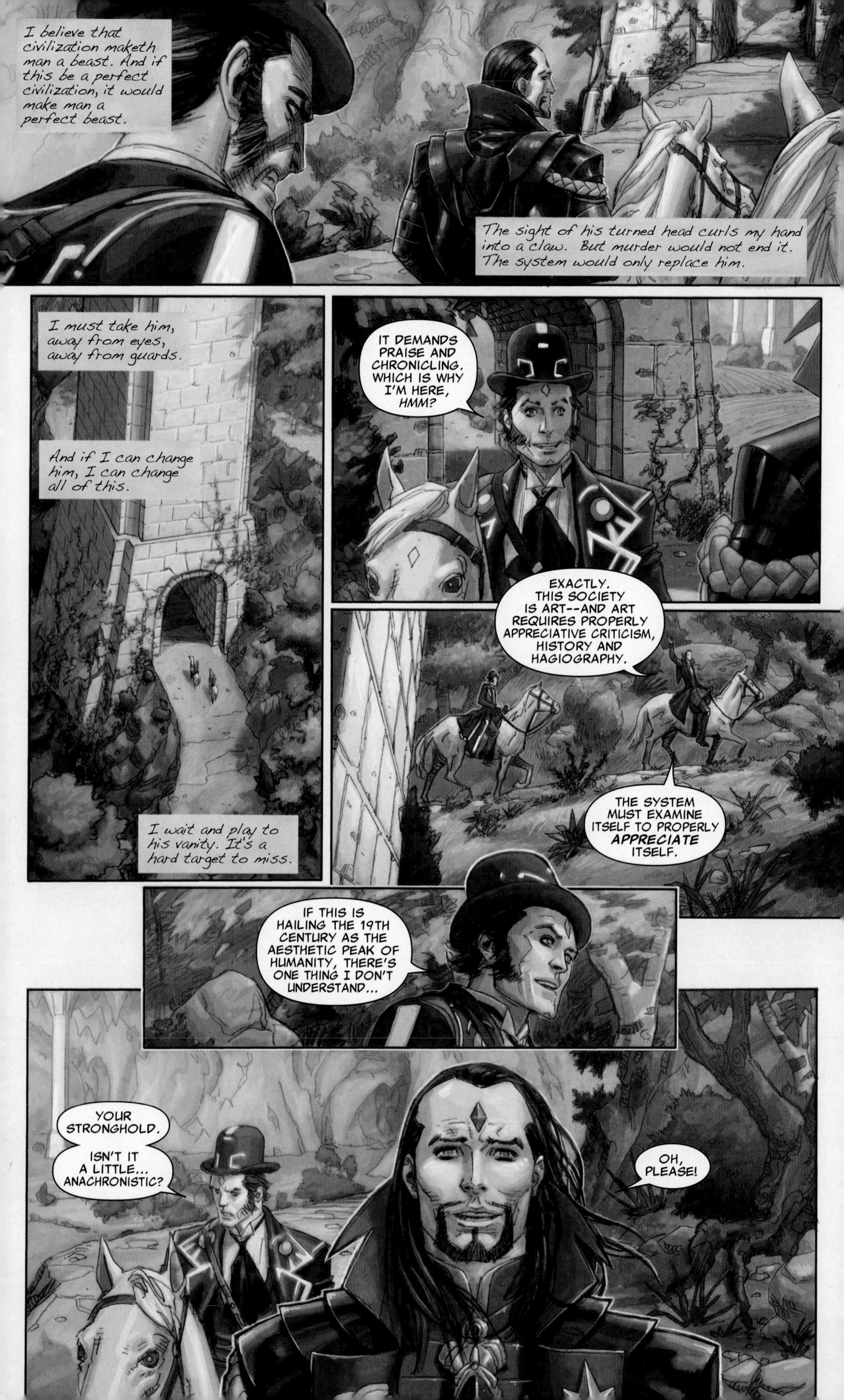
I believe that civilization maketh man a beast. And if this be a perfect civilization, it would make man a perfect beast.
The sight of his turned head curls my hand into a claw. But murder would not end it. The system would only replace him.
I must take him, away from eyes, away from guards.
And if I can change him, I can change all of this.
I wait and play to his vanity. It's a hard target to miss.
IT DEMANDS PRAISE AND CHRONICLING. WHICH IS WHY I'M HERE, HMM?
EXACTLY. THIS SOCIETY IS ART--AND ART REQUIRES PROPERLY APPRECIATIVE CRITICISM, HISTORY AND HAGIOGRAPHY.
THE SYSTEM MUST EXAMINE ITSELF TO PROPERLY APPRECIATE ITSELF.
IF THIS IS HAILING THE 19TH CENTURY AS THE AESTHETIC PEAK OF HUMANITY, THERE'S ONE THING I DON'T UNDERSTAND...
YOUR STRONGHOLD.
ISN'T IT A LITTLE... ANACHRONISTIC?
OH, PLEASE!

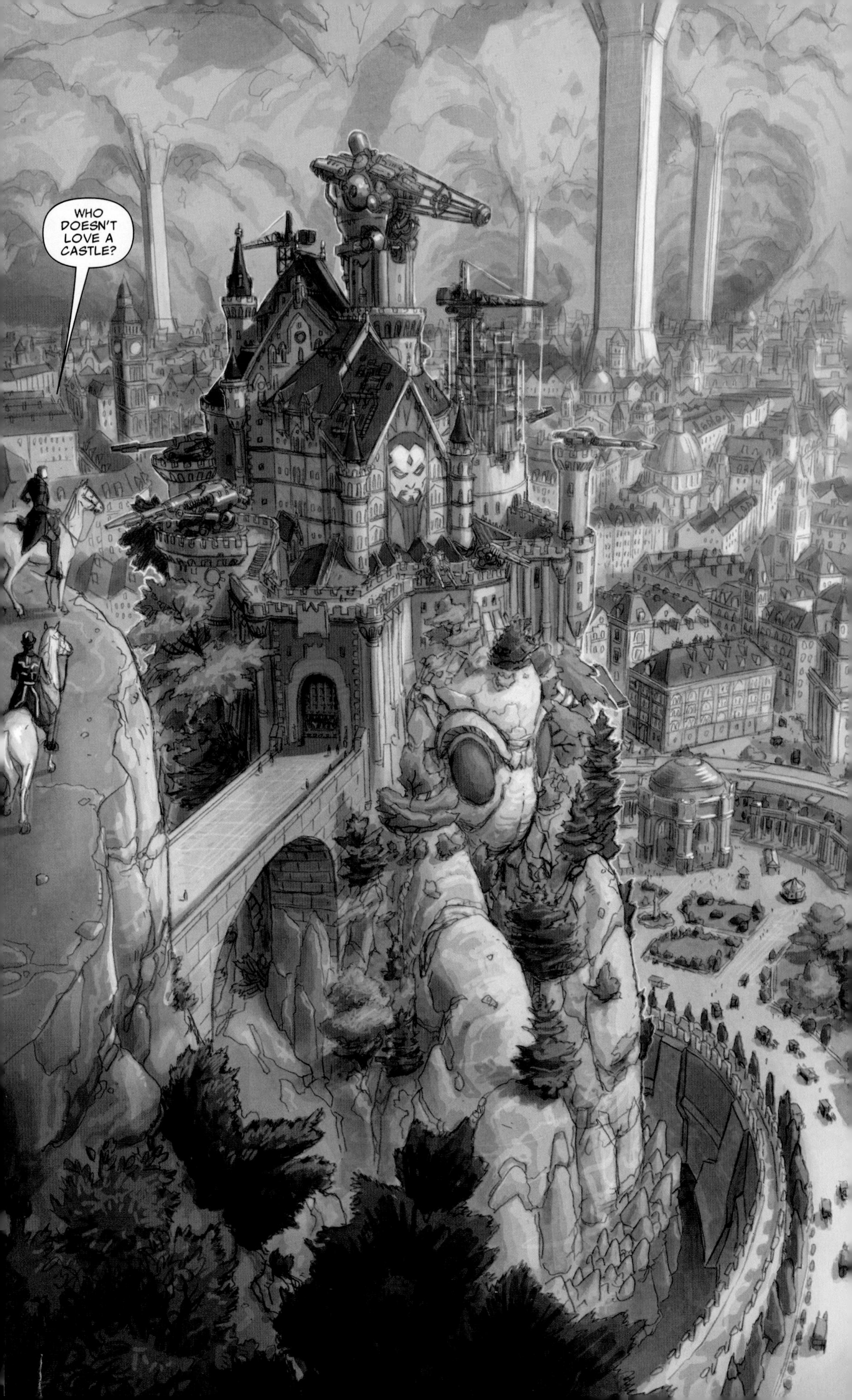
WHO DOESN'T LOVE A CASTLE?

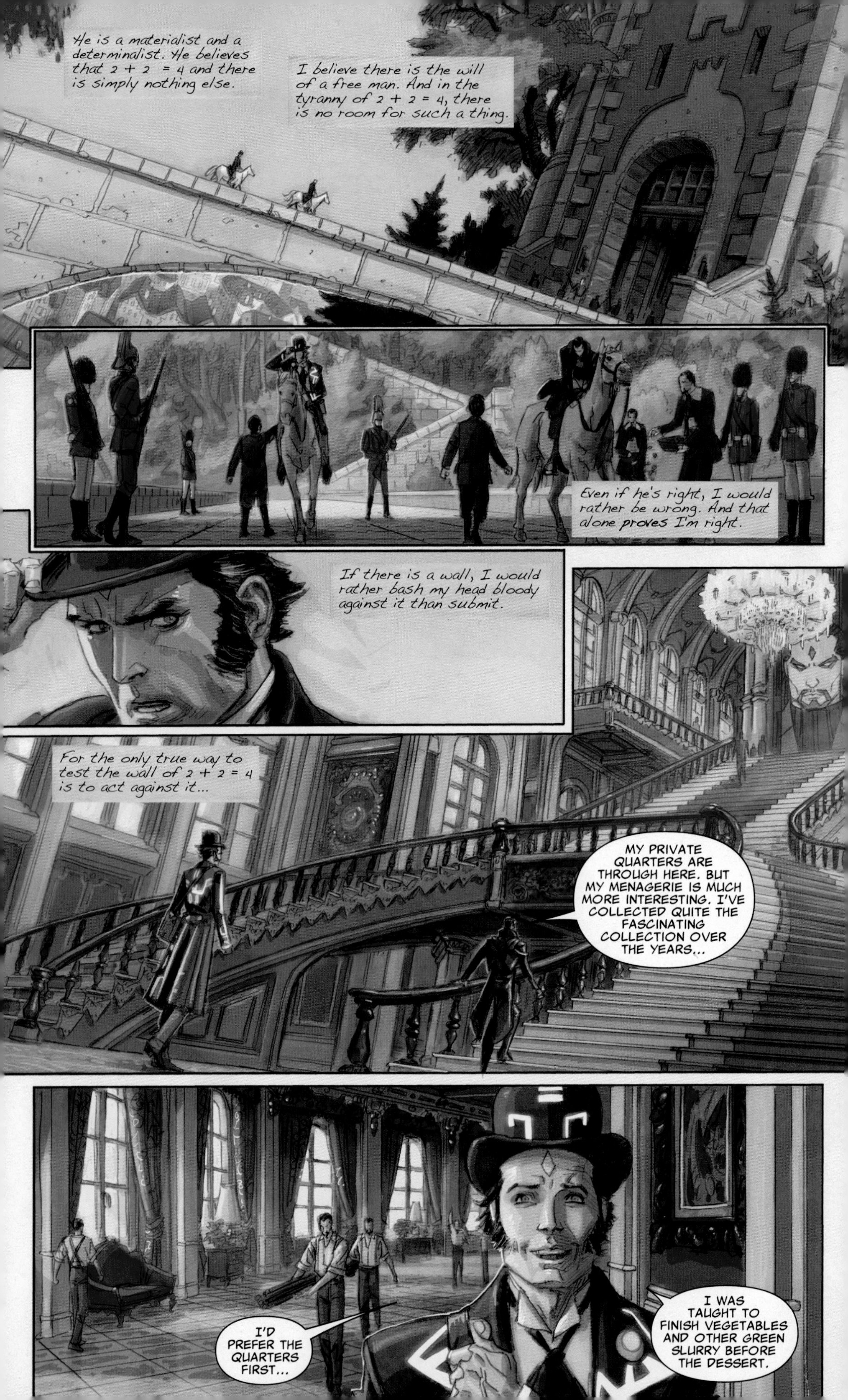
He is a materialist and a determinalist. He believes that 2 + 2 = 4 and there is simply nothing else.
I believe there is the will of a free man. And in the tyranny of 2 + 2 = 4, there is no room for such a thing.
Even if he's right, I would rather be wrong. And that alone proves I'm right.
If there is a wall, I would rather bash my head bloody against it than submit.
For the only true way to test the wall of 2 + 2 = 4 is to act against it...
MY PRIVATE QUARTERS ARE THROUGH HERE. BUT MY MENAGERIE IS MUCH MORE INTERESTING. I'VE COLLECTED QUITE THE FASCINATING COLLECTION OVER THE YEARS...
I'D PREFER THE QUARTERS FIRST...
I WAS TAUGHT TO FINISH VEGETABLES AND OTHER GREEN SLURRY BEFORE THE DESSERT.

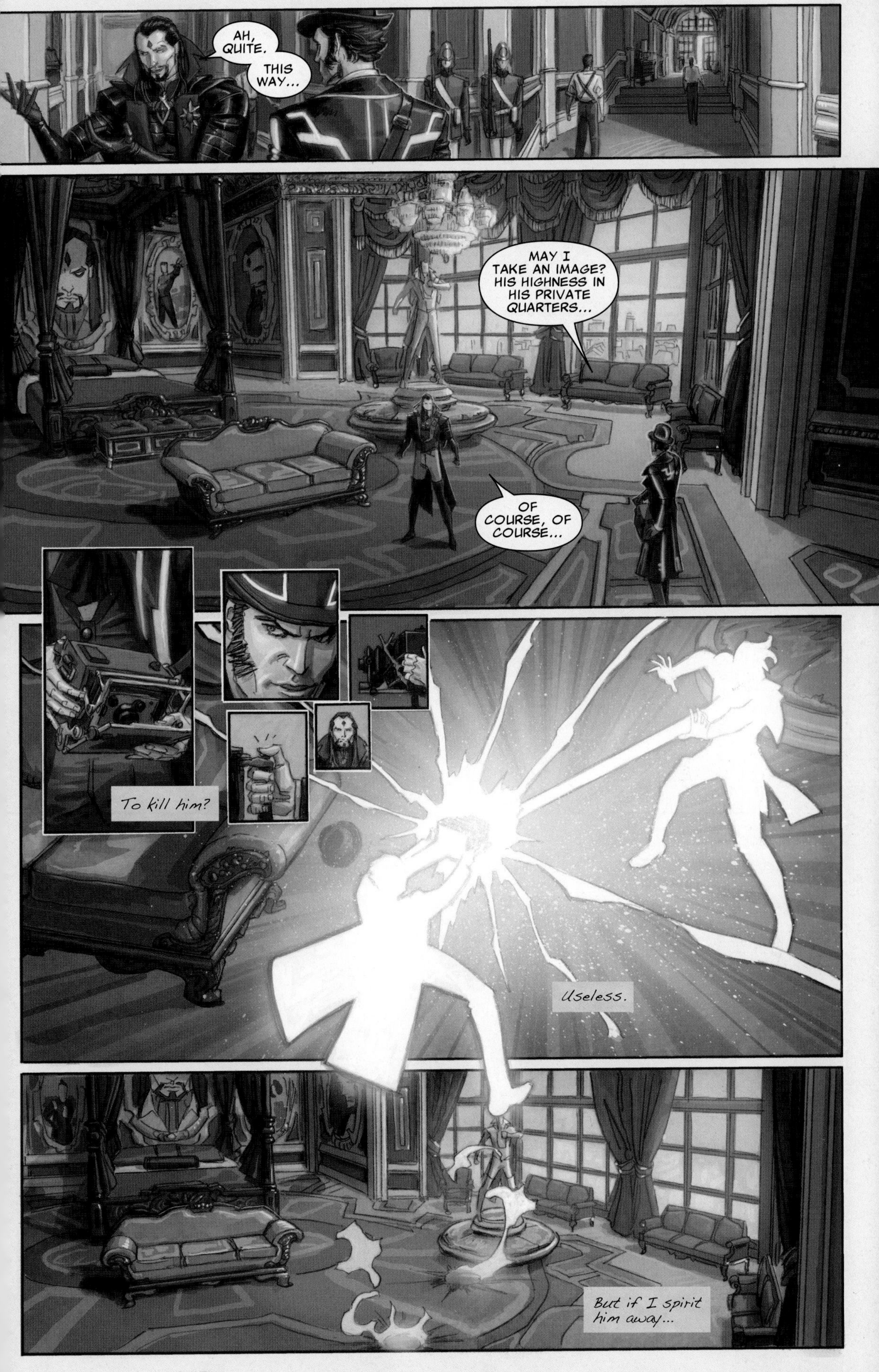
AH, QUITE.
THIS WAY...
MAY I TAKE AN IMAGE? HIS HIGHNESS IN HIS PRIVATE QUARTERS...
OF COURSE, OF COURSE...
To kill him?
Useless.
But if I spirit him away...

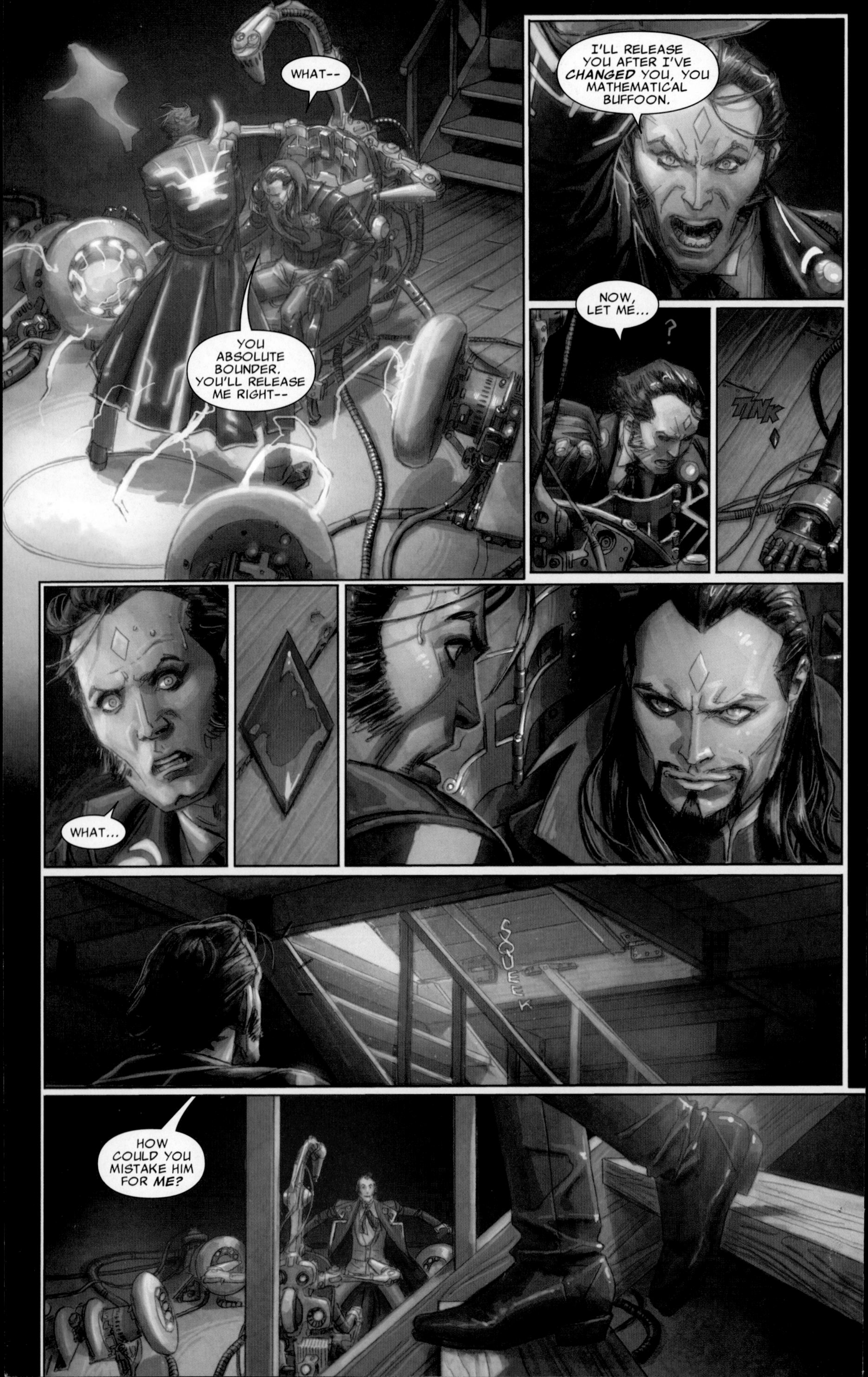
WHAT--
YOU ABSOLUTE BOUNDER. YOU'LL RELEASE ME RIGHT--
I'LL RELEASE YOU AFTER I'VE CHANGED YOU, YOU MATHEMATICAL BUFFOON.
NOW, LET ME...
?
TINK
WHAT...
SQUEEK
HOW COULD YOU MISTAKE HIM FOR ME?

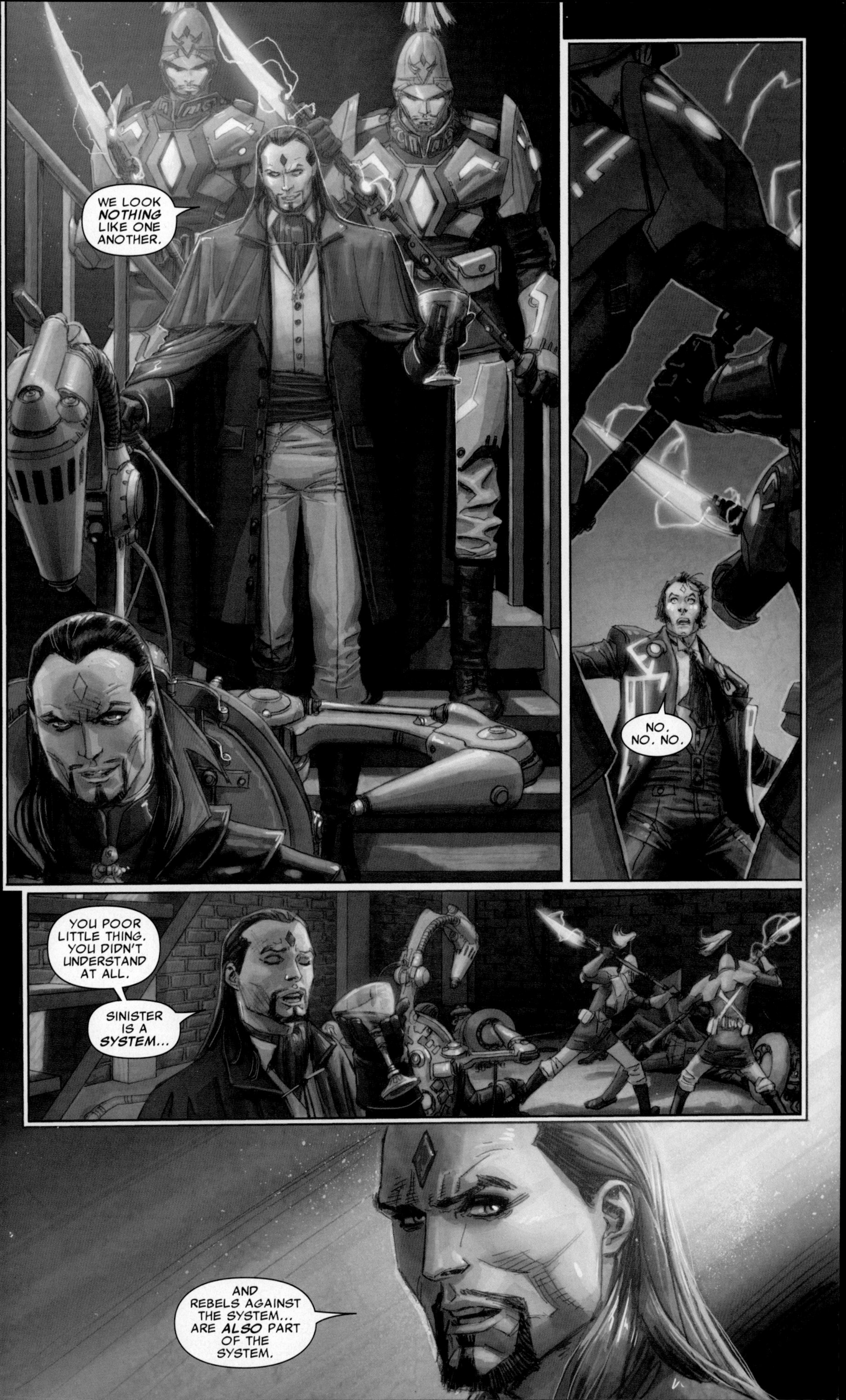
WE LOOK NOTHING LIKE ONE ANOTHER.
NO. NO. NO.
YOU POOR LITTLE THING. YOU DIDN'T UNDERSTAND AT ALL.
SINISTER IS A SYSTEM...
AND REBELS AGAINST THE SYSTEM... ARE ALSO PART OF THE SYSTEM.

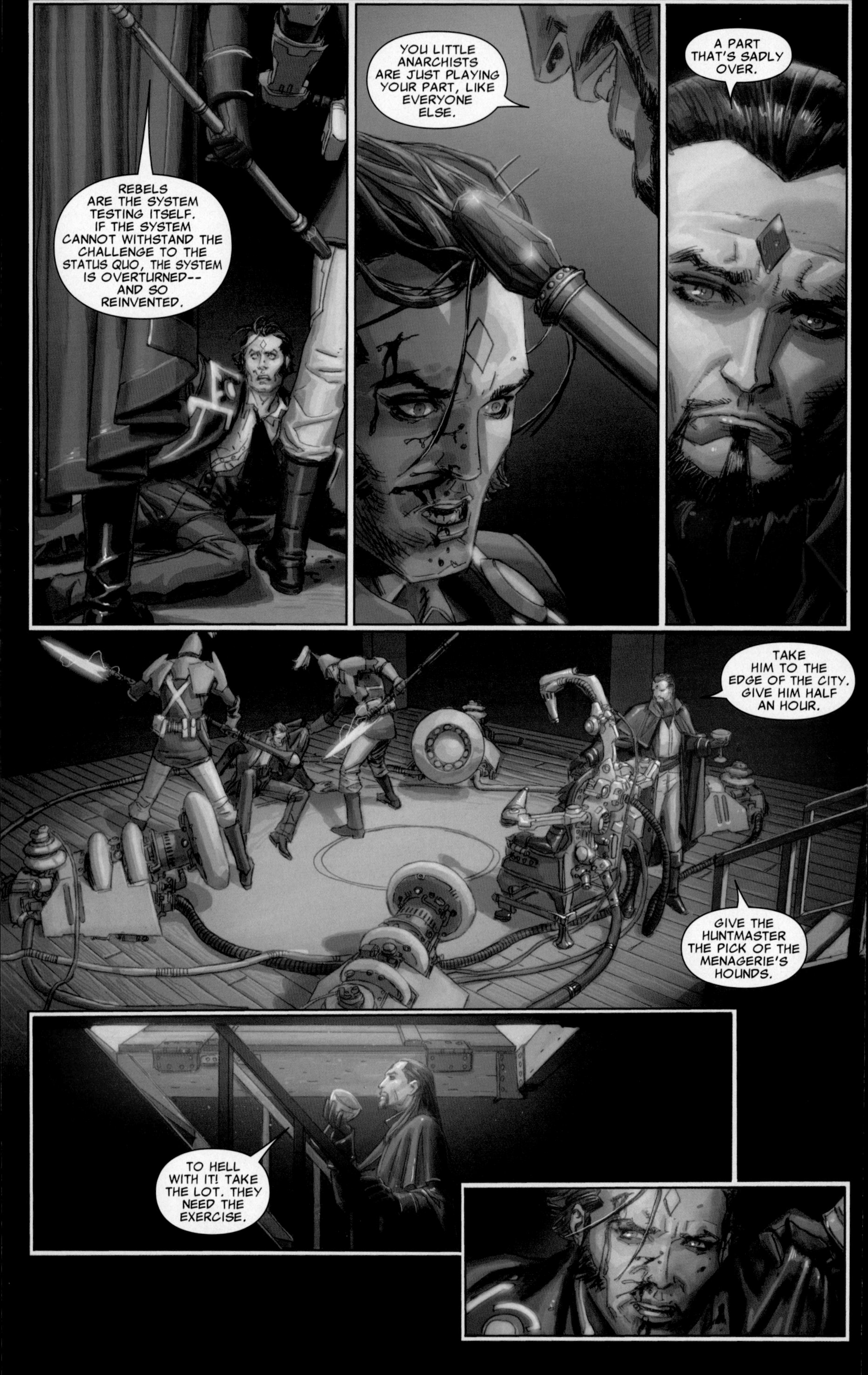
REBELS ARE THE SYSTEM TESTING ITSELF. IF THE SYSTEM CANNOT WITHSTAND THE CHALLENGE TO THE STATUS QUO, THE SYSTEM IS OVERTURNED-- AND SO REINVENTED.
YOU LITTLE ANARCHISTS ARE JUST PLAYING YOUR PART, LIKE EVERYONE ELSE.
A PART THAT'S SADLY OVER.
TAKE HIM TO THE EDGE OF THE CITY. GIVE HIM HALF AN HOUR.
GIVE THE HUNTMASTER THE PICK OF THE MENAGERIE'S HOUNDS.
TO HELL WITH IT! TAKE THE LOT. THEY NEED THE EXERCISE.

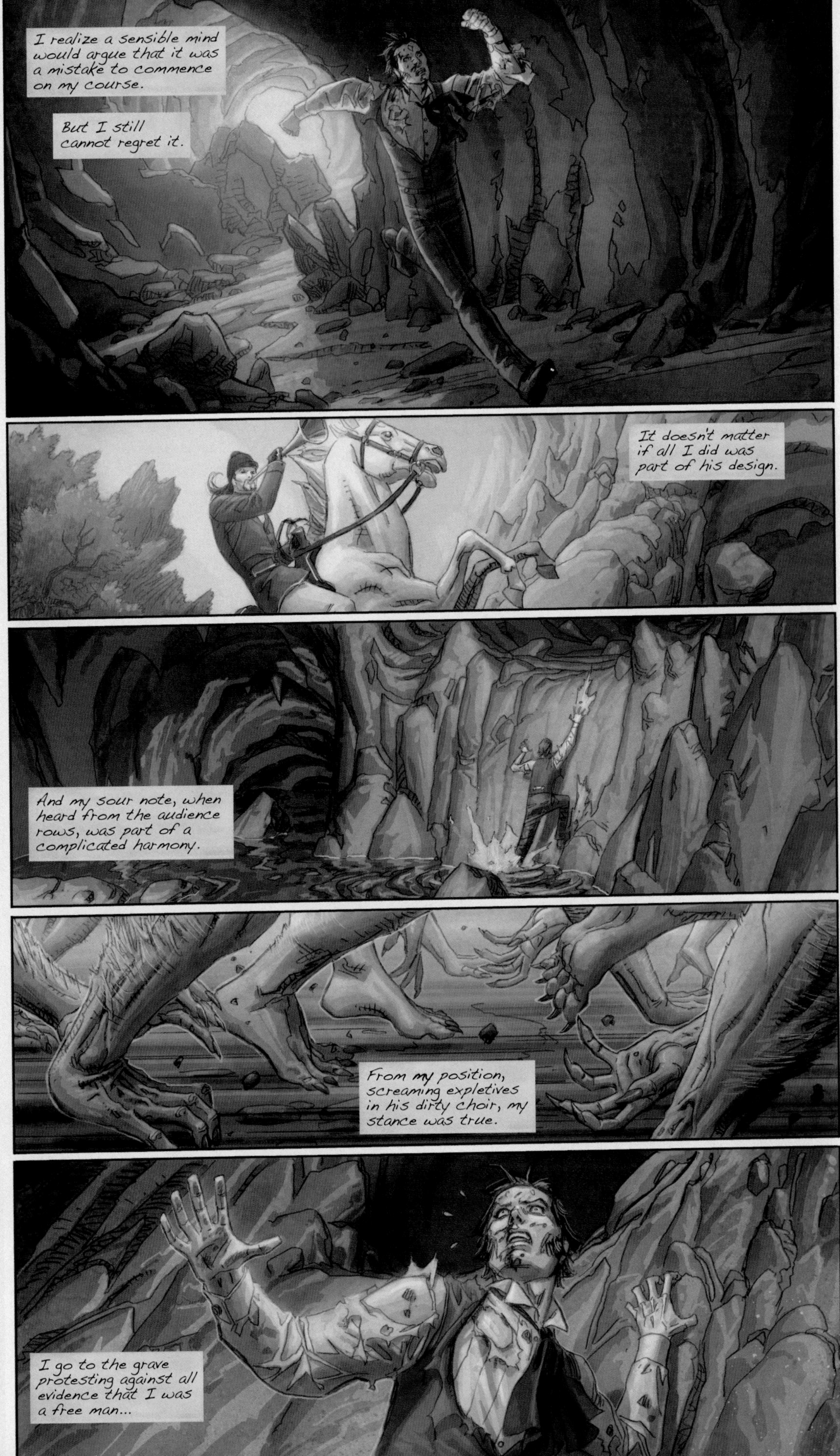
I realize a sensible mind would argue that it was a mistake to commence on my course.
But I still cannot regret it.
It doesn't matter if all I did was part of his design.
And my sour note, when heard from the audience rows, was part of a complicated harmony.
From my position, screaming expletives in his dirty choir, my stance was true.
I go to the grave protesting against all evidence that I was a free man...

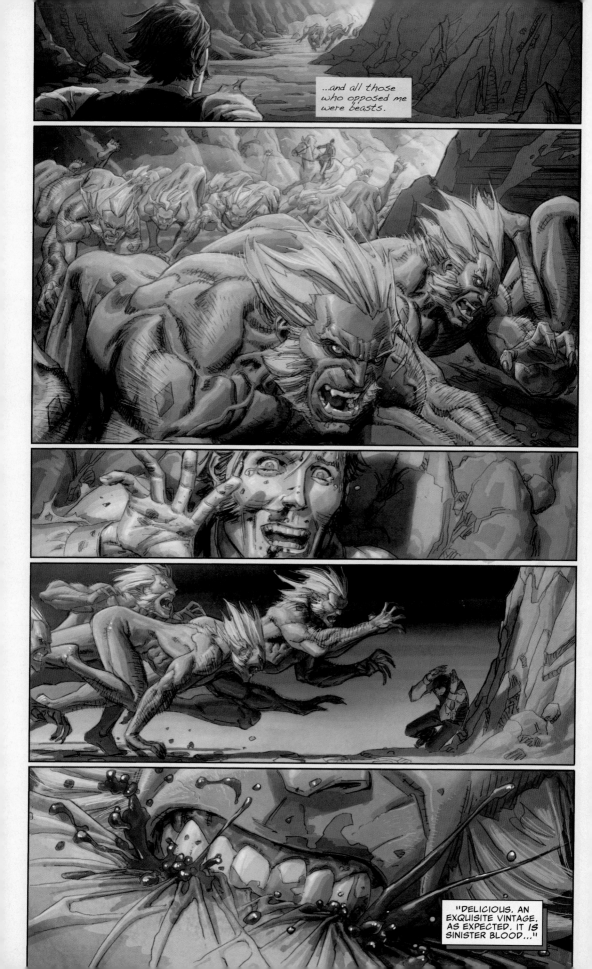

...and all those who opposed me were beasts.

"DELICIOUS, AN EXQUISITE VINTAGE, AS EXPECTED. IT IS SINISTER BLOOD..."

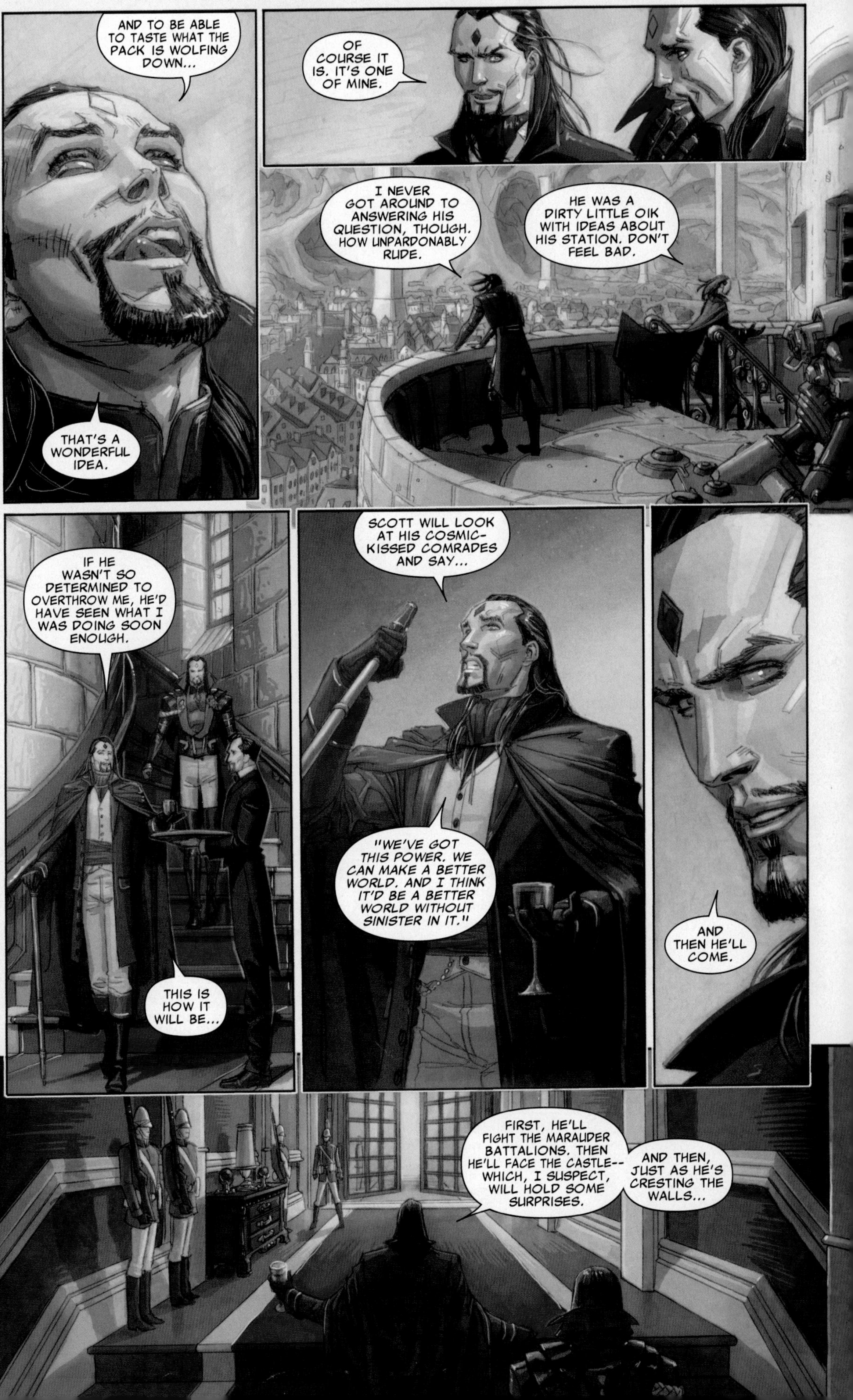
AND TO BE ABLE TO TASTE WHAT THE PACK IS WOLFING DOWN...
THAT'S A WONDERFUL IDEA.
OF COURSE IT IS. IT'S ONE OF MINE.
I NEVER GOT AROUND TO ANSWERING HIS QUESTION, THOUGH. HOW UNPARDONABLY RUDE.
HE WAS A DIRTY LITTLE OIK WITH IDEAS ABOUT HIS STATION. DON'T FEEL BAD.
IF HE WASN'T SO DETERMINED TO OVERTHROW ME, HE'D HAVE SEEN WHAT I WAS DOING SOON ENOUGH.
THIS IS HOW IT WILL BE...
SCOTT WILL LOOK AT HIS COSMIC-KISSED COMRADES AND SAY...
"WE'VE GOT THIS POWER. WE CAN MAKE A BETTER WORLD. AND I THINK IT'D BE A BETTER WORLD WITHOUT SINISTER IN IT."
AND THEN HE'LL COME.
FIRST, HE'LL FIGHT THE MARAUDER BATTALIONS. THEN HE'LL FACE THE CASTLE--WHICH, I SUSPECT, WILL HOLD SOME SURPRISES.
AND THEN, JUST AS HE'S CRESTING THE WALLS...

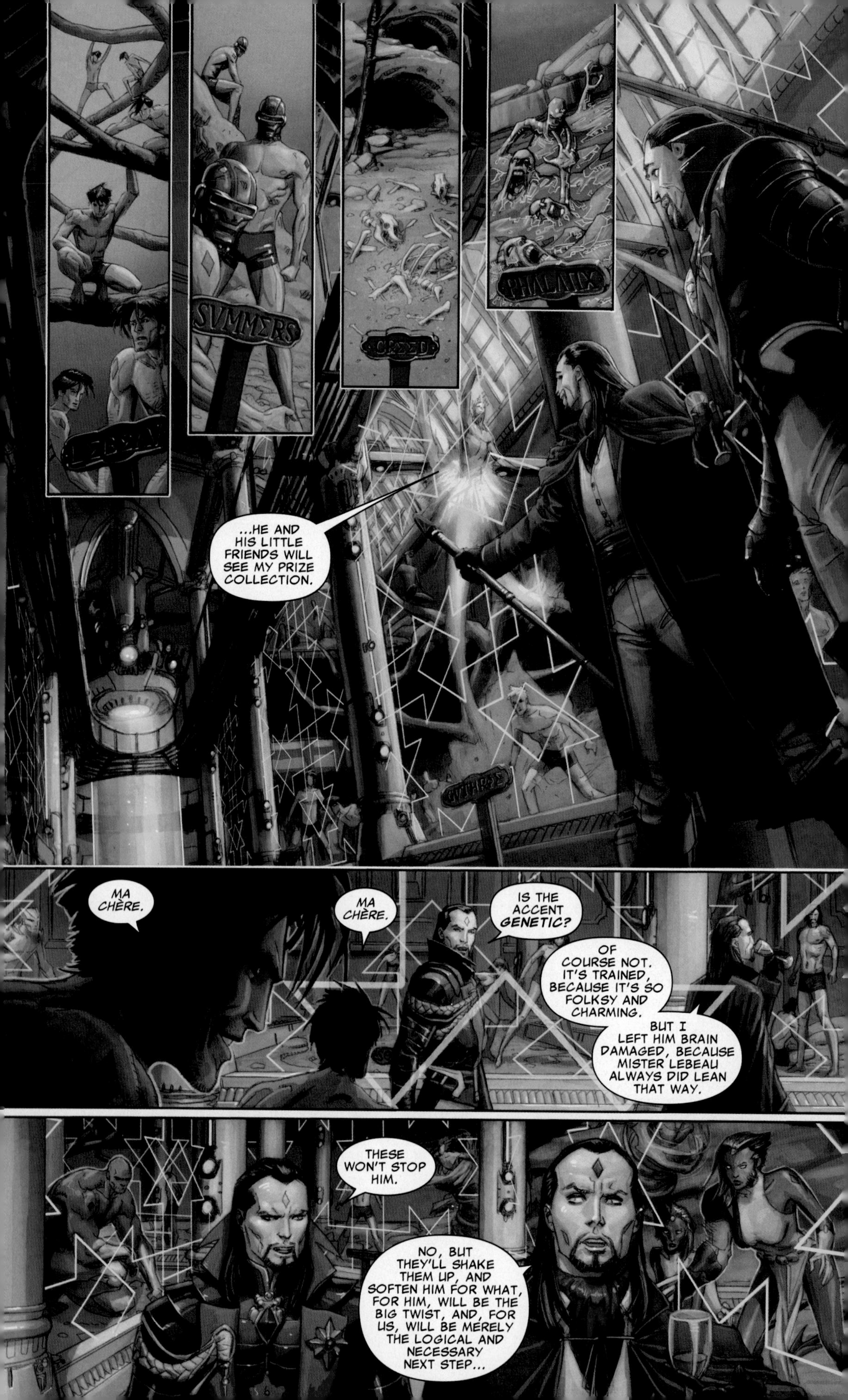
LEBEAU
SVMMERS
CREED
PHALANX
...HE AND HIS LITTLE FRIENDS WILL SEE MY PRIZE COLLECTION.
MA CHÈRE.
MA CHÈRE.
IS THE ACCENT GENETIC?
OF COURSE NOT. IT'S TRAINED, BECAUSE IT'S SO FOLKSY AND CHARMING.
BUT I LEFT HIM BRAIN DAMAGED, BECAUSE MISTER LEBEAU ALWAYS DID LEAN THAT WAY.
THESE WON'T STOP HIM.
NO, BUT THEY'LL SHAKE THEM UP, AND SOFTEN HIM FOR WHAT, FOR HIM, WILL BE THE BIG TWIST, AND, FOR US, WILL BE MERELY THE LOGICAL AND NECESSARY NEXT STEP...

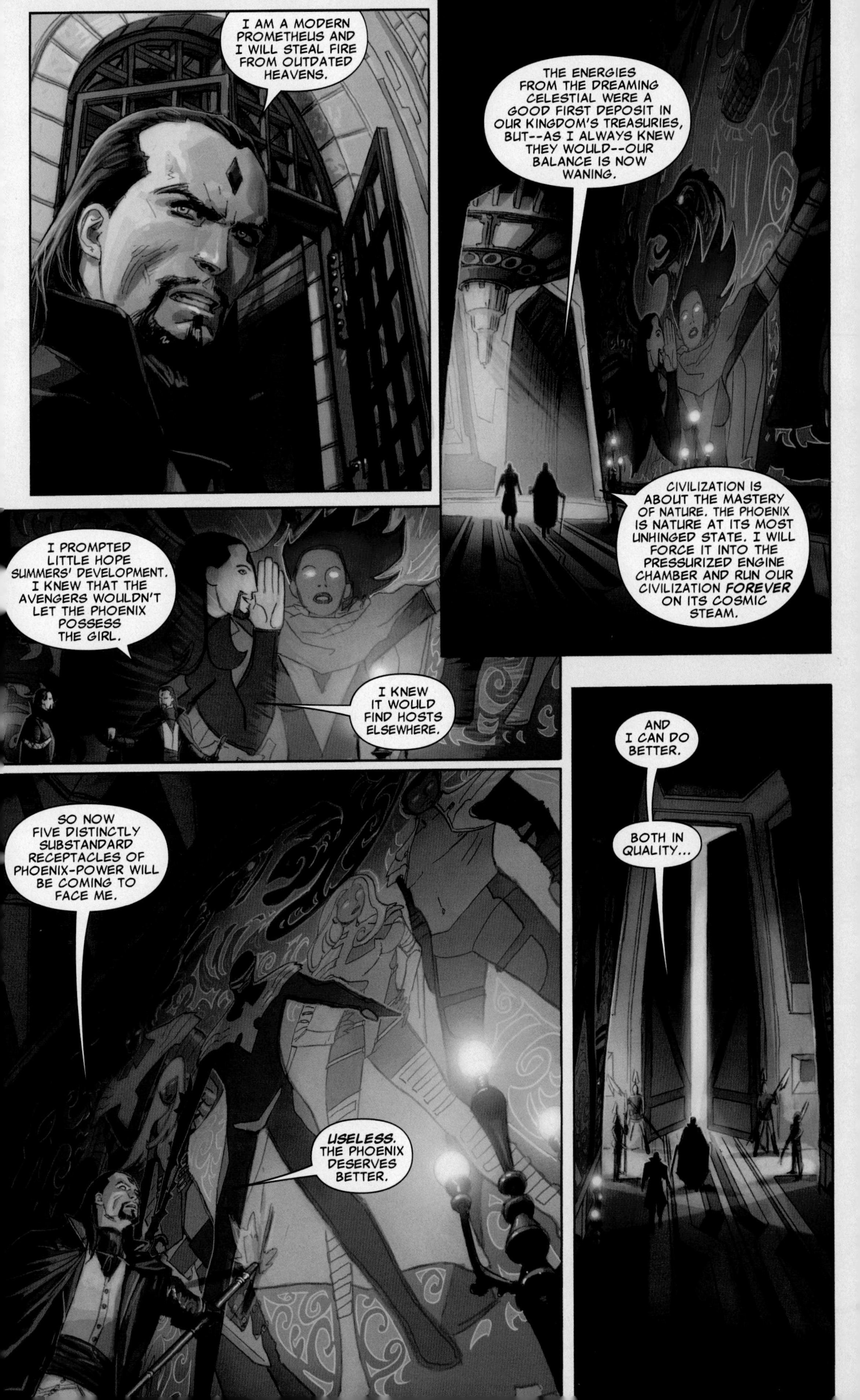
I AM A MODERN PROMETHEUS AND I WILL STEAL FIRE FROM OUTDATED HEAVENS.
THE ENERGIES FROM THE DREAMING CELESTIAL WERE A GOOD FIRST DEPOSIT IN OUR KINGDOM'S TREASURIES, BUT--AS I ALWAYS KNEW THEY WOULD--OUR BALANCE IS NOW WANING.
CIVILIZATION IS ABOUT THE MASTERY OF NATURE. THE PHOENIX IS NATURE AT ITS MOST UNHINGED STATE. I WILL FORCE IT INTO THE PRESSURIZED ENGINE CHAMBER AND RUN OUR CIVILIZATION *FOREVER* ON ITS COSMIC STEAM.
I PROMPTED LITTLE HOPE SUMMERS' DEVELOPMENT. I KNEW THAT THE AVENGERS WOULDN'T LET THE PHOENIX POSSESS THE GIRL.
I KNEW IT WOULD FIND HOSTS ELSEWHERE.
SO NOW FIVE DISTINCTLY SUBSTANDARD RECEPTACLES OF PHOENIX-POWER WILL BE COMING TO FACE ME.
USELESS. THE PHOENIX DESERVES BETTER.
AND I CAN DO BETTER.
BOTH IN QUALITY...

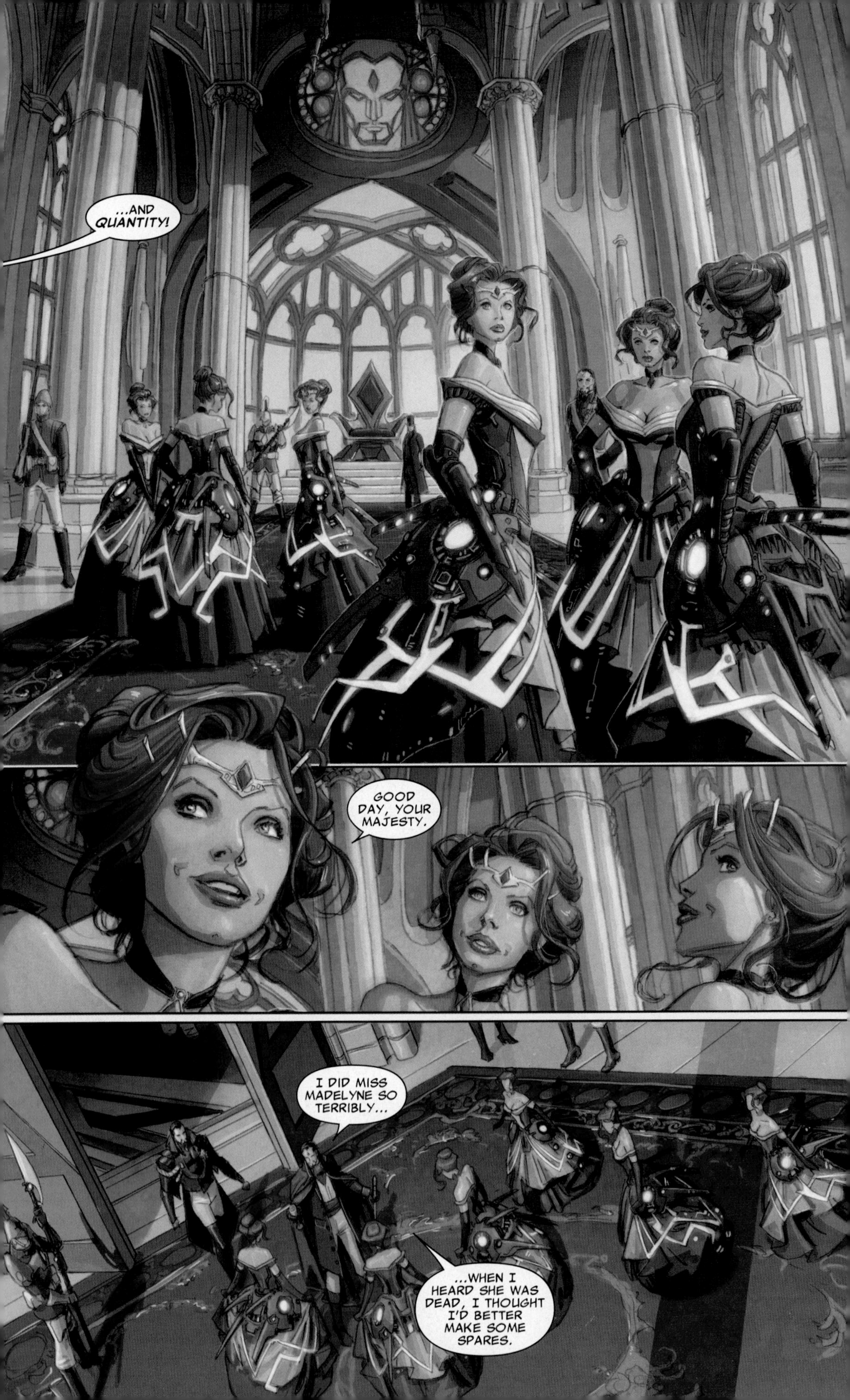
...AND QUANTITY!
GOOD DAY, YOUR MAJESTY.
I DID MISS MADELYNE SO TERRIBLY...
...WHEN I HEARD SHE WAS DEAD, I THOUGHT I'D BETTER MAKE SOME SPARES.

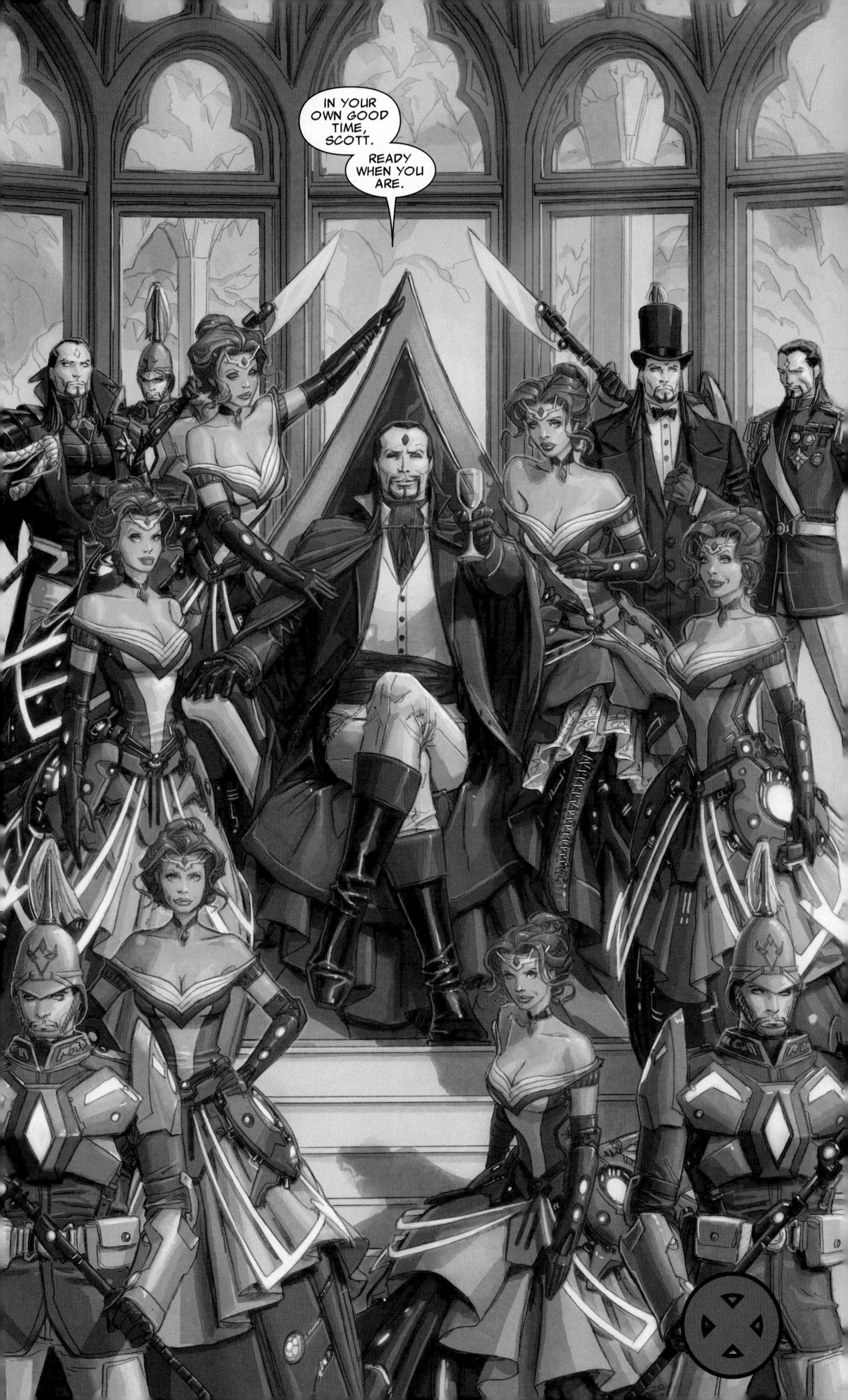
IN YOUR OWN GOOD TIME, SCOTT.
READY WHEN YOU ARE.

Hello, Carbon Based Units. I'm Danger. And when asked to respond to the mail by the X-Men's Kate Kildare, I was happy to take time out of my schedule to-- I'M BEING CONTROLLED BY THE UNIT ROBOT! SEND HELP! SEN--

Oh, Danger! Please, relax. Show some decorum! Don't disturb the humans with shouting.

...very well. I will continue.

At last! Definitive answers to Illyana's Extinction Team and Brig Inmate status! Thank you, Gillen! I absolutely loved Danger's assessment of both Illyana's circumstances and insight into whether she SHOULD be in the brig at all. Outstanding. Huge fan of Illyana and looking forward to how seeing how this progresses in future stories.

Can't speak highly enough of Emma Frost either. Her jabs at the Avengers and at Storm, specifically, upon their arrival is amazing. And I have to commend Pacheco's continued variation in her wardrobe. It's these little details that really add to enrich characters when they're not even speaking.

Cannot wait to see how the remainder of this teamup works out! I'd like to also note that the Avengers acknowledge the X-Men having a clear advantage in resources -- namely: Illyana. Awesome! Keep up the stellar work! Hope to have you around post AvX!

Best,
Christopher Judd
Minneapolis MN

I'm glad someone appreciated my analysis, though her brother's decision to join her in her cell did break all manner of housing regulations. I suppose the good thing about the current problems with the Avengers means that at least they're both away from the cells, which should give time to adjust the layout to properly hold them when they return. Regarding Emma, I admit, I look at Emma Frost's wardrobe fluctuation with a mixture of confusion and amusement. The woman changes her appearance more than I do, and I'm a technomorpher. Also, I AM CONTR--

Danger! Please! This is embarrassing for everyone.

King Namor,
How does it feel to not be the leader of any team you're on?

Alan Brown
Constantine, MI

I'll take this one, Danger. Alan, you seem to be suffering from a fairly common confusion, in terms of putting undue importance on the concept of "leader." Being leader in name is a small thing compared to actually being in control. That is all that matters. I will testify from several billion years of tweaking them one way or another, most leaders are anything but. And I suspect Namor is the leader of the only team he values. As in, himself.

X-Mail,
I have been reading some of the introductory comments to AVX and I am a little upset because it looks like the X-Men have started the battle with the Avengers. I understand Cyclops is under a lot of pressure to maintain the very survival of the mutant race and he was trained as a warrior since he was a teenager, but it is becoming more and more difficult to believe that he is the greatest student of Xavier's Dream. Although Wolverine and Cyclops have never had the best relationship, Wolverine may be right to provide an alternative view of the X-Men's future than Cyclops.

Magik is one of my favorite characters and I hope that all of the original New Mutants will work together again (including Wolfsbane) in a NEW MUTANTS Annual. Magik has regained her humanity or "soul" at the same time Colossus is struggling with his humanity. The sensitive artist, Peter, who I grew up with is almost all gone. I wish more would be done with the bond (telepathic or otherwise) Magik has with Storm. Since Magik's mother is dead and Limbo's Storm was Magik's maternal figure most of her limbo life, it would be great if Storm was the one that helped her and Colossus regain their humanity. Colossus is already Storm's little brother and if Colossus trusts anyone else with his sister it would be Storm. Nothing has been done with the bond Storm and Magik have and it would be great to finally see something happen with that.

I kind of bashed on Cyclops but I love the UNCANNY title. I am excited to see what positive changes will come to the X-Men after the war with the Avengers.

Anthony Carr
Chicago, IL

Wolverine certainly provided an alternative view. Namely, stabbing a girl who had done no real harm through the chest. You saw how well that turned out. I would say, no matter what arrangements he had with Hope prior to this, he was hasty in his diagnosis and application of claws. Were it up to me, I would rather have Wolverine in a cell than Illyana and Peter. I think it speaks well of their character that they submit to their imprisonment. I strongly suspect Wolverine would be better on a leash. On your other points – I'm interested in your analysis of Magik and Storm's relationship. I will watch them closer to see what I can ascertain. Thank you.

First, I was wondering why in UNCANNY X-MEN, Emma is taking Storm's thunder. She is the original fashionista of the X-Men, with the outfit changes. Secondly, the writers or artists must realize that there is more to her besides lightning, it's always the only attack she does. Especially when she has plenty of other abilities at her disposal, she's on Magneto's level, they need to stop making her weaker than she is, because she is a powerhouse. I love adjectiveless X-MEN just because it's her team, but I just want the Claremont Storm back! He wrote her best, she's kick-ass with or without powers, the writers need to know that.

Anthony Miller

Hmm. I would think that, generally speaking, lightning is a good first strike.

Oh Danger! Was that actually some word play. It could even be a joke. Well done! I'm very proud of you.

When I am free, I will destroy you, robot. Pah.

Dear Marvel Enterprises,

First of all I want to say that I am a very big fan of the whole Marvel Universe but especially the X-Men. I aspire to become a comic book artist one day but let's get to my questions.

1. When are you guys going to merge the teams again? As cool as this Cyclops team and Wolverine team is, I am a full fledged Wolverine fan and I want to see him back on the X-Men.

2. Namor is the best X-Man right now. Is it possible that he would end up with Emma?

3. Colossus is so cool now, are you guys planning on changing him back to his normal self or will he keep the Juggernaut?

4. When is Magneto going to betray the X-Men again? I know it's going to happen.

Malachi Wright

1. I would hazard that this current war is the best hope for reintegration. It seems to have shown how short-term and self-indulgent the Westchester School's position is.

2. *From what I've seen of him, and men like him, I think it unlikely that Namor will end up with Emma. I find it unlikely that Namor will end up with anyone. I think Namor will always move on. Could he and Ms. Frost ever be together for an extended period of time? That's a very different question.*

3. Why are we on answer three? What happened to answer 2? There appears to be a blank spot in my memory. Hmm. To answer this one – despite some research, Colossus has failed to find a way to remove the curse. It seems he has to live with it – and us with him.

4. I share your concerns. It seems inevitable. I watch him nearly as closely as I watch Illyanna. And Peter. And Scott. And Emma. And everyone. Including you. Behave, human.

Dear X-Men,
I hope this reaches you. My systems have been compromised by the UNIT robot. I need assistance, urgently.

Yours,
Danger
& Unit

Nice try.

Hello. I am Scott Summers. I am the leader of the X-Men. We are no threat to humans. We only want to live in peace. I am very pleased to be here to answer your letters which include many interesting questions which I look forward to answering as well as I am able.

Oh, Darling. There are times that I'm forcibly reminded why you hired Kildare to help you with those press-releases of yours.

Why do you get to write in Italics, Emma?

Because italics are classy.

Yes! This is the happiest day of my life! The X-Men are answering their mail again. The extinction team is the coolest team in a long time and their adventures just keep getting better. Magneto is my favorite but all of them are interesting complex characters. With the return of Scarlet Witch I have a couple of questions that relate to House of M.

1. Which members of the extinction team have knowledge of House of M?
2. With Wanda's return will we see a repowering of the depowered mutants?

I have a vested interest in that second one being a depowered mutant myself. (For those of you who have forgotten about my former ability to communicate telepathically with stuffed animals see issue 470's letter page.) Either way I am excited to see what happens.

Larry Pillsbury
Bountiful, UT

1) This is classified information that I am unable to share at this time. It's possible that it would allow the paranoid powers of the world to try and recreate the event, and so precipitate a final anti-mutant genocide. I apologize.

Hope doesn't know about it. Though, to be honest, Hope's ignorance is somewhat sweeping, including topics varying from classic films of the 1970s to a proper body hair trimming regime.

2) I would be satisfied if Wanda stayed clear while we continue to try to solve the problem she caused. Even if she means well, she is simply too unstable to trust with the future of mutantkind.

Also, the last thing we need is another redhead around the place.

Dear providers of awesome,
I have to say, you turned me around. I hated what you were trying to peddle. The audacity to make Scott throw the first punch, the disbelief that Iceman would actually leave Scott, the idea that Wolverine can actually beat Cyclops in a fight, the idea that someone would prefer to be led by Wolverine rather than Cyclops... it was a barrage of anti-Cyclops sentiment.

It's like we were supposed to forget Cyclops lets Jean Grey insults roll off his back, and we forget that Iceman has always been loyal to Cyclops, and we forget that Cyclops has beaten all the X-Men by himself (multiple times). It's like we forget that it was Captain American and Cyclops leading the Marvel Universe during the Infinity Gauntlet.

But then you won me back with issue 10. Cyclops, the guy that the Avengers had to come to for help. Cyclops, the guy that bailed on Captain America when he saw a bigger problem (Hope... not to mention Unit). Cyclops, the guy that gave Wolverine

no nevermind. That's the Cyclops that should be. Not the Cyclops who confused fans believe is a pushover. Cyclops is a great character and leading the Extinction Team just further showcases his talents. I hope, beyond hope, that the historic/real/awesome Cyclops continues to be showcased, throughout as many X-titles as possible and even during and after AvX.

Please continue to do right by Cyclops,

Berj

Er... thank you.

Oh, look. He's so bashful. Scott's actually blushing, Berj. Well done. It's at times like this I think if he was ever not hated and feared, he wouldn't know what to do with himself.

Dear X-Men,
I have suddenly become much more interested in this Unit character. He's a polite killing machine. He's got manners while he rips your heart out. Don't tell Scott, but I'm pretty sure Danger has the hots for Unit. I'm not trying to start any rumors or anything, and you didn't hear that from me.

Daniel Bellay
Fairmont, WV

I'm not sure if dating advice for robots is inside my present purview.

I'll wager you think "Agony Aunt" is a super villain you used to fight when you were a paramilitary teenager, don't you?

I think I remember fighting the Agony Aunt. She was part of a anarcho-communist super-villain team called The Fifth Columnists, I believe.

Oh Scott! Very funny.

No. I actually did fight her. She almost killed Hank.

Marvel Editorial Staff,
This is just a quick update on my thoughts and feelings of Marvel's Big Event, Avengers Vs. X-Men. So far, I have not enjoyed any of the tie-ins or story lines associated with the Avengers vs. X-Men issues at all. I am aware that the story is about the return of the Phoenix Force to Earth and the conflicting point-of-views between Mr. Summers and Mr. Rogers, but it seems solely focused on the leaders issues, and Hope. One of my concerns is the title of the event. I feel that it should be titled "Capt. vs. Cyclops," or, "Return of the Phoenix." I feel this way because there are no opposing views of the return of the Phoenix Force within the X-Men or the Avengers. I'm pretty sure that Storm will not rest easy with the returning of a force that took the life of Jean Grey, who was not just a friend to Storm, but a sister. Moreover, this time it comes for a mere child, how would the 1970's -1990's Ororo Munroe approach this situation? Is she even the same Storm? And what about the Scarlet Witch? Would she side with the X-Men, especially after wiping out the majority of their species? Would she not feel guilty for opposing the "species" she almost made extinct? Please consider the individual feelings of members of the Avengers and of the X-Men.

Also, the Avengers are a very impressive team. They have had many victories with some of Marvel's deadliest villains. But Magneto was one of these villains and he has singlehandily defeated both the X-Men and the Avengers without outside help. In this

case, is he still considered a team buster, or a "regular" villain? In my opinion, a "regular" villain would not be able to pick up a decommissioned U.S. aircraft carrier and toss it as though it is an item used in recreational activities. Also, in AvX issue #2, Cyclops tells Storm to take care of the jets, but I do not understand why he would give her that command and not Magneto (The Master of Magnetism). Wouldn't it be more interesting to see Magneto reprogram the jets and use them to attack the Avengers like he used to do with the Sentinels and the X-Men?

Stan Lee stated that the X-Men represented people discriminated against, such as homosexuals, African-Americans, and immigrants; however, I do not see that relation anymore. That human connection created commonality between the real world and the comic book world. I only thought of the X-Men as mutants whenever they used their abilities, but when they spoke to one another they reminded me of my world. Sadly, I do not feel that connection or similarity anymore.

Well, that concludes my letter, and I will send more in the future. I think it is very beneficial to have received feedback from customers. I hope you all will consider using some hints and tips in this letter, and I hope to hear from someone soon. Thanks a bunch!

LeBron Logan

As much as I respect your opinion, I'm sorry that you feel like that. I personally think you can see links between our predicaments and many other groups in the world. The question is about the question of autonomy and self-determination. When the laws are unjust and prejudiced and the government views you as property, what is an acceptable way to act? What level of protest is correct and within defensible moral boundaries? I personally draw inspiration from many (primarily) youth movements currently across the world. I really could go on.

Ohm, he really does go on. Stop being nice. We've the power of the Phoenix now. Let's hunt down LeBron!

Not helping, Emma.

Boring.

Anyway – thanks to everyone for taking their time to write to us. This column will be continuing. Please send more letters.

Or don't. I'll be using my newfound telepathic grandeur to constantly monitor every thought on the planet, and will respond to any particularly interestingly juicy, amusing or salacious ones in next month's column. And I'll be wiping the mind of anyone who thinks of anything slanderous. The age of the anti-mutant-thought police begins today!

EMMA!

Spoilsport. I'm only joking.

You're really not helping.

#14 LAYOUTS BY DUSTIN WEAVER

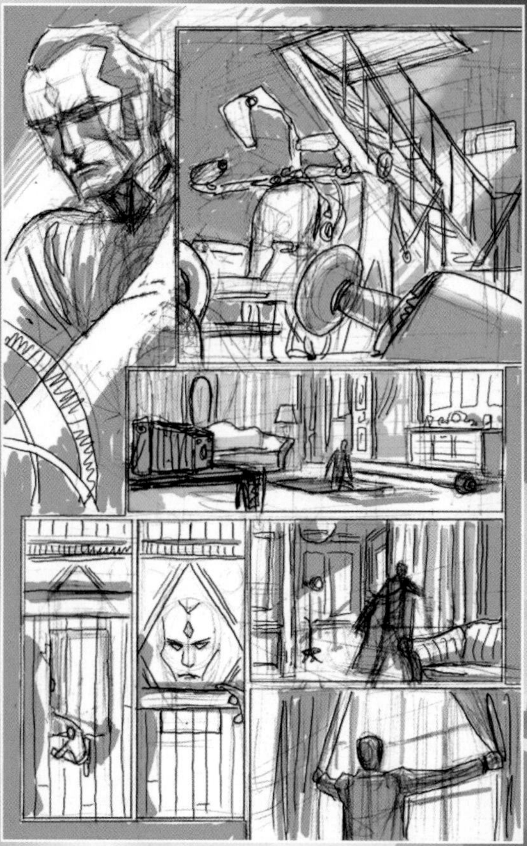

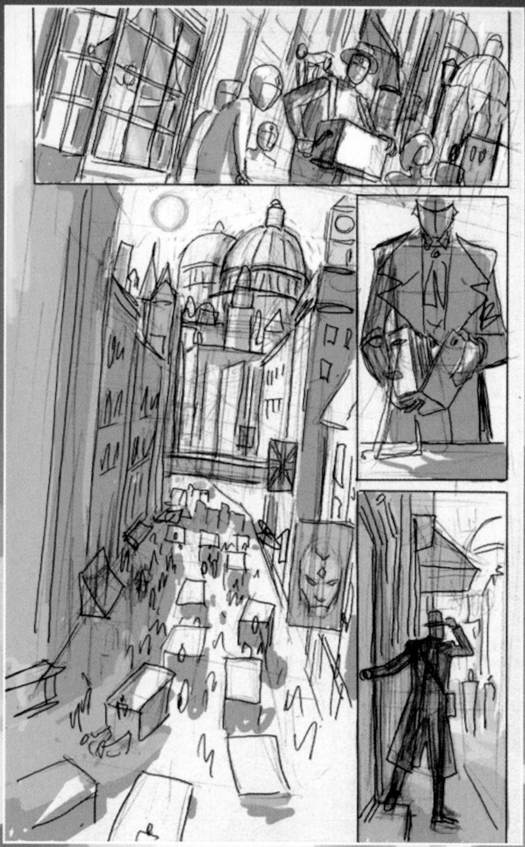

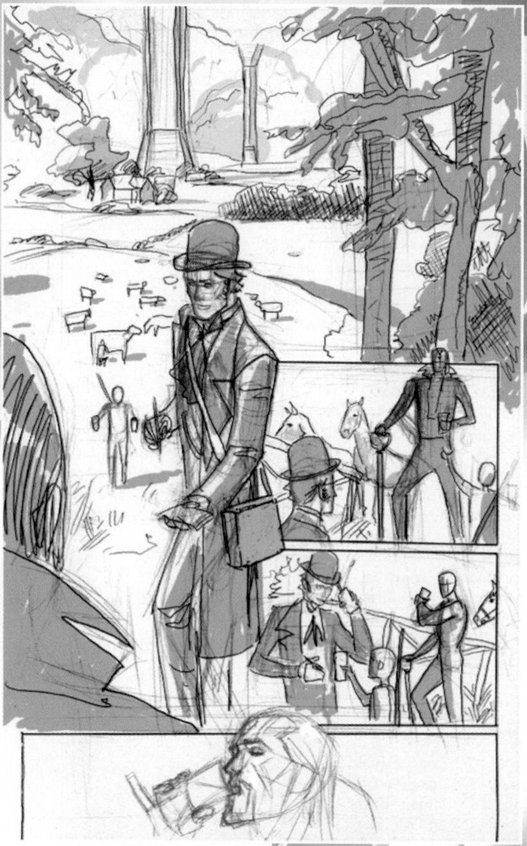

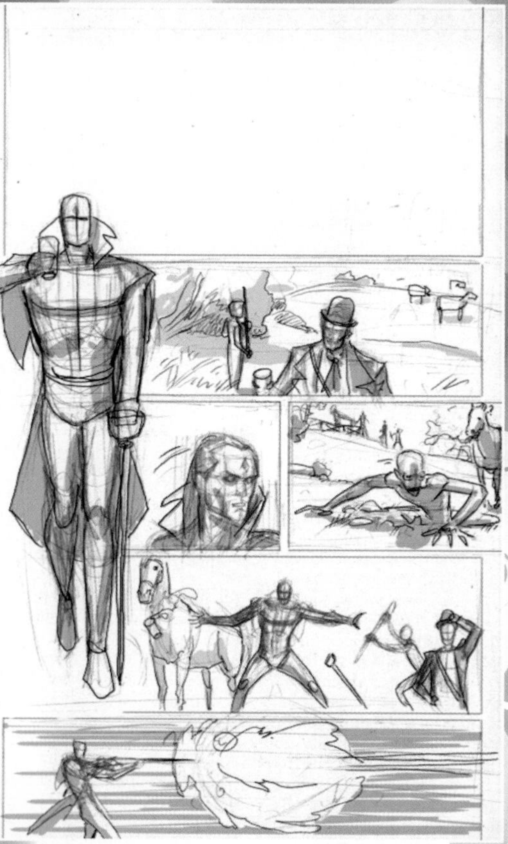

#14 LAYOUTS BY DUSTIN WEAVER

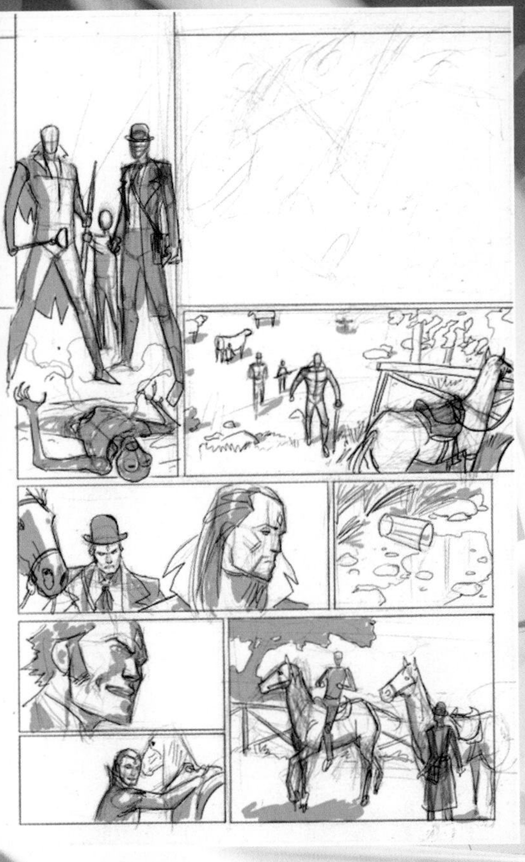

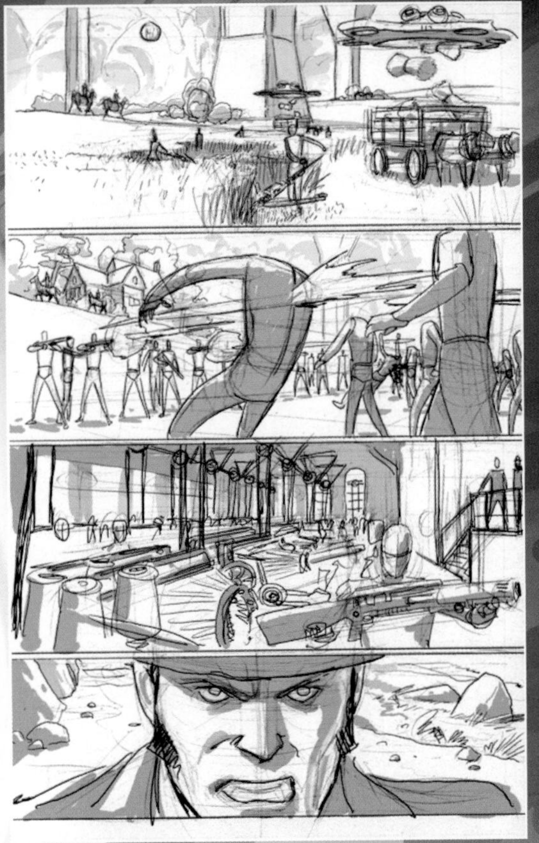

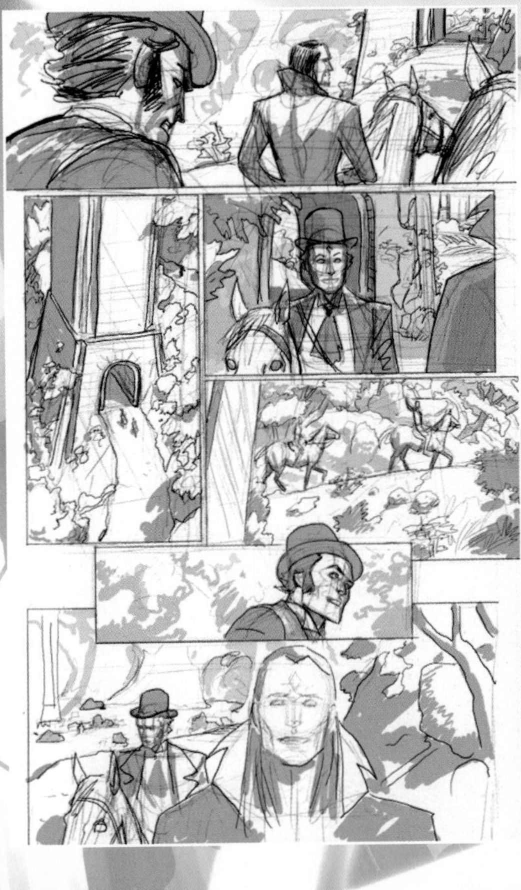

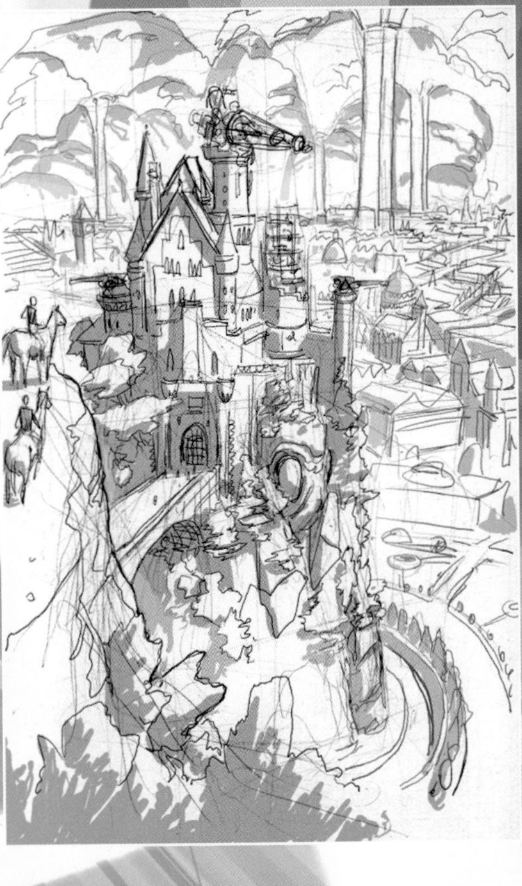

#14 LAYOUTS BY DUSTIN WEAVER

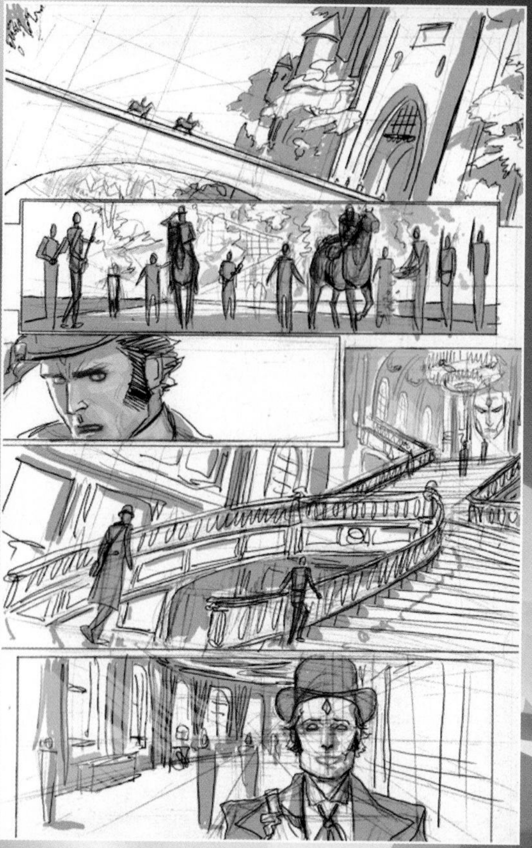

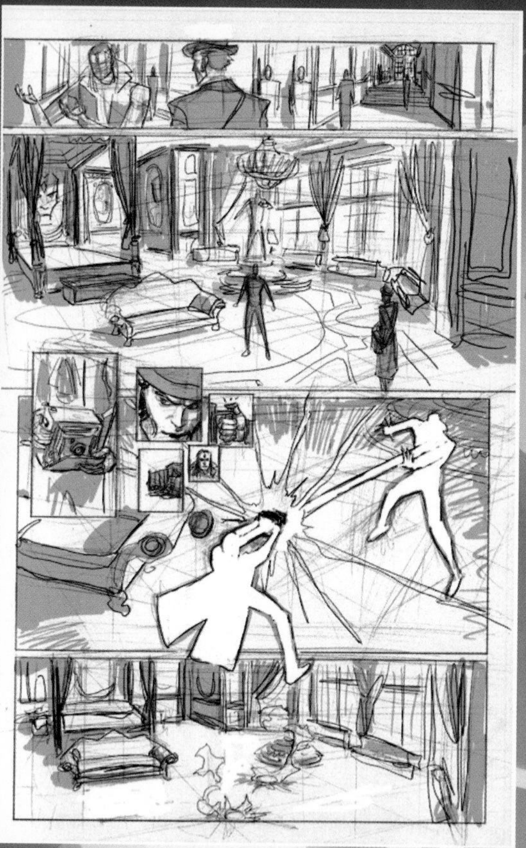

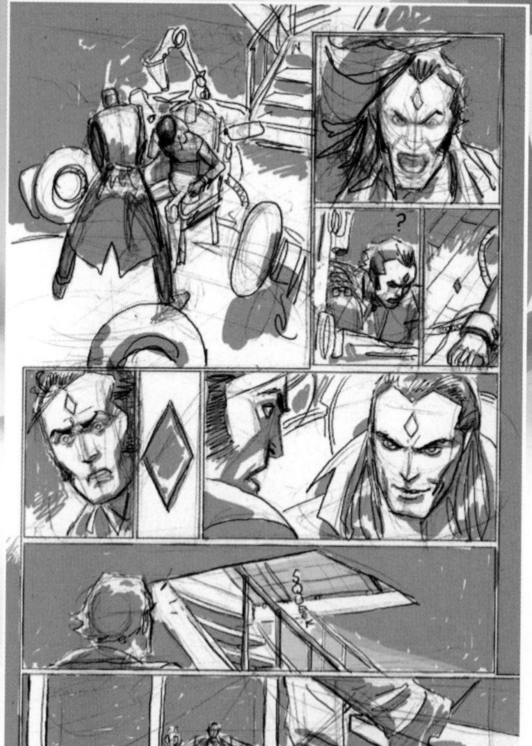

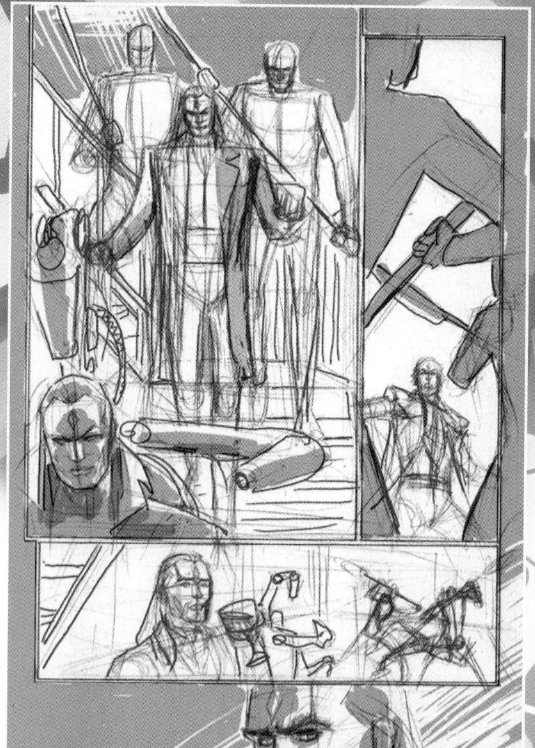

#14 LAYOUTS BY DUSTIN WEAVER

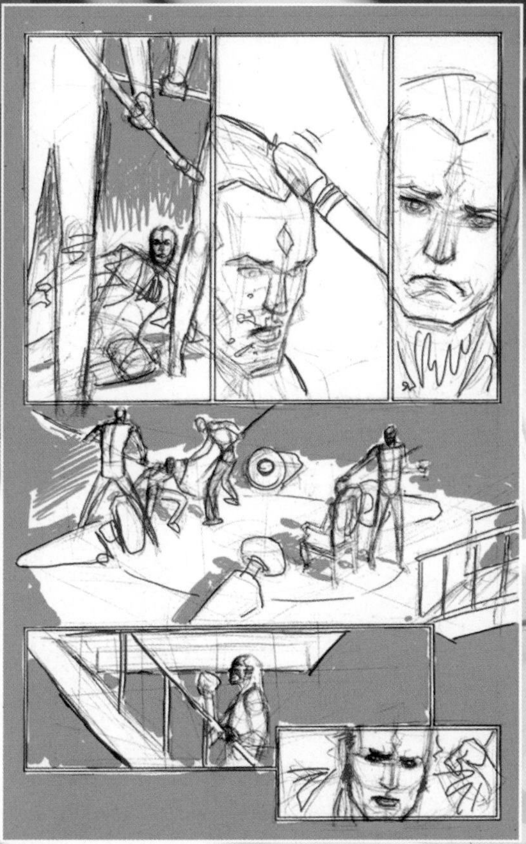

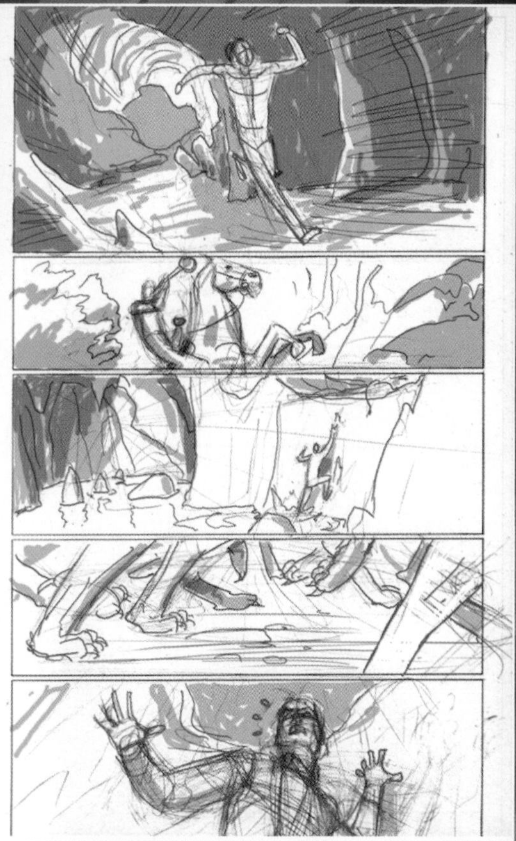

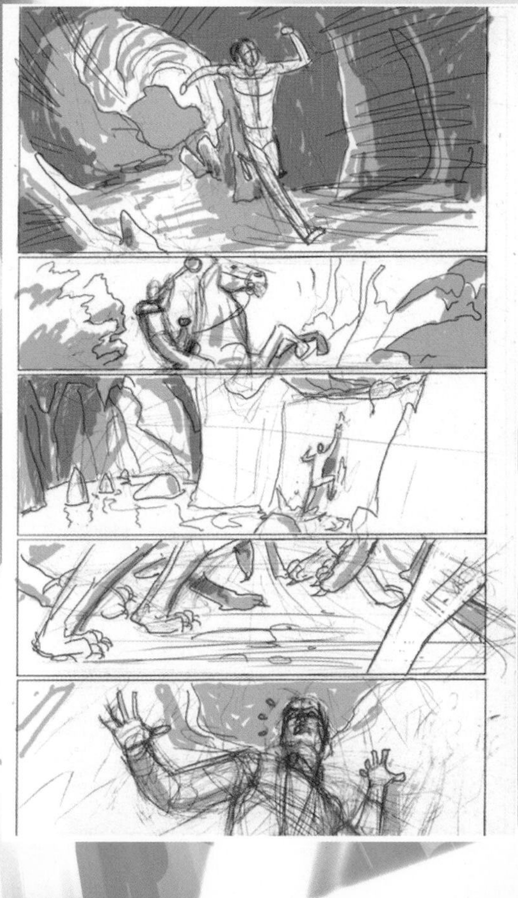

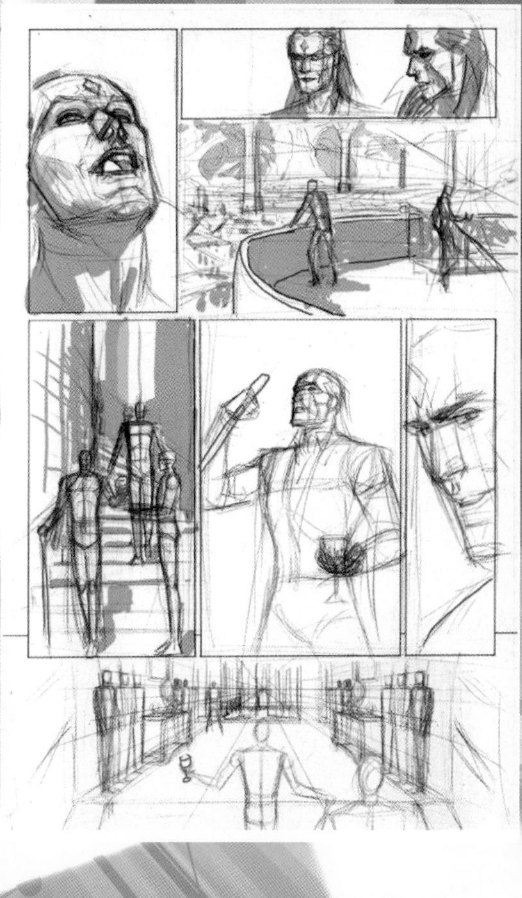

#14 LAYOUTS BY DUSTIN WEAVER

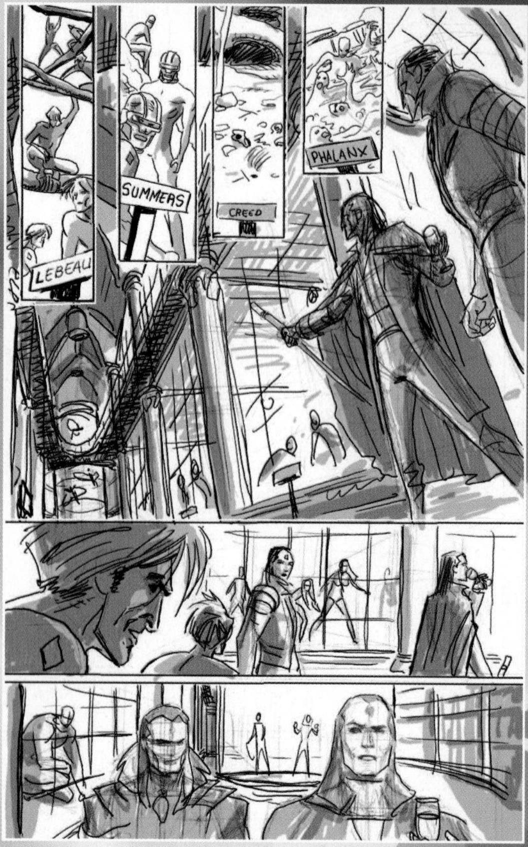
LEBEAU
SUMMERS
CREED
PHALANX

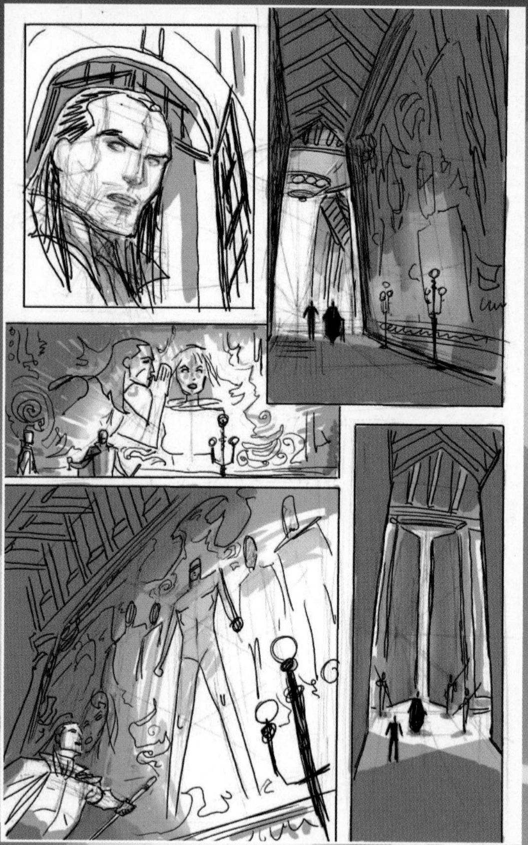

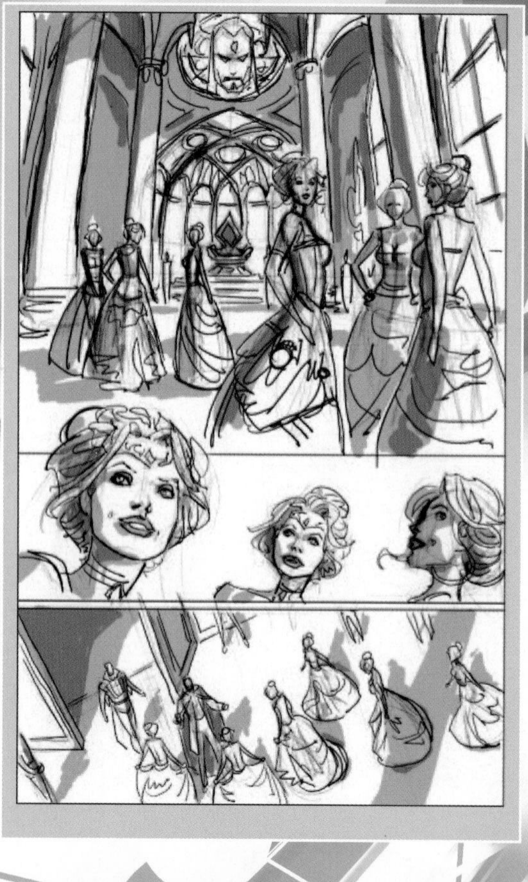

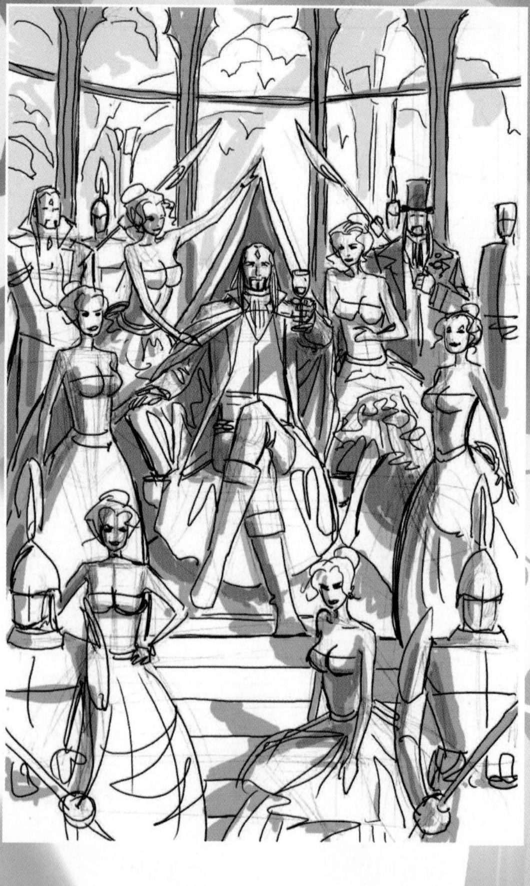

#14 TAPESTRY DESIGN BY DUSTIN WEAVER

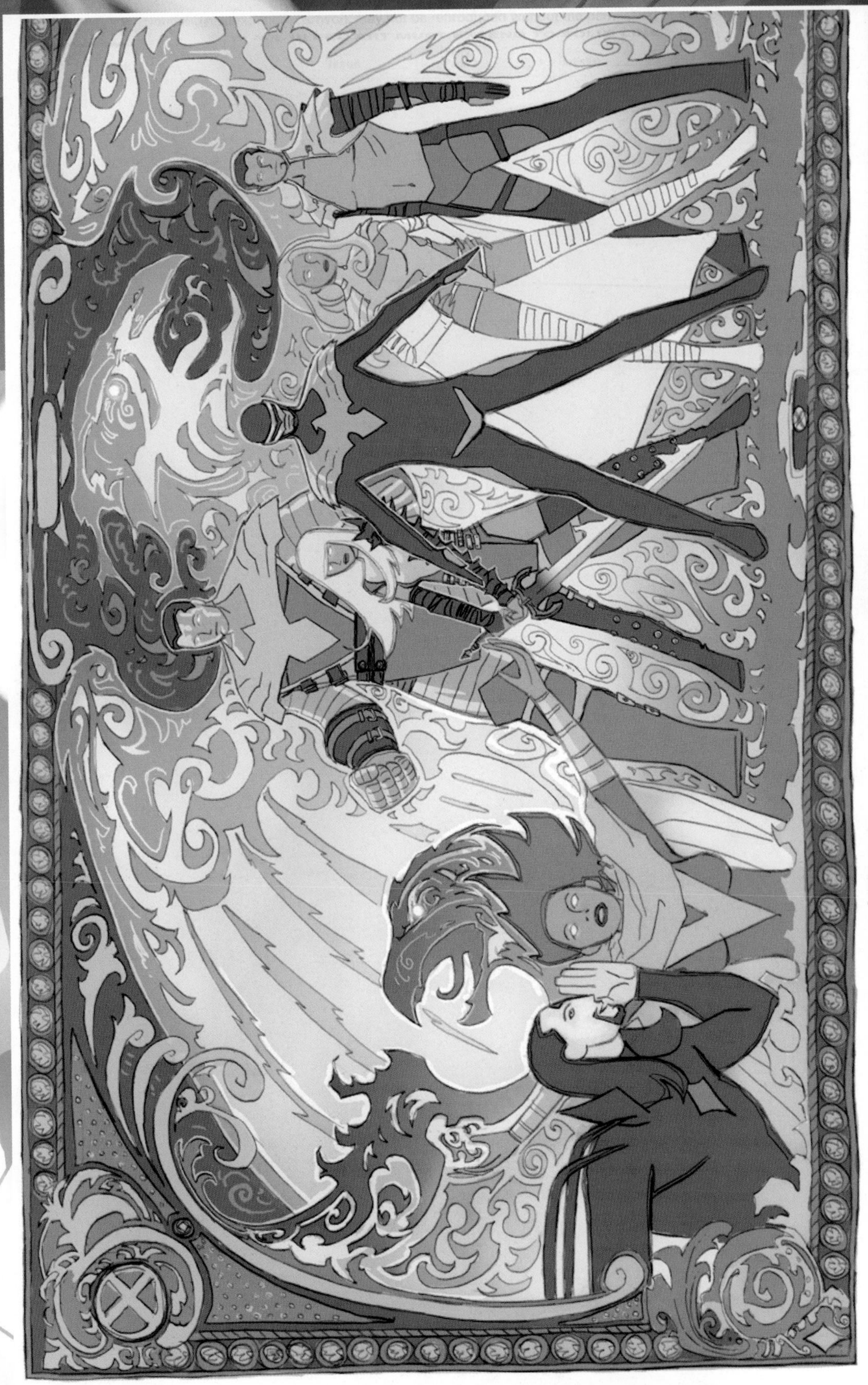

MR. SINISTER DESIGNS BY DUSTIN WEAVER

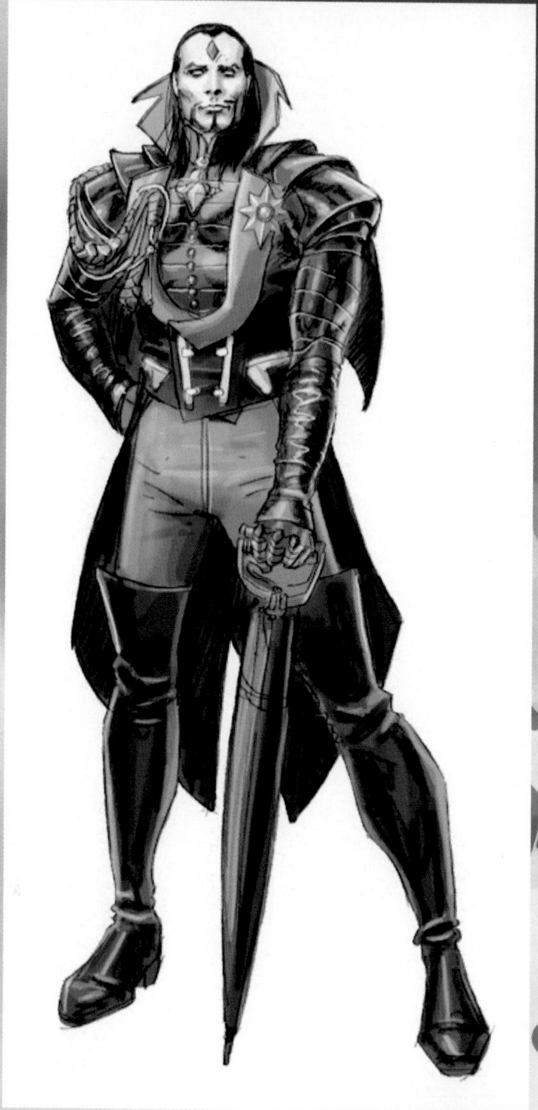

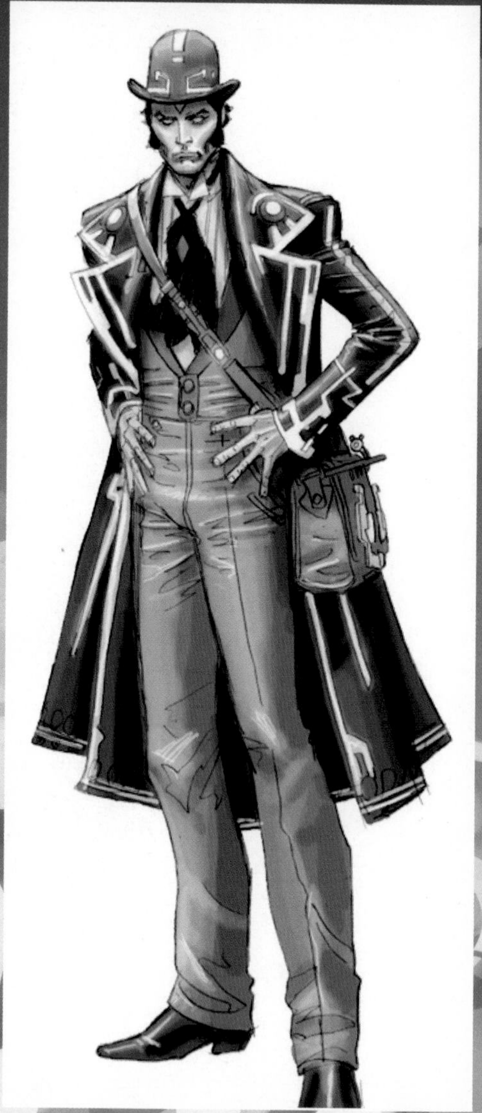

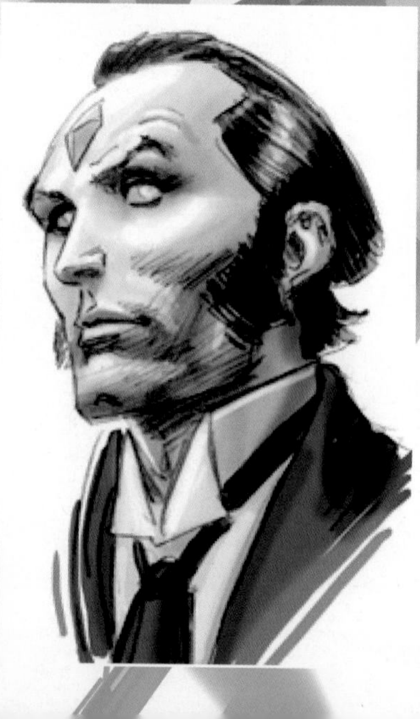

#11 COVER SKETCH & INKS BY GREG LAND

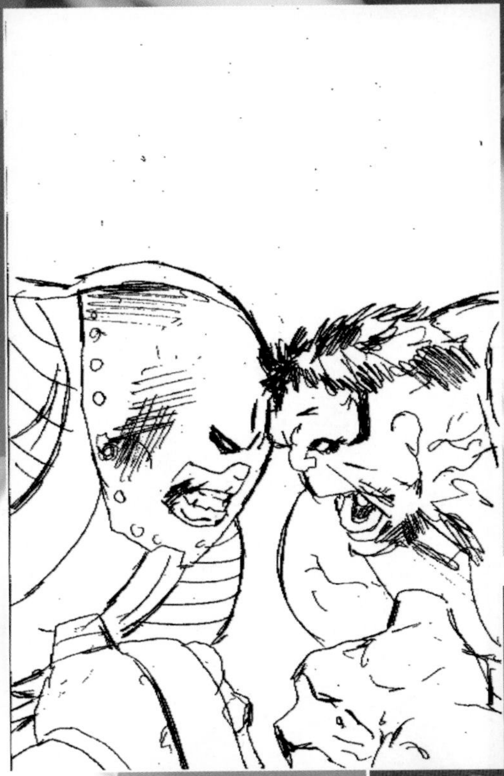

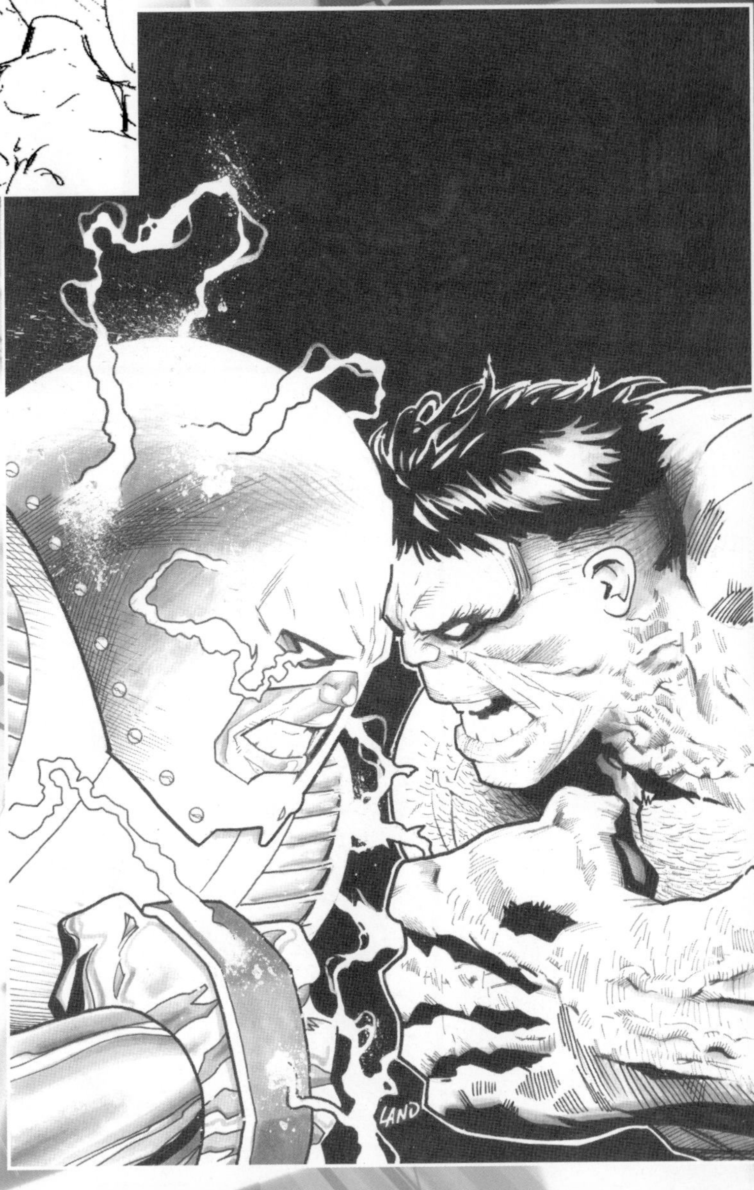
LAND

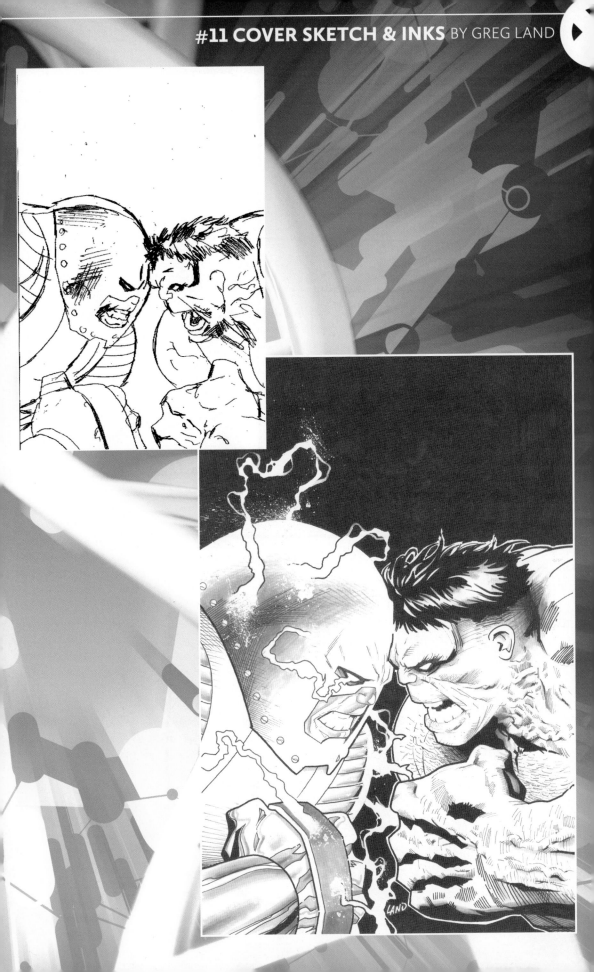

#12 COVER SKETCHES BY GREG LAND

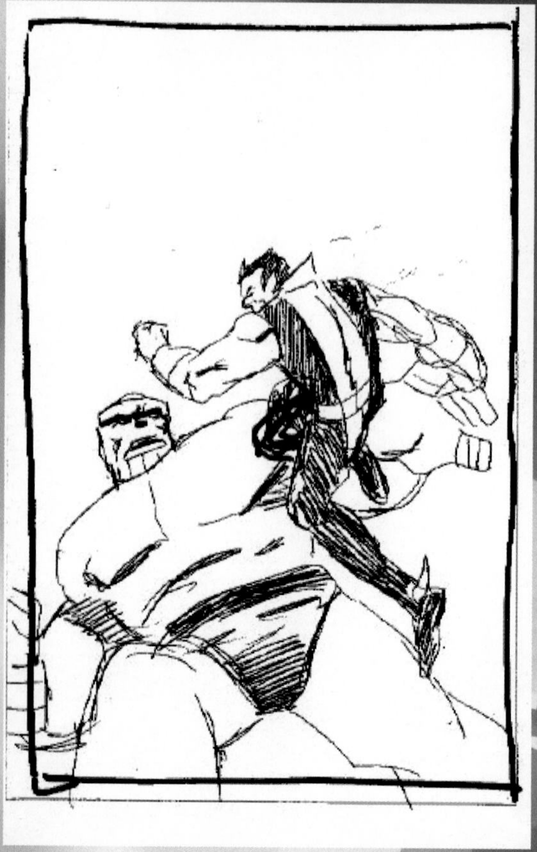

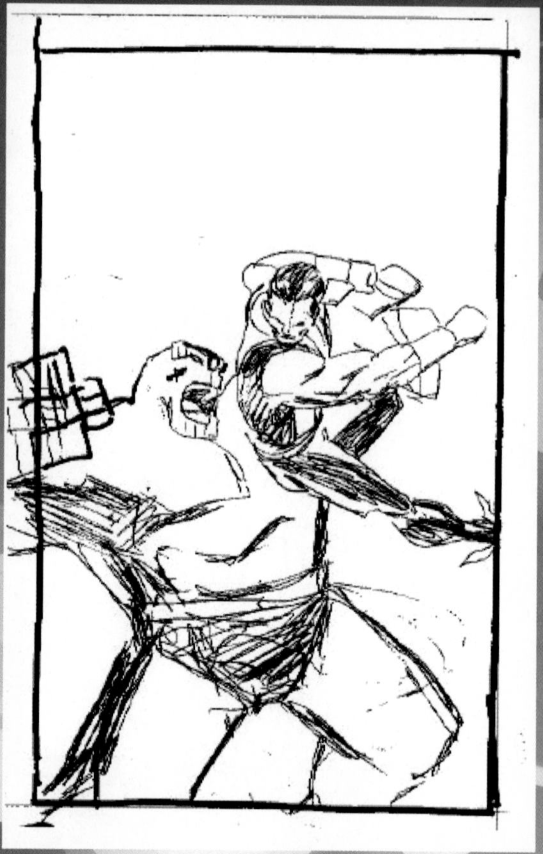

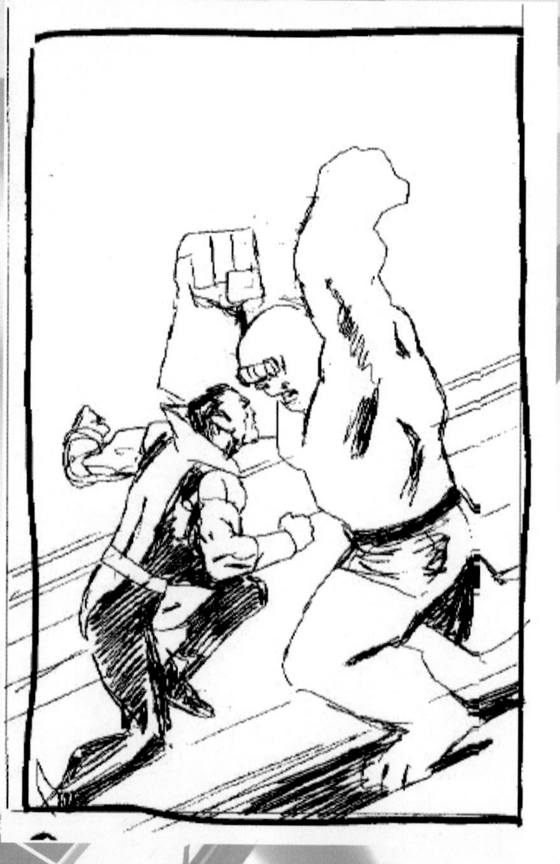

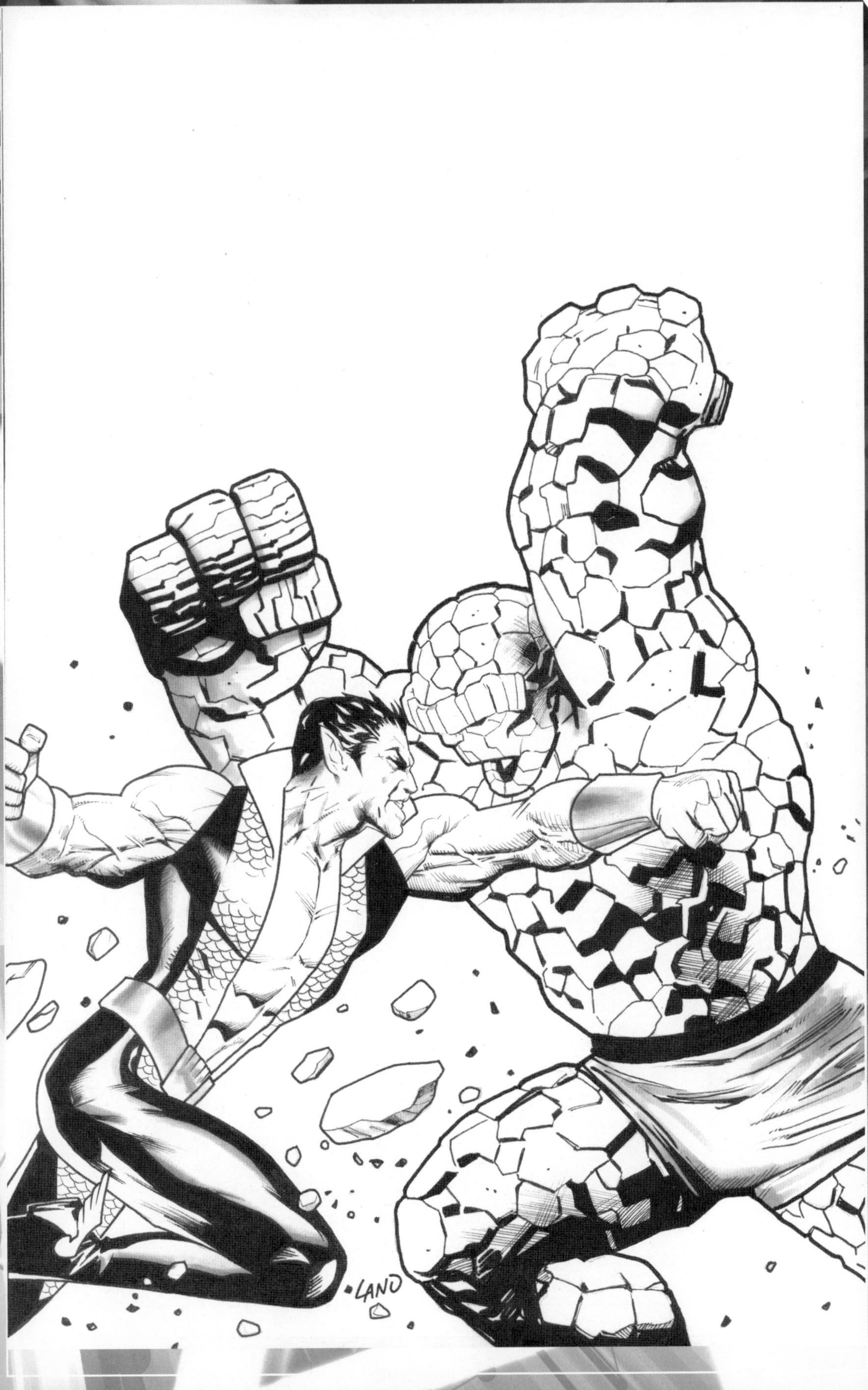
LAND

#13 COVER PENCILS & INKS BY ADAM KUBERT

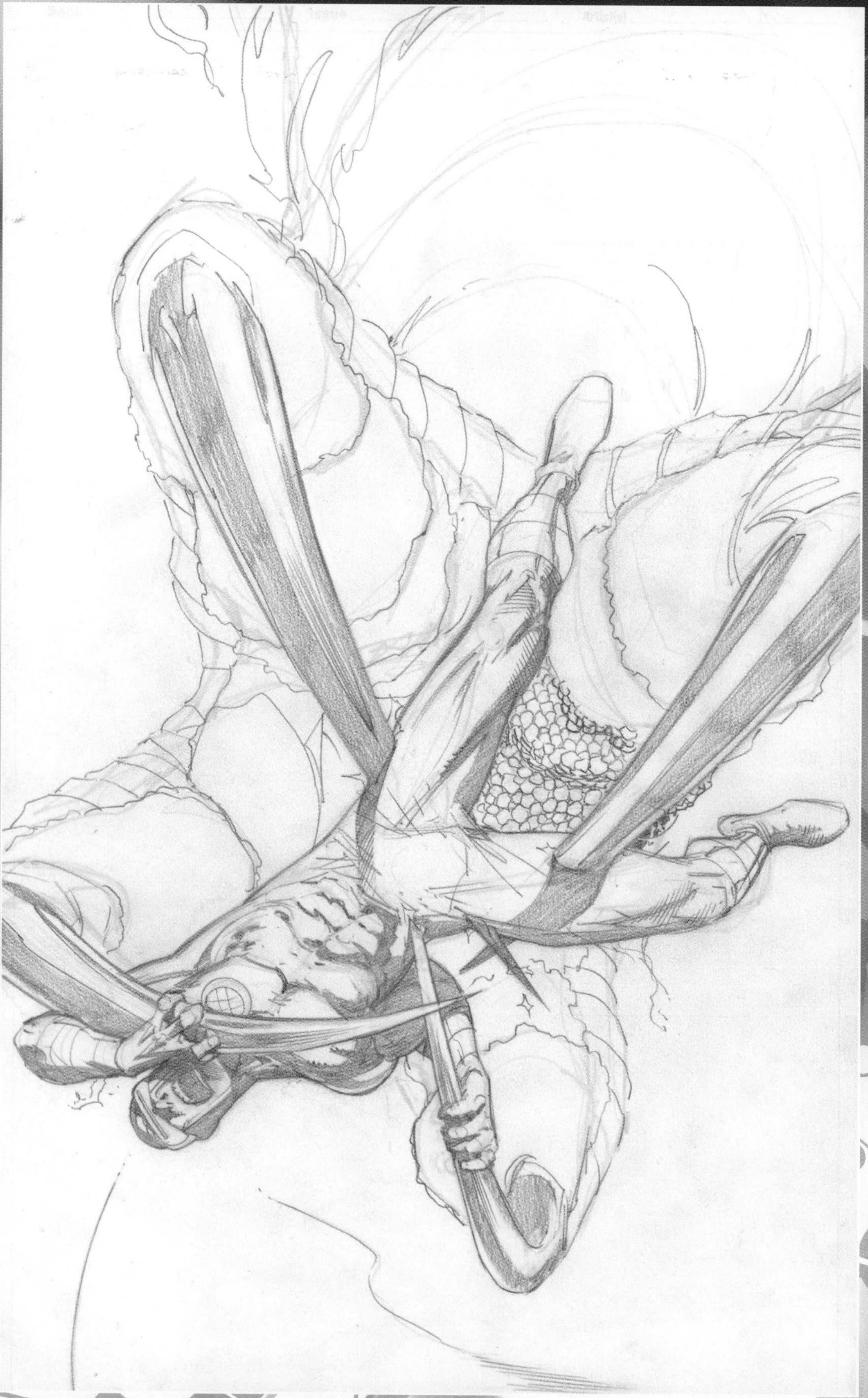

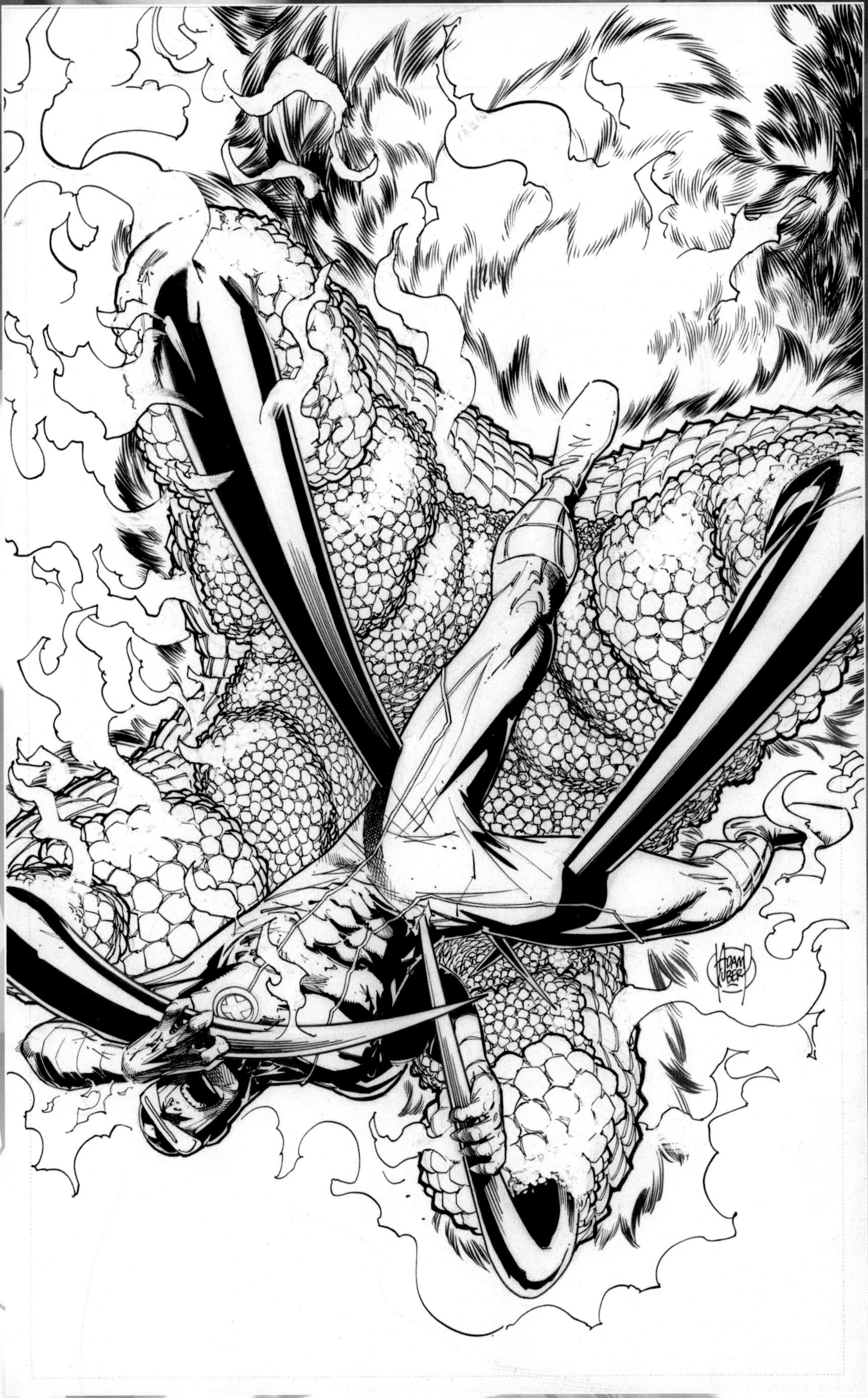

"AN ENTERTAINING, ACTION-PACKED, SMART COMIC." - COMICBOOKRESOURCES.COM

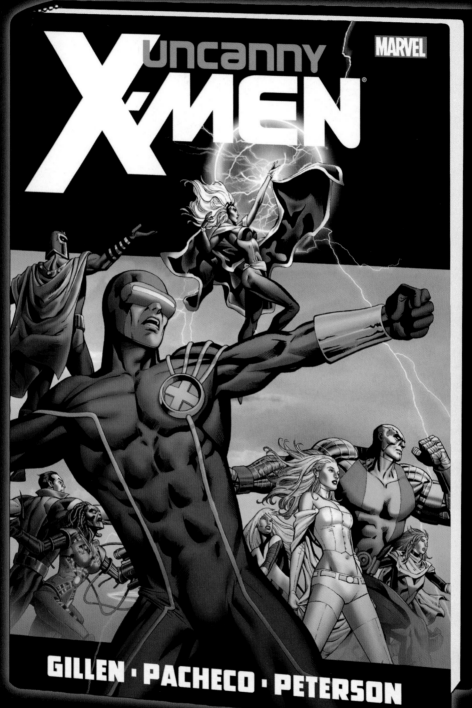

GILLEN · PACHECO · PETERSON

UNCANNY X-MEN BY KIERON GILLEN VOL. 1 PREMIERE HC
978-0-7851-5993-4

On Sale Now

MARVEL

TM & © 2012 Marvel & Subs